SUCCESSFUL BUSINESS STRATEGY

SUCCESSFUL BUSINESS STRATEGY

HOW TO WIN IN THE MARKET-PLACE

LEN HARDY

Kogan
Page

To Iris

Copyright © Len Hardy 1987
All rights reserved

First published in Great Britain in 1987
by Kogan Page Ltd, 120 Pentonville Road, London N1 9JN

British Library Cataloguing in Publication Data

Hardy, Len
  Successful business strategy: how to
  win in the market-place.
  1. Strategic planning
  I. Title
  658.4'012   HD30.28
  ISBN 1-85091-174-6

Printed and bound in Great Britain
by Billing & Sons Ltd, Worcester

Contents

sell? 180; Physical distribution 181; The trade 183; Trading pricing policy 184; The national promotion plan—for and against 186; Trade development 187

PART 4

PART 5

Acknowledgements

The author thanks the following copyright owners for permission to reproduce extracts from the works cited.

The Boston Consulting Group Limited for 'The Product Portfolio'; The Boston Consulting Group, *Perspectives* 1970.

Professor ASC Ehrenberg for 'How Advertising Works' by ASC Ehrenberg and GJ Goodhart in *Understanding Buyer Behaviour*, J Walter Thompson, 1980.

AC Nielsen Co Ltd for 'Why Advertise Established Brands?', *The Nielsen Researcher*, 1976.

Harvard Business Review for excerpts from 'The Product and the Brand' by Burleigh B Gardner and Sidney J Levy (March-April 1955) and 'Good Managers Don't Make Policy Decisions' by H Edward Wrapp (Sept-Oct 1967). Copyright © 1955 and © 1967 respectively by the President and Fellows of Harvard College; all rights reserved.

Pan Books Ltd and the Crown Publishing Group for *Ogilvy on Advertising* by David Ogilvy. Text copyright © 1983 by David Ogilvy. Compilation copyright © 1983 by Multimedia Publications Ltd. Used by permission of Crown Publishers Inc.

John Wiley & Sons Inc for *The Art of Problem Solving* by RL Ackoff. Copyright © 1978 John Wiley & Sons.

Preface

One of the best ways to learn about strategy formulation is to take part in the planning process, and then to have to live with the results as the plans become reality in a highly competitive market-place.

I have been particularly fortunate in this respect. My earlier appointments were in medium-sized businesses where, even as a more junior manager, I was able to take part in strategy formulation.

My study under a Leverhulme Research Fellowship was very much of a practical nature. Although it was carried out many years ago I still appreciate the discussion sessions the research gave me with a number of practising business executives. Many of them were very successful strategists, and their comments most valuable to me.

I had the privilege to be a board member of Lever Bros for over 20 years, including six years as Marketing Director, and over 10 years as Chairman. Within the company strategy was argued fiercely and frequently. I am greatly indebted to my Lever colleagues over the years for their lively discussion, stimulating argument, and most important of all, their willing help. Business in Lever was serious, challenging, and most enjoyable.

The views and opinions expressed in this book are, of course, mine. They do not necessarily represent the views of the Lever company or the people in it. The details in the quoted case studies are based on my personal recollections.

This book is intended to help business executives develop a practical approach to successful business strategy formulation. It is also intended to help students who are preparing to face the great challenge of business: to create and satisfy customers *and* make profit.

Len Hardy

PART 1

Introduction

Business strategy is a fascinating subject. It is interesting, demanding, stimulating, at times very exciting, and vitally important for success in business.

My first contact with the theory of business strategy came during my days as a student of accountancy and then of business administration. Later, when I was awarded a Leverhulme Research Fellowship to consider the financial aspects of marketing I was able to make it, in effect, a study of business strategy.

To consider the theory of business strategy from the position of a researcher can be helpful, but the real challenge, and the real excitement for anyone interested in the subject, must come from actual experience in the market-place.

In the mid-1950s I had the opportunity to work in the breakfast cereal industry. This gave me a 'feel' of a very competitive consumer market in operation in both the United Kingdom and the United States. In 1961 I moved into Lever Bros, the UK soaps and detergent operating company, and one of the major 'base' companies of Unilever.

The soaps and detergents market held a great attraction for me. I knew the industry was a vigorously competitive one—the major players had won outstanding reputations for their business skills in the markets of the world. Procter & Gamble were recognized as probably the foremost consumer goods company in the USA, and in the UK their company had an enviable reputation as a highly effective business unit. Colgate-Palmolive were clearly very able operators; Lever, too, had achieved considerable success.

If you played in this market you were certainly in the First Division.

This was most definitely a place where getting the business strategy 'right' was clearly crucial.

In 1963 I became Sales Director of Lever Bros. As a board member I was involved in the various strategy discussions, although at this time much of my effort was devoted to winning the day-to-day operating battle in the market-place. This was an excellent experience, helping me to develop a 'feel' for the market and for the consumer and trade behaviour within it.

Late in 1967 I became Marketing Director with responsibility for all the Lever brands in the UK. For a company such as Lever its brands represent the very strength of the business, so here I was deeply concerned in the planning and implementation of strategy.

Within some three months of my becoming Marketing Director of Lever the major competitor, Proctor & Gamble, launched a brand which was to become probably their most successful UK operation. Lever's fortunes were at a low ebb. It was a good time to become deeply involved with the Lever strategy.

I took over as Chairman of Lever Bros in the UK in late 1973. The whole business was now my responsibility. Strategy was clearly one of my top priorities. I was Lever's Chairman until I retired in early 1984.

The broad strategy objectives we set for the business through this period were reasonably straightforward—to return an increasing level of trading profit and cash through the shorter-term periods, and to become leader in every market in which Lever competed actively and so provide for a strong and profitable business into the longer term.

These were tough objectives. They required that in highly competitive markets the company should become what might be termed a 'growth cash cow'.

Developing strategic plans and putting them into operation was an exciting task in Lever during this period. The company was most fortunate in having within it people of a particularly high calibre. Their commitment and attitude may be summed up in one phrase, 'Who is going to be second?'

Many of the strategy concepts and approaches discussed in this book featured in planning sessions within the Lever business at this time. A number of the case studies quoted are based on the actual market-place experience of translating the strategy into operation.

One of the great satisfactions which came from working in the UK soaps and detergents industry centred on the fact that, out of the vigorous and continuous competition, the record shows that the UK consumer received a remarkably good deal. The 'value for money' of soaps and detergents in the UK compares favourably with that of *any* other developed country in the world.

Formulating a business strategy, making it happen in a highly competitive market-place, providing the consumer with what she/he considers to be 'best value', and making satisfactory profits is a most stimulating challenge—it can also be enjoyable and very worthwhile.

A winning strategy

At one time the generals seemed to have a monopoly of the term 'strategy'. They used it frequently, argued about it, and wrote about it in their memoirs—it was very much a military expression.

Over recent years 'strategy' has become a well-used term in the business world. Businessmen, too, have argued about it, probably at even greater length than the generals. They have debated and discussed its place within the field of business management, and like the generals they have found it difficult to reach any clear agreement.

However, through all the argument there seems to be one point on which both the military and businessmen agree—*if you want to win then you'd better get your strategy 'right'*. In business, as in war, if you want to survive and prosper winning is all-important—to win a good operation will be necessary, and a winning strategy absolutely essential.

The Oxford dictionary defines strategy as 'Generalship, the art of war...' and goes on to talk about the 'Management of an army or armies in a campaign, art of so moving or dispersing troops or ships or aircraft as to impose on the enemy the place and time and conditions for fighting preferred by oneself'.

In many ways, of course, business *is* a form of war. For real success in business it is necessary to out-think and out-manoeuvre your competitors (the enemy), when appropriate to move faster than they do, and to get yourself into an advantageous position from which to dictate the course and outcome of the action. It is also necessary in business, as in war, to have the skill and ability to follow through and deliver results against your strategy.

In business, the action (the battle) is fought primarily in the market-place. The territory over which the battle is waged is the market itself and the winner's reward is a major share of the customers' money.

While a general may lose certain battles, if he is to win the war he must win the key encounters. Similarly, the businessman may have periods when he suffers setbacks in the market-place, but if he is to survive and prosper, he must, in the longer term, succeed in the market.

This all argues that the Oxford dictionary definition of the term strategy is well suited for business strategy, and indeed it is. The businessman has available certain resources, and he needs to plan their use in such a way as to ensure that he 'wins the war'.

Business—the purpose and the objective

Business must be competitive. The whole free enterprise system only works satisfactorily when there is strong and vigorous competition for the customers' money. It follows that businessmen must create and satisfy customers. This is the purpose of business.

However, for real success in business, fulfilling the purpose alone is not enough. The business organization must have an objective. Again the free enterprise approach has a requirement: it is that the business objective should be to make profit. Stated more fully, the objective should be to make at least a satisfactory profit return on the resources invested in it.

This is the important double requirement for success in competitive business. The need is both to fulfil the purpose and achieve the objective. *Customers have to be created and satisfied—and a profit must be made.*

A businessman who achieves merely a reasonable profit return on his resources will hardly be considered an outstanding success however. *Real success demands superior results*—results which are well ahead of those of competitors, and in this context competitors are all those other companies which may be competing for additional resources.

A winning business strategy will be designed to get superior results. It will be competitive and plan to 'win the war'. It will accept the importance of creating and satisfying customers—without customers there is no profit, and ultimately no business. In effect, a winning business strategy will be concerned with the making and taking of business opportunities.

Making and taking business opportunities

Successful companies create and develop business opportunities, and then exploit them to the full.

Major business opportunities are invariably concerned with customers, and with their needs and requirements. The discovery of a customer need or requirement which is not being met adequately by a brand or product already in the market is the discovery of a business opportunity. Discoveries of this kind, often referred to as *marketing opportunities*, are at the very centre of the development of a progressive business.

An enlightened management realizes that while the solving of problems within the business is of importance, problem-solving has limitations. There is a limit to the recovery which can be made from the value analysis of the formula of a particular brand, for instance, or from the detailed study of a production process. Eventually the effort outweighs the potential savings.

However, the record shows there is no limit to the growth of the customers' appetite for new developments which provide additional and superior benefits. There may, of course, be limitations to customers' ability to afford the products which provide the additional benefits, but part of the business opportunity is contained in the challenge to meet the new requirements at an acceptable and viable price.

Management attitude

Much of the business strategy formulation process should be concerned with the creation and development of business opportunities. This involves skill and effort, but even more important is a positive management attitude. 'There is always a better way' should be the accepted approach, immediately followed by the resolve 'to find and exploit it before anyone else'.

It is noticeable that a number of companies have a similar recruitment policy. They recruit from the same schools and universities, each accepting personnel of high potential only, and yet one or two of the companies always seem to achieve consistently better results. The systems and methods employed may explain part of the difference, but an additional factor is most certainly the management attitude which is encouraged and developed within the companies.

Real business success requires an attitude which accepts that improvements are *always* possible. It is an attitude which searches for and finds the opportunity, makes sure it is worthwhile and suited to the business, and then works skilfully, positively, and vigorously to develop and exploit it.

Often the requirement is to add to the factual marketing research findings a degree of creative flair—a flair which can come as much from a rigorous and analytical examination of the facts as from an artistic approach.

An additional factor which is always present in a successful business is *enthusiasm*. This is not a wild and uncontrolled emotion, but an approach which is a form of controlled enthusiasm. It is manifested as an eagerness to obtain superior results in a business-like manner.

Strategy objectives

'They were here in January and all they could talk about was making more profit. They came in June and it was all about improving market share. When they come in December the chances are the only subject to rate discussion will be the cash position.' Remarks of this kind by chief executives are not uncommon. They refer to the visits of the owners, or their representatives, and although they may appear very cynical, they will often be encountered in organizations which are recognized as well-managed businesses.

In all competitive organizations there will be shorter-term pressures to meet particular requirements; indeed an active management in pursuit of superior performance may well take deliberate action to create pressure within the business. However, the need for short-term activity should not be allowed to obscure the long-term strategic aims. The fact that there will always be short-term pressures highlights the vitally important need for the management to be completely clear as to just what its strategic objectives are, and not to lose sight of them under pressure.

The business owners (the shareholders) will normally be interested in a flow of increasing dividends, and a satisfactory uplift in the value of their share holdings. A substantial increase in profits earned, year on year, would normally be the key factor in meeting these objectives. It is, of course, always possible that the owners may decide they are prepared to sacrifice short-term profits for market share growth, or that they require a high level of dividend payment irrespective of the level of profit earned.

In practice the shareholders of a public company are rarely in a position to decide the strategic objectives for the business. In effect, they delegate this task to the individuals they appoint to run the company. In particular, they delegate the responsibility to the appointed Chief Executive who will need to decide just what the strategic objectives should be and also the timing of their delivery.

If his company is a public one with a Stock Exchange quotation he will need to be aware of the price movement of the company's shares. A lengthy period without dividends as market share is developed is unlikely to be appreciated by the stock market—all the benefit of the hard work on market share could accrue to a predator.

Where the business is the subsidiary of a multi-national or a conglomerate the strategic objectives may need to be closely linked to those of the parent company. The performance of the business in other parts of the world will be significant, and the Chief Executive may find he has to 'wait his turn' to make a new brand launch, or 'get out and get some cash' if the parent wants to invest heavily elsewhere.

The Chief Executive will invariably be involved in a balancing act. Growth and a bigger business, winning in the existing markets: such factors will be important for the long term, and also for staff morale. Producing satisfactory levels of short-term profit and cash may be of consequence for the stock market and for shareholders.

Part of the skill of the Chief Executive is getting the balance of objectives right for his business. Most important of all, he should be clear in his own mind what his objectives are. This does not mean that he should necessarily have in mind exact levels of profit and market position. It does mean that he should be clear where he believes the main opportunities for the business are and how they can be best exploited.

Although he may not spell out his objectives to the staff of the business in terms of exact figures and specific positions, it will be essential that he conveys to them a sense of purpose and direction. A business without a sense of purpose and direction is like a ship without a rudder.

Business strategy—the folklore

Good folklore is based on the record, and is established over time and from experience. Business strategy formulation is a relatively young practice; nevertheless already it has developed a number of 'strategy folklores'.

'Always play on your home ground', more recently expressed as 'Stick to the knitting', is an established lore. The record shows very clearly that companies do better in those markets where they have developed special skills and experience. New markets (away grounds) can often bring unforeseen trouble.

'If it's worth doing, it's worth doing well—if it isn't worth doing well, then don't do it.' A half-hearted approach to a business venture rarely ever succeeds. A full commitment is essential for a good result, and if the project is not worthy of this then the business would be well advised to drop it.

'A leader must enforce market discipline, he must be ruthless in dealing with *any* competitive challenge.' If you make a price move and a competitor undercuts it, then he should be shown that his action has been noticed and will be punished. If he is not punished, he will repeat the move—and soon your leadership will be eroded.

A maxim borrowed from the military is: 'Always attack your competitor where he is weakest, and never mount a full frontal attack against a strongly entrenched leader.' To this may be added, 'Before you make your attack be sure your competitor has been softened up, and thrown off balance.' Again the record shows this to be very good advice.

The lore for new markets is simple: 'Get leadership early, and make sure you grow with the market.' When you decide there is a market in which you wish to invest you should do everything possible to discourage your competitors from investing in it. One way would be to see that their profit prospects from the market are at best very low indeed.

To these established folklores the experienced and successful strategist will add others. Examples of the lores at work can be seen in many of the case studies in this book. Should they always be followed? Most of them are, in fact, good business common sense. In the majority of cases they are certainly worthy of attention. In the majority of cases—but not always. There have been a limited number of instances where a business has deliberately chosen to 'buck the lore' and has gone on to record outstanding success. Judging correctly just when it is wise to 'buck the lore' is a considerable skill.

Strategy and operations

A statement which makes clear the vital importance of a sound strategy reads: 'The army was highly trained and superb at fighting in the mountains; unfortunately it was positioned in the wrong mountains and lost the war.'

This statement, however, and others like it, tends to underplay the major significance of an effective operation in obtaining business success. It is a truism that a skilfully designed strategic plan is of little avail if nothing happens to make it come to life in the real world of business. An incompetent and ineffective army would probably lose the battle even if it were positioned in the right mountains.

A simple but nevertheless relevant example of the importance of effective operation is often to be seen when a company holds a superior volume position in a market. The superiority should bring lower unit costs, but they will not just happen, they have to be worked for. And if they are not obtained then the superior volume can become a form of competitive disadvantage.

Shrewd observers of the business scene in recent years have commented that the truly effective business organizations have managements which concentrate their attention on a limited number of activities, and ensure that they keep their operations simple. 'If the proposition cannot be justified on one sheet of quarto, then the chances are we should not accept it for action' is an approach that has gained wide application. Concentration and simplicity are considered to be among the key factors necessary for business success and both tend to be referred to in terms of business operation.

But it will be extremely difficult to attain the necessary concentration and simplicity in operation if the strategic plans have not been formulated to provide for it.

Strategy and operation are complementary. A winning strategy needs the backing of an effective and efficient operation for real business success.

Responsibility for strategy

Much has been written of the need for more delegation within business management. At the same time it has to be recognized that many of the more successful businesses are in fact managed in what is known as a 'hands on' manner.

The arguments for and against more delegation within a particular business are rarely worthwhile unless they consider *specific* situations. In most businesses there are probably some decisions which could be safely delegated further down the organization. Equally there are a limited number of 'key' decisions which should certainly not be delegated.

Strategy is concerned with the use of the total resources of the business. Every part is involved, and a successful strategy is vital to the future of the business. Getting the key strategic decisions right is all-important—clearly these should not be delegated.

The Chief Executive should be responsible for the business strategy. The title of his position may vary from company to company: he may be called Chairman, President, or Managing Director. Regardless of the title, the man who is responsible for the overall management and leadership of the business should take responsibility for strategy. If he neglects to do this, if he delegates it to someone else, then he may carry the title of Chief Executive but he will not be doing the job.

The very essence of strategy formulation is contained in the judgement decisions as to which opportunities the business should pursue, and the manner in which this pursuit should be carried out. These are the key decisions and the Chief Executive should take them. He may receive advice and guidance from other members of the business, but the key decisions should be his responsibility. Getting them right for his business is probably the most important task of any Chief Executive.

The development of the strategic approach

Progressive businesses have always been aware of the importance of having a successful strategy. They may not have called their deliberations strategy planning, and they may have worked with very rough volume and financial estimates. They may, indeed, have been working on 'hunches', but they were in fact using a strategic approach, looking for business opportunities and for the competitive advantages with which to exploit them.

In the 1950s and 60s long range planning was adopted on a wide scale throughout industry. Much of it centred on the development of the business itself and was not strongly directed towards competitive issues. This is, in part, understandable in that through the 1950s and part of the 60s many companies had a relatively easy time and were concerned mainly to meet an expanding demand for their products.

Through the 1970s the economic climate changed dramatically. Most developed countries experienced deep recessions. In many cases survival became the major preoccupation of management. Earning an adequate level of profit and generating necessary cash flows in these new circumstances demanded a more skilful and competitive approach to business. In this new environment, competitive strategy formulation became of major significance.

This new development received considerable impetus from two particular sources—the business schools within the universities, and the business consultants.

Much of the literature coming from the business schools tends to concentrate on the more fundamental aspects of strategy formulation. This is to be expected and it is appropriate that the basic theories and concepts within the field of strategic development should be considered. The universities are well suited to this task and have clearly been very active.

For many of the business consultants the developments of the 1970s represented a significant business opportunity. In their attempts to gain a competitive advantage in their markets the consultants have been most active in bringing new strategy concepts forward, and there can be little doubt that the best of these have had a strong influence on the strategic thinking of many businessmen.

It is understandable that the consultants' presentations and publications tend to concentrate on particular aspects, and on the use of specific techniques, within the strategy formulation process. Normally the publications cover areas in which the consultant concerned believes he has a lead over his rivals.

The younger manager, making his way up the business ladder, is likely to recognize that the literature available to help him form a practical approach to strategy formulation is indeed very limited. A prime aim of this book is to provide a series of 'guidelines' to construct a practical approach.

An approach to business strategy formulation

This book starts from the basis that the right strategy for any individual firm must be *specific to that firm*. There is no single strategy which is right for a particular industry or for the various firms competing in that industry.

There is no single technique, formula, or concept that will provide a successful strategy. The most advanced computer does not have the ability to provide the right business strategy. Of course, this is not to say that certain techniques, specific concepts, and the computer, may not have a helpful part to play in the strategy formulation process.

The right strategy for a particular business will depend upon a series of factors including the position of the business, its objectives, the competitors in its markets, and the business environment. These factors will change from time to time and so it may be necessary to make adjustments to the strategy.

The view taken here is that formulating a successful business strategy requires:

1. A realistic analysis of the current position of the company and its competitors in a series of key areas. These would include:
    - The markets in which the company competes.
    - The position of the various brands and products within these markets, including an appreciation of their strengths and weaknesses.
    - Management performance and ability.
    - Financial strengths and weaknesses.

- Research and development resources and abilities.
- Production performance and capabilities.
- Operating performance and ability.

2. The compilation of a series of forecasts of future developments in the key areas, including changes in the environment and in consumer behaviour.

3. The search for, and assessment of, the business opportunities which can be expected to develop during the period of the strategic plan. Also necessary is an assessment of the ability of the business, and of its competitors, to develop competitive advantages which will provide the base for the exploitation of the opportunities.

4. The selection of those opportunities which the business expects to be able to develop and exploit more effectively than its competitors.

5. A plan for the marshalling of the resources of the business, and the concentration of those resources on the development and exploitation of the opportunities selected.

When considering the business opportunities which are expected to develop, it is important to have estimates of their extent and timing. The business must be sure that each opportunity it intends to develop is worthy of the time, effort, and resource it will consume. In many cases timing will be of real significance — a market can be lost if entry is unduly delayed. Equally, a move made too early can mean a considerable waste of effort and resource.

While research data can provide very useful guidance to the probable value and extent of business opportunities, the assessment and selection processes are ones where sound judgement will be all-important. It is in the assessment and selection of those opportunities which are right for the particular business concerned that the basis for a successful strategy is founded.

The order of discussion

This book is divided into five parts. In this Introduction (Part 1) a number of the basics with which we are concerned have been discussed. It has been a brief discussion, but it is hoped it has been sufficient to set the scene for the more detailed reasoning which follows.

Part 2 is concerned with a series of strategy considerations — concepts and subjects which may be of particular significance in the formulation of a specific business strategy.

Some of these considerations are fundamental, and therefore of significance in the strategic planning of all companies. The concepts involved in the chapters on the Best Value approach, Competitive Advantage, and Market Leadership come under this heading.

There is also a series of chapters on subjects which might be termed 'basics'. The Market, Economic Climate, and Opportunities in the Market are included in this section. Again, these are likely to be concerned in all strategic planning approaches. They tend to be more factual and less conceptual than the fundamentals.

All strategy considerations must ultimately be linked to the brands or products of the business. These are the pillars on which the business is built, and so their development and progress is of vital importance. In Part 3 a series of subjects including Pricing, Advertising, Product Costs, Promotions, Distributor Brands, and Capacity is also discussed. In many strategic plans they will all be of significance, in others they may not all be of consequence. Part of the skill of the strategist will be contained in his ability to know when a particular subject is significant to his plan formulation, and when it is less important.

The ownership, financial structure, and the management, of competitors is clearly of consequence and is considered in Part 4. A study of their strengths and weaknesses under these headings can make a major contribution to a plan which aims to out-manoeuvre and eventually defeat them.

Part 5 is concerned with the actual formulation of the business strategy, and the final chapter sets out a stage-by-stage approach for a medium-sized company. It is very much a 'rough outline' for it is accepted that strategy formulation, its method and form, as well as its general approach, is a matter for the individual Chief Executive.

Highly successful strategies have come from very unusual formulation approaches—the style and manner should be that of the responsible executive. There is only one all-important requirement: for the welfare of the business, and everyone associated with it, the resulting strategy must be a winning one.

This book is primarily concerned with the formulation of strategy in businesses engaged in the manufacture and marketing of consumer goods. A company engaged in the production of engineering tools is unlikely to be interested in consumer advertising or household sampling. However, it is strongly suggested that many of the fundamental strategy issues discussed here do apply to industrial companies, and also to businesses operating in the service industries. They should certainly be interested in the movements of their markets, the search for marketing opportunities, the development of competitive advantages, and the other strategy formulation considerations. Indeed, it can be argued that the various basic strategy issues discussed in this book apply to all businesses although, of course, there may be differences in the degree, the form, and the manner in which they apply.

PART 2

CHAPTER 1

The Best Value Concept

When the housewife walks along the supermarket aisle and studies the various detergents on offer you can be sure of one thing: when she decides to buy she will select the brand from those available which she believes to be 'best value'. The same basic point applies when she buys cake mix, breakfast cereal, biscuits, or any other item.

Housewives are not alone in this respect. All buyers—that is, all customers—behave in exactly the same way. When they buy, they buy what they personally believe at that time to be best value.

The manufacturers of branded goods, or any manufacturer in fact, had better recognize this very simple and fundamental factor if they want to succeed in business. If their business is to survive and prosper they must make sales. They must create and satisfy customers. To do this they must ensure that their brands or products represent best value to a satisfactory number of the potential customers to whom they are directed.

'Value' is, of course, subjective. Each individual has his/her own appreciation of the value of any given brand or product and these appreciations are unlikely to be identical. As an individual's needs and requirements tend to change from time to time, it follows that his/her appreciation of the value of a particular brand or product will not necessarily remain constant. It will also change.

It is important to appreciate that the customer's best value test isn't just for the first purchase. Every time a purchase is made the test must be passed. The real requirement, of course, is that the brand passes the customer's best value test and goes on to make a profit. The business purpose may be the creation and satisfaction of customers, but the objective is to make profit. Business success demands achievement of both purpose and objective.

It follows that it is vitally important that the manufacturer should have a very keen appreciation of what represents best value in his markets, in the market segments, and in particular for those customers to whom his brands are primarily directed.

What is 'best value'?

'Value' is an entirely subjective quality, and for a particular item it may differ from person to person. In some instances an individual's appreciation of value can take a most unusual form—some people place a much higher value on a brand with a yellow package top than one with a blue top. For some, a particular colour or form of product is all-important to its value, even when the colour or form makes no real difference to the product's performance.

Such slight variations in package top colour, for instance, are normally key value issues for only a small minority of customers. For the majority more reasoned brand attributes are the key value factors.

Clearly, the manufacturer, if he is to appreciate what is 'best value' for his market, will need to have a thorough understanding—what might be termed as a 'sound feel'—for what are the key value considerations the consumer has in mind when making a brand purchasing decision.

Are there certain attributes which are key to meeting the consumers' best value requirements? Can these attributes be applied across all markets, or do they differ from one market to another?

Extensive research, and considerable practical experience, suggest that there *are* certain key value attributes which apply for a large majority of consumers in a wide range of consumer goods markets. Indeed, there is a good case for saying that the key value attributes apply beyond consumer markets and into the industrial and service fields.

A very broad classification of consumer markets often employed defines buying within them as either emotional or non-emotional. This can be misleading in that it can be argued that there is a degree of emotion in every purchase. Buying a perfume, for instance, may be a highly emotional act, but there is also a degree of emotion, normally at a much lower level, involved in the purchase of a household product such as washing powder.

It is suggested that the difference in consumers' value appreciation between the various markets, or within the sectors of a given market, is not so much a change in the key attributes but rather a change in the emphasis, or weight, accorded to them.

Within this book it is reasoned that the key value attributes applied by the majority of consumers will be basically the same for a household product as for an item such as a perfume. When purchasing the household brand, however, the consumer is likely to apply a very different degree of emphasis between the attributes as compared with the one she will apply when buying a perfume.

The 'key' attributes in the consumers' 'best value' equation are:

Purpose
Performance
Price
Presentation.

Purpose

Purpose here refers to the consumer need the brand meets, or the consumer benefit it provides. A brand that does not meet the basic purpose for which the consumer requires it will clearly have only limited value to him/her. A man who has a need for a business shirt will expect his purchase to meet that requirement. A shirt styled and coloured for beach wear would have little value to him on this occasion. A shirt styled and coloured in a manner he considers appropriate for business will have a much greater value.

The same reasoning applies to the housewife when she makes her purchases. If she has a family which produces dirty shirts, sheets, and so on, then she will have a need for a product which meets the requirement to clean them. To have value to her the washing powder must meet this basic purpose. If she needs a product that 'cleans and softens' her skin, then the brand of toilet soap which represents best value to her will almost certainly promise and deliver this benefit.

As people become more prosperous and sophisticated their requirements develop and their needs become wider in nature. Thus, the washing powder may need to 'clean, whiten, and *soften*' and the toilet soap may need to 'clean, soften and *deodorize*'. In the toilet soap market the perfume contained within the product is invariably of major consequence. The consumer's requirement may be that the product should provide the main cleaning benefit, and in addition it should leave her skin with what she considers to be an attractive smell. The growth of these various additional consumer requirements is, in effect, the development of a form of segmentation within the market.

There is considerable skill in defining and expressing a brand purpose, in the right words and manner. The consumer must both understand and accept it. At one time in the UK it was thought to be important that a washing powder's purpose should be expressed as getting clothes *white* rather than clean. The housewife believed that whiteness was more totally embracing than cleanness. This was at a time when much of the wash was made up of white clothes. The expression of the consumer benefit, or purpose, is part of the presentation factor considered below.

There is also a skill in discovering a consumer need that is not adequately met by existing brands. Consumers frequently have difficulty in defining their requirements with clarity. Knowing how to structure and conduct a consumer research exercise which will open up the consumer's thinking, and enable her to state her need more precisely, can provide the base for a valuable marketing opportunity.

The basic fact is that to have a value to the consumer, a brand must meet his/her need or requirement. It must promise and provide the benefit for which he/she purchases it.

Performance

A brand's value is markedly influenced by how well it performs in meeting the purpose.

Many brands have the same basic purpose, but they are unlikely to have the same level of performance. The manufacturer's skill in formulation, in processing, and the quality of the ingredients he is prepared to use, are significant factors in determining brand performance. Frequently, but not always, the level of performance may be reflected in the brand formulation cost.

Performance is, of course, very much a competitive consideration, and the manufacturer who has a superior performance may well take active steps to inform the consumer of his superiority over other brands.

In the value equation the brand performance rating which really matters is the one given to it by consumers, and this will not necessarily be the same as that shown in the manufacturer's laboratory. Specific ingredients that have advanced technical qualities, but which do not show through to the consumer in *results*, are unlikely to affect performance appreciation and in turn the consumer's view of the brand's value.

In practice, consumers often have their own approach to performance rating. Many women judge their washing powder, for instance, on the occasion they have a particular kind of wash, possibly one where the clothes are heavily soiled. Others make their judgement only when they wash in higher water temperatures, and so on. It is part of the skill of a manufacturer to know the ways in which consumers judge performance, and to formulate his brands accordingly.

Frequently it is necessary to get from the consumer a comparative rating of performance. In the competitive battle the brand requirement is often to obtain not just better, but significantly better performance. If the consumer rates the new development as only marginally better, it may not be worth a major exploitation effort. A significant improvement, one that the consumer recognizes readily, could be a very different proposition, and warrant a substantial backing.

The wise manufacturer never underestimates the consumer's ability to make a sound judgement of a brand's performance. There is considerable evidence from many product fields to show that, over time, the consumer can be a very good judge of performance.

The ability to research the consumer and to form an accurate view of comparative performance ratings is a valuable skill. It can be a vitally important factor in the development of the most cost-effective formulation to meet a particular brand requirement.

There are a number of product categories in which consumers find it extremely difficult to judge performance merely by using the product. Toothpaste is a good example. The purpose may be to prevent tooth cavities, but this benefit can require a lengthy period of use before it is effective, and even then other factors may make the performance difficult to judge. In these circumstances, skilled presentation can play a major part in influencing the consumer's acceptance of a particular performance level.

In cases of this kind it can be helpful to get performance verified by a recognized authority—for a toothpaste, a prominent and widely recognized association of dentists, for instance, or for a washing powder a well-respected washing machine manufacturer.

Price

It is an elementary fact that the money the consumer pays for the brand is its price. Money is a measure, and so price is very much part of the value equation.

Given two brands with the same purpose and the same level of performance, the one with the lower price would get the consumer's vote as the best value. (This, of course, ignores the value of brand *presentation* which could affect the buying decision and is considered later.)

The price in the value equation is always the one which applies on the particular occasion when the buying decision is made. This means that if a brand is enjoying a special price reduction in a store the probability of it attracting the consumer's custom is enhanced because its value has been improved. At the lower price level it is more likely to be rated as best value.

Similarly, if a special pack containing an extra quantity of the product is offered without any increase in price, the value of the brand will rise and its prospect of being considered best value improved.

As with performance, skill in judging what level of price differential the consumer considers significant is important. 'What level of differential will motivate her to change her buying decision? Would a move of 1p per pack make any worthwhile difference to competitive value? Is 5p per pack the minimum adjustment required to make an impact and to get a buying decision change?' In theory, with the help of a series of tests, it should be relatively easy to plot the movement of brand demand with varying levels of price adjustment. Useful guidelines can be obtained from research. However, in the real market-place competitive prices rarely remain unchanged and so an exact plot is seldom possible.

It is important that the manufacturer should have research which guides him to the most favourable price position for his own brand compared with those of his major competitors, and beyond this to an indication of the movement of demand with various levels of brand price differential.

The manufacturer should also have a worthwhile guide to the relationship between performance and price in his particular market, or market sector. When once he has clarified and settled on his brand purpose, it is with the attributes of *performance* and *price* that he will be primarily concerned in any attempts he may make to change his brand value to the consumer.

Of the key attributes in the brand value equation, price is the one which can be moved most rapidly. A change in the other attributes invariably requires considerable time in preparation.

The consumer's reaction to price can often be aligned to his/her own financial position at the time of purchase. Given a liberal supply of funds, the position of price in the best value equation is likely to change and performance become of greater significance. However, this is certainly not to say that the purchase of low priced brands is necessarily concentrated in the lower income section of the population.

Presentation

In presenting his brand the manufacturer should be concerned to inform his prospective customer of the brand's purpose, its performance and—as appropriate—its price. The presentation will have as one of its main objectives the task of getting the consumer to try the brand and, in the case of regular users, of ensuring further retrial.

Obtaining brand trial and retrial, and in this way building sales volume, is the major task of presentation. One of the best ways of convincing consumers that a brand offers best value is to get them to try it. Only in use can they really judge the brand's standard of performance.

It should always be remembered that there are only two ways in which the sales volume of a brand can increase. One is by increased penetration and that means increased trial. The other is by persuading existing users to increase their consumption. Getting consumer trial is fundamental to ultimate success.

'A fully effective brand presentation can have a marked effect on the pace of development of a market and of the brand within that market.

In the mid-1960s Lever launched Comfort into the UK fabric softener market. Despite substantial investment in advertising and promotion the market, and the major brands within it, were very slow to develop.

The television advertisement used for Comfort at the time of the launch was thought to be a particularly good one. It used a very gentle tone and style of presentation and was considered extremely persuasive.

In view of the slow development of the brand Lever decided to conduct a very detailed research into the consumers' reception of the Comfort advertisement.

One of the surprising facts coming from the research was that many consumers were confused as to how Comfort worked, what it was (some thought it was a water softener), and the results it could bring. Lever had apparently underestimated the need to explain this new product, its use, and its benefits in simple terms.

A new television advertisement was developed to put this right. It explained in a simple manner the need for Comfort, just how it worked, and the results it could provide. In showing the results a novel presentation feature – a glass drawer – was used. Through the glass drawer the consumer was shown how, before the use of Comfort, clothes would be flat and the drawer close easily. After the use of Comfort the same clothes would be so soft and springy that the drawer would not close. This new advertisement was very well received by consumers and it was most effective in encouraging them to try Comfort.

Many factors were involved in the rapid development of the UK fabric softener market in the 1970s, and in particular in the growth of Comfort. The 'drawer' presentation certainly played a valuable part.'

No matter how he sets about the task of presenting his brand, no matter what style, manner, or environment he chooses, the manufacturer is bound to make a brand impression. The package can be designed with loud, gaudy colours, or with soft, pleasing colours. The style of the presentation can be loud and aggressive, or it can be quiet and unassuming. The manufacturer must decide which approach he wishes to use.

The presentation will automatically build a brand personality or, as it is sometimes termed, a brand image. It is clearly better to build a personality which is helpful to the progress of the brand rather than one that is damaging.

This means that the manufacturer should decide on the type, style, and form of personality he wants for his brand. He should decide this well before it enters the market, and then he should ensure that his brand presentations work to develop and maintain that personality.

There is no good reason why a skilled presentation should not do the required double job. That is, it should do an outstanding selling job, encouraging the consumer to try and retry the brand, and it should do this in a style and manner which play their full part in building the desired brand personality.

There is considerable evidence to show that where a brand has built the right personality it can have a beneficial effect on the brand's value, and it can be a helpful factor in enabling the brand to pass the consumer's best value test.

Judging the effect of personality on the brand's value is extremely difficult. For the 'emotional' buy markets it can be very significant. In the less emotional fields it may be less pronounced but still of real worth.

It is possible, with the use of skilled research, to get an indication of how strongly the brand personality is established, just how the consumer thinks of it, and how it is likely to affect her value judgements. However, it will always be difficult to be precise as to the effect of the brand's personality on its value, and it would be unwise to build a premium on this account into strategic plans.

Synergy of the best value attributes

In practice there is undoubtedly a synergy between the key best value attributes. The record shows that for real brand success the requirement is to get the right purpose, the right balance of performance and price, and then to add to this the right presentation.

The right purpose will depend upon consumer requirements within the market, or market sector, at which the brand is directed. With the balance of performance and price, a high level performance (ie high when compared with other brands in the market) can normally command a higher price, whereas a lower level performance would normally need a lower price.

A low level of performance with a high price is very unlikely to succeed. A higher level of performance with a low price clearly has value advantages.

A strong and acceptable personality is unlikely to bring a brand success if the purpose is wrong, or if the balance between performance and price is wrong. It will, however, be helpful, and indeed may cover to some extent a very slight imbalance between performance and price.

If all the key attributes are right they will build on each other, and this will act to increase their total value.

'Persil must rate as one of the greatest successes in brand marketing in the United Kingdom.

Through three decades into the 1970s Persil lead the highly competitive UK washing powder market. It was strong enough to withstand almost continuous attack from the synthetic detergents. Its position of leadership was lost only when the composition of the total market changed from purely high sudsing powders to a mixture of high and low sudsing products. Persil is a high sudsing powder – Persil Automatic is a low sudsing powder and took over the total market leadership position from Persil in the late 1970s.

The Persil success is often attributed to its advertising. It has certainly been supported by very skilful advertising, particularly during its leadership period. However, closer examination shows that Persil, throughout its highly successful leadership period, conformed very closely to the best value approach.

Persil's purpose was to provide 'superior whiteness' for the wash: this was clearly the right benefit for a main sector product at a time when most of a typical household's wash was in fact white. Beyond this, the benefit of whiteness was believed to have a higher overall value to the housewife than, for instance, cleanness.

The Persil formulation was a particularly effective one, providing a very high level of performance. Persil contained a large quantity of soap which is known to be a most efficient detergent and also a relatively high level of perborate. Perborate is a particularly effective ingredient in removing stains when used in a high temperature wash. Through the 1950s and 60s it was very common for the housewife to do her wash in very hot, often boiling, water.

Persil also packed a slightly higher weight of powder in its packets (thereby encouraging heavier use) than did its major competitors.

Persil prices were normally below the price levels of the competitive synthetic detergent brands.

To a very strong position in purpose, performance and price Persil added particularly effective presentation – the Persil personality was extremely well developed and clearly very 'right' for the brand. Little wonder, then, that Persil should have been such a great success and have represented 'best value' to so many people buying washing powders in the UK during the 1950s and 60s.'

The 'best value' equation in strategy

The 'best value' approach contains a number of important lessons for the strategist. An examination of the successful brands in the household product markets (and the same considerations will apply in many other of the fast moving consumer brand markets) shows that a remarkably high number of them conform to the basic reasoning of the best value approach. They are providing the right benefit, and where they are obtaining a premium price they do provide a superior performance. If their product performance is near to the middle of the market, so too is their price.

In an established market there may be the exceptional brand which is successful because an outstanding presentation has supported a somewhat inferior product. Such brands are likely to be found in the more 'emotional' markets.

For new brands entering established markets, success for an inferior product attempting to obtain a premium price is indeed rare. When established brands are strongly placed within a market, a new brand will frequently require a significantly superior performance with either an equivalent or a lower price, if it is to make progress.

It is very important that these considerations should be faced in strategic planning. A brand plan based on superior presentation alone is unlikely to bring success in the market-place. This kind of plan makes the elementary mistake of underplaying the consumer's ability to make a realistic judgement of performance. Experienced and successful operators never underestimate the consumer.

In many consumer goods markets both in the UK and Continental Europe, distributor brands have recently made considerable progress. In some instances, in particular multiple chains, they have become brand market leaders. (A distributor brand is one that carries the name of the store, sometimes referred to as an 'own label' brand.)

The fact is that to many consumers the distributor brand has become best value—better value than the competing manufacturer brands.

Distributors frequently produce a product slightly below the manufacturer's brand in quality, and then give it a lower price. Where the distributor is the clear leader it would seem that the manufacturers are either misjudging the value to the consumer of any product superiority they may have, or are overvaluing the contribution to brand value of their presentations. The argument that the manufacturer has an advertising cost to carry is not acceptable. If the advertising is doing its job properly it is bringing additional volume which in turn should mean lower unit costs. It is always possible, of course, that the manufacturers may have misread the market and have allowed the distributors to move into what is really the main sector, and not just one of the smaller segments.

The basic point is that the best value concept, and the reasoning behind it, are backed by considerable market experience. It is relatively simple in approach, and in many respects can be considered good business common sense. Plans for brand developments within the business strategy which disregard the best value concept should be very closely questioned. They may, for special reasons, be sound plans and bring business success. However, a strategy which accepts the best value concept, and provides for it in the expenditures and revenues it plans, will be much more soundly based.

CHAPTER 2

Competitive Advantage

In all markets there are winners and losers. The winners invariably have some form of competitive advantage over the losers, and they are able to use this advantage to obtain superior results. It follows that business strategy—which is competitive and concerned with winning—should be directed towards the development and exploitation of competitive advantages.

Successful businesses are engaged in making and taking opportunities. The development of a competitive advantage automatically creates an opportunity, and so the reasoning may be modified to: 'successful businesses are engaged in the creation and exploitation of competitive advantages.'

Many factors are involved in the formulation of a winning strategy. Planning for the creation, development, and eventual exploitation of competitive advantages is most certainly at the very heart of the process.

What is a competitive advantage?

A competitive advantage is quite simply an advantage your competitors do not have. Once they have access to the special formulation, the new process, the high speed machinery, or whatever your advantage is, then it is no longer a competitive advantage.

If an advantage is to become a *competitive* advantage as defined here, it should have a particular feature: if it involves an additional cost—for example, an extra formula ingredient—it should have the ability to recover that cost from the customer. The recovery may be in the form of a higher unit price, or in the ability to generate a higher volume which will bring a bigger revenue, and in this way recover the additional total cost involved. The aim should always be for the competitive advantage ultimately to do much more than recover its cost: recovery is a minimum position.

Competitive advantage and the successful business

Finding, developing, and exploiting competitive advantages are at the very heart of the truly successful business. The management drive to exploit the business opportunity which the competitive advantage brings will be fundamental to the success of the business and should permeate every part of it.

Everyone throughout the whole organization should be made aware of the need to create and develop competitive advantages, and should be encouraged to play their full part in the creation, development and exploitation process.

All competitive advantages are worth having. However, the skill and the drive of the business should be aimed at developing those which are of real significance. Such an advantage should be big enough in its content and value to motivate customers and to enhance the brand's position in its market.

Where does the organization find a competitive advantage?

A competitive advantage can be developed in any sector of the organization. It can, for instance, come from the introduction of a new production process that removes certain expensive operations generally employed in the industry. It can come from the development of a new formulation that maintains product quality at an unchanged level but which brings a significant reduction in cost. The value analysis programmes which are now widely employed within industry can often produce a competitive advantage.

The aim should always be to obtain the most significant competitive advantage possible, and to develop and protect it in such a manner that it cannot be copied.

Patents are particularly important in this respect in that if the patent is a strong one, it will protect the competitive advantage for many years.

In practice a manufacturer is fortunate if he can maintain a competitive advantage over the long term. His competitors will be working to render it ineffective, or at least to remove its exclusivity, from the time it first becomes known to them. However, an effective operator will invariably be able to make a significant advantage work well for him even if he has it for only a short period. If he is clever he will ensure that, as his competitors copy him, so they also compliment him, and strengthen his position. ,

The most valuable competitive advantages, the ones that are big enough to make an impact directly on the market-place and on the competitive positions within it, are normally associated with the key brand attributes contained within the best value concept. This is understandable. These key factors bear directly on the brand's value to the consumer, and any favourable movement in them can immediately enhance the brand's attractiveness.

Purpose

As consumers become wealthier, better educated, more travelled, and so on, so their needs tend to widen and develop. For instance, they are no longer satisfied with a powder scourer, they want a liquid cleaner which will protect their new plastic baths. They have tasted foreign foods on their travels and want to enjoy them on occasions in their own homes. These and similar developments are very natural, and they have accelerated in recent years.

A consumer need not fully satisfied by the brands currently competing in the market is a marketing opportunity. If a marketing opportunity is discovered before competitors have appreciated its existence then it can become a competitive advantage.

The search for new marketing opportunities should be non-stop. This requires a close and continuous exchange of views with consumers about the weaknesses and strengths of current brands, and about the consumers' unfulfilled needs and requirements.

In a free enterprise competitive system it is the consumer who makes the final decision as to which brand is best value. Retail and wholesale traders can influence the consumers' ability to buy certain brands by their stocking and pricing policies, but in the main the consumers' view is all-important.

A manufacturer who has developed an effective approach whereby he has a continuous and productive dialogue with consumers, and in particular with those consumers who are interested in his markets, will have constructed a most valuable asset. If this asset is markedly more effective in operation than the efforts of his competitors, then he should be able to gain a competitive advantage in terms of brand purpose.

> ❛When questioned about their lavatory and the requirement to clean and maintain it in a satisfactory condition, many people talked of the need to 'kill germs' and 'remove stains'. Very few people talked of the need to remove smells.

> More detailed consumer research revealed that the removal of smells was a major requirement with many people; however, they found it a very difficult subject to talk about.
>
> This simple fact was one of the discoveries which contributed to the development and eventual launch of Frish lavatory cleaner. The benefits provided by Frish are that it 'Kills germs, cleans stains, smells fresh too'.
>
> Frish was the first major lavatory cleaner to provide this threefold benefit. Within one year of its launch into the UK lavatory cleaner market it became the leader with a share of over 50 per cent.

The requirement is not only to find the new and unfulfilled consumer needs — a major requirement in itself — but also to classify them in terms of significance to the consumer. Are they of real importance or are they merely marginal? Significant new needs may be worthy of a new brand, marginal new needs would normally go towards the relaunching of an existing brand.

There will, of course, be a need for further research to decide whether or not the consumer requirements can be met in practical development and manufacturing terms. The costs involved also have to be fully considered. However, the important first requirement is to highlight the worthwhile marketing opportunity. Once this has been achieved, skill and determination can normally turn it into a business proposition.

> The UK scouring powder market, with brands such as Vim and Ajax, is a long established one. The products within the market are excellent cleaners in many ways and particularly well suited to the houses of the 1940s to 60s. However, in the 1970s the composition of the sinks, hand basins, and baths in many households changed — stainless steel and plastic were introduced and became widely accepted.
>
> With the changes the consumer made clear that she had a new requirement: she needed a product that would 'clean without scratching' her new stainless steel sink or plastic bath. The established scouring powders could not provide this new benefit.
>
> Jif was the first brand to identify the new requirement and to provide the new benefit — Jif's purpose was to 'clean without scratching'.
>
> Introduced nationally in 1974, Jif quickly established a dominant leadership of the liquid scourer market. In the early 1980s the number of UK households buying liquid scourers moved ahead of the number buying powders. Jif continued as a dominant market leader, outselling its nearest competitor by over 2 to 1. Identifying and meeting the marketing opportunity that the new consumer need provided, and doing this ahead of competitors, was clearly a valuable competitive advantage for Lever.

Performance

Most marketing managers, when questioned on competitive advantages, would tend to discuss brand performance. This is to some extent understandable. The exploitation of a performance advantage is readily appreciated; in recent years there have been a number of 'classic' brand performance advantages demonstrated in television advertisements. It is also probable that the majority of businessmen would prefer to compete through performance rather than, for instance, with price.

How should performance be judged? Wherever possible, the judgement should be that of the consumer who is to make the best value decision. Ideally, consumers should be able to notice the product advancement in a 'blind product' test against their normal brand. Product performances which are noticed in this form of test are normally of consequence, and when they are supported by advertising prompting they can become significant. If it is necessary to provide a prompt in the consumer test to get any form of favourable reaction, then the real life result is likely to be more marginal.

In cases where the laboratory has achieved a performance advantage in its test, but this advantage is not appreciated by the consumer as it cannot be experienced easily, the manufacturer may need to enlist the help of a recognised and respected testing authority. The use of the dental authorities in the case of toothpaste has already been mentioned in this respect.

Advertising can play its part to the full when it is given the opportunity to inform the consumer of a significant product advance which can be demonstrated. A persuasive demonstration can be a most effective way of encouraging brand trial, and television advertising is particularly well suited to showing comparative demonstrations.

Many of the product performance changes are marginal, and it can be extremely difficult for the consumer to notice them individually. Bringing a series of marginal changes together can produce significant results. Manufacturers differ in their approach to this situation. Some use the marginal advances as they come from the laboratory, others hold them until they are in a position to make a significant change which is worthy of advertising and promotional investment.

Hitherto, reference has been to the brand product. Brand packaging is included under this heading. Competitive advantages in packaging can be of great significance. The manufacturer who was first with the introduction of plastic containers for washing-up liquids (as against glass bottles) had a marked competitive advantage for a period. The same position applies to the plastic tubes which have been replacing metal tubes in certain markets, and so on.

In terms of getting consumer acceptance of a product development, performance and presentation are very clearly linked. A performance advantage that is capable of clear and simple demonstration to the consumer is normally much more valuable to a manufacturer than one of a similar dimension which is not demonstrable.

'An excellent example of a performance competitive advantage is provided by the Domestos relaunch in 1971.

Domestos competes in the household bleach market. It is a particularly strong bleach and its strength is its main performance lead over other brands. However, as it was very difficult to demonstrate this superiority, many consumers were unaware of it.

In the late 1960s the Lever research and development unit found a means of thickening Domestos. This provided the brand with an important performance competitive advantage – the thicker product remained on lavatory walls and similar areas for much longer than its thinner and weaker rivals and so it was able to perform more effectively.

The thickened product had a further great advantage – its superiority could be demonstrated very clearly in advertising, and in a competitive manner against the thinner bleaches.

Lever was able to obtain patent protection for this development and so its value was further enhanced.

The thicker product was a great help to the Domestos brand through the 1970s. It proved to be a very real competitive advantage and the brand was able to consolidate its position as a dominant market leader and move forward to become one of the most successful brands in the UK.'

However, it is most important to ensure that the product changes do, in fact, bring benefits to the consumer, and that the additional revenue they are expected to bring does outweigh any extra costs involved. Expensive formula changes which provide very marginal advances that can be featured in advertising, but which cannot be appreciated by the consumer, can prove to be a competitive *disadvantage*. Their cost can be beyond their worth.

In markets where consumers are buying and using products frequently they can become very able judges of product formulation performance. If the consumer does not value a new and expensive ingredient and is unwilling to pay for it, then the manufacturer may lose volume, or he may need to reduce his price to hold volume. Beyond this he will have wasted part of his advertising investment.

Price

In many markets price can be a very potent marketing weapon, particularly over the shorter term. It works immediately in the market-place on the value of a brand and, unlike the other key factors in the best value concept, it can be moved rapidly and without undue administrative or technical problems.

However, one manufacturer's move can be followed by all the others in the market within 24 hours or less. If the moves are all of the same proportion the competitive positions within the market would be unchanged. If the move is a price reduction, all would be receiving lower revenues. It follows that considerable care is required in using price competitively.

Price can become a competitive advantage where it is backed by a superior cost performance. If all the competitors in a market, with the exception of firm A, have a product cost of £100 per ton for similar performance products, and firm A also for the same performance, has a product cost of £90 per ton, then firm A has available to it a price competitive advantage of £10 per ton.

A lower price for a product that is not backed by superior cost performance merely means that the manufacturer has chosen to invest in price rather than in, say, service, promotion, or presentation, or in the other avenues for investment which are open to him. Many manufacturers are prepared to use price in this way and it may well be wise for them to do so. However, while a move of this kind may give the manufacturer a price advantage in the market, it will not be a competitive advantage in the terms of the approach outlined above.

A manufacturer may obtain a superior cost performance in two ways: (a) through effective and efficient operation, and (b) through volume.

Effective and efficient operation should apply throughout the business. With direct brand costs it can, for instance, follow a skilful blending of formula ingredients which provides a higher level of performance at a lower cost, or the introduction of packaging which is more effective and yet less costly, and so forth. An approach which first aims to get the desired level of performance, and then concentrates on reducing the cost, can often result in a competitive advantage.

With indirect costs, a lean and efficient administration is much less costly, both in itself and in the additional work it generates, than is the swollen and inefficient one. Within the physical distribution system, cost advantages may be gained by the skilful arrangement of order sizes and delivery journeys. Beyond this, all sections of the business should be reviewed periodically. The profit improvement or cost reduction programmes mounted by many companies to cover indirect expenses (or overhead) can make valuable contributions to a cost advantage under this heading.

It is often difficult for a manufacturer to be sure how his indirect costs compare with those of his competitors. With direct brand costs comparison is easier, as formulas and ingredient costs should be available from product analysis. For indirect costs comparative estimate statements are worth compiling. Details of personnel numbers can usually be obtained, and many other cost factors can be estimated with reasonable accuracy from intelligent observations. The form and type of unit cost reductions which can come from brand volume are discussed in more detail in Chapter 8 on product costs.

Where a manufacturer has a volume advantage—particularly if it is substantial—over his competitors, it is vitally important that it works for him. Right through the operation of the business, from the initial buying to the final selling, comparative unit cost savings should accrue. Savings through volume and efficiency are clearly linked. The more efficient an operator is the more he can save, in absolute terms, as his volume increases.

While a manufacturer continues to hold a dominant position in a market the volume advantage is exclusive to him. The cost savings the volume advantage should bring clearly represent a competitive advantage. In the case of a brand which is a dominant leader of a big volume market the unit cost advantage could be substantial and represent a highly significant competitive advantage.

'In the second half of the 1970s the annual volume of Persil Automatic was in excess of 100,000 tons — a volume more than twice the level of any other UK-produced washing powder brand.

Persil Automatic was manufactured in a modern, well equipped, efficient plant, which concentrated on the production of the brand.

In view of its high volume and effective purchasing policy, the brand had good reason to believe that it was obtaining its raw materials and packaging at very competitive prices — prices which were lower for equivalent quality than those paid by competing brands.

Persil Automatic was a dominant market leader outselling its nearest competitor by over 2 to 1. This meant that it was frequently featured by the grocery trade, often at particularly competitive prices.

Through the late 1970s and into the 80s Persil Automatic clearly had good reason to believe it held an advantage in unit cost terms over its competitors, a position which could have substantiated a real competitive advantage in price.**'**

Presentation

Brand presentation has two major aims, first to inform the consumer of the brand's name, its purpose, its performance standard, and how it can benefit her/him. When appropriate it should also show the brand's price. It should do this in a way which encourages the consumer to try the brand, to put the brand to her own best value test. If the consumer is already a user then the aim is to ensure that there should be continuous retrial.

The second aim of the presentation is to carry out the first requirement in a style and form which help to develop the desired brand personality, or brand image as it is sometimes called.

While the two aims are clearly linked, they are of a different nature and this should be appreciated. The first requirement is particularly concerned with encouraging the consumer to try the brand. For this part of the presentation to pay off for the manufacturer it is essential that the other key factors (ie the purpose, the performance, and the price) measure up as best value with a satisfactory number of consumers. The presentation works on these factors. In effect, it makes them known to the consumers. When the consumer tries the brand she/he must form the view that it represents best value, and come back for a repeat purchase. The repeat purchase is all-important. Without it there can be no future for the brand.

There are many creative skills involved in the presentation of brand purpose and performance characteristics. A brand competitive advantage can clearly come from a highly skilled presentation. However, it is important to appreciate that the highest level of creative skill in presentation will not get repeat purchase without the help of the other key factors. This does not always seem to be understood when the ability of advertising to generate sales is considered. Advertising normally plays a major part in getting the first purchase but to blame advertising for failing to get repeat purchases can be unjust.

The second aim of presentation is concerned with what is, in reality, an attempt to add value to the brand. In the presentation of his brand the manufacturer is bound to make an impression, he will automatically give his brand a personality. He should ensure that it is one that favours the brand's development.

In developing the 'right' personality for his brand the manufacturer will need to use considerable skill. First, he will need to be sure just what is the right personality, and second he should be careful to ensure that what he actually produces is in line with the requirement. Sometimes the feelings and impressions consumers take out of an advertisement differ widely from those intended. Research can help with this requirement but good judgement will be at a premium.

The record shows very clearly that if a market has two brands with the same purpose, performance and price, then the brand personality can be the vital factor in deciding the consumers' best value choice.

> 'The UK soaps, detergent and household cleaner markets have seen a number of outstanding brand presentations which have helped to build competitive advantages.
>
> It is widely agreed that the skilful presentation of Persil, and later Persil Automatic, has given the brands very favourable personalities which have enhanced their value. In particular, the Persil and Persil Automatic advertising, always in a style and tone which is caring and friendly, always well produced, always simple in approach, and always consistent in its message, has been able to command a conspicuous position within the field of washing powder advertising.
>
> Fairy Liquid has been the most successful UK dishwashing liquid. Its brand strength has centred on its high level performance and its mildness. Over the years its presentation has always followed a distinctive style – a style and a tone which have emphasized the mildness benefit.
>
> Ariel was the first enzymatic washing powder in national distribution in the UK. Enzymes are chemical ingredients which are very effective in removing certain stains from fabrics, and they work particularly well when used in a soak. The television advertising which introduced Ariel to many consumers in 1968-70 featured a comparison of the performance of Ariel and a non-enzymatic powder in stain removal in a soak situation. This outstanding performance demonstration definitely acted to enhance the aura of efficiency which was an important part of the Ariel brand personality.
>
> The main benefit supplied by Comfort, the UK's leading fabric softener, is softness. The Comfort brand advertisements have always featured this, and softness is conveyed not only in the message but also in the style of presentation. This skilful presentation has certainly helped Comfort to maintain the dominant leadership of its market. '

In those markets where the purchase decision is strongly emotional presentation can clearly have a more marked effect on the buying decision. In the cosmetics market, for instance, presentation in its widest form, including package design, is often of particular significance to the consumers' appraisal.

Putting an accurate value to this form of competitive advantage is indeed difficult. The advantage normally takes time to develop, and it would be foolhardy to count on it until it is established. It is certainly not advisable to include it in strategy forecasts before it has been developed.

The value of a well constructed brand personality often becomes most apparent when a market enters a mature stage. In the absence of any major new purpose or performance introductions, the established personality tends to remain unchallenged.

Evaluating a competitive advantage

The competitive advantage should be at the centre of planning to exploit the marketing opportunity. The competitive advantage should be a key factor within the operations which are mounted in the market-place. It should be at the centre of the manufacturer's main effort, and vital to his investment plans. It follows that he should be completely confident that the competitive advantage he has developed, and proposes to use, is big and strong enough to carry through successfully the particular job he assigns to it.

Each competitive advantage should be assessed realistically. Where the advantage is one of superior product performance then consumer research can clearly be very helpful, and a worthwhile measure of the consumers' view of the performance advance should be possible. If it is intended to adjust the brand's price to help pay for the advance, it is worth testing the consumer's willingness to pay the additional money to ensure that the proposed performance/price balance is sound.

In many cases it will be extremely difficult to value a particular competitive advantage. Nevertheless an effort should be made to get at least a rough check on the value. This is an area where it is very easy for enthusiasm to take over. Enthusiasm based on ignorance can prove very costly.

Once established, it is important to *protect* the competitive advantage. Can it be exclusive for six months, one year, two years, or ten years? Clearly, the extent of the protection available to a particular competitive advantage will greatly affect its value.

CHAPTER 3

Market Leadership

It is a fact that by far the majority of consumer product companies make the bulk of their profit from those markets where their brands hold a commanding share position.

Taking this one stage further, it is also a fact that the dominant brand leader of a market is invariably the brand which makes a major part of the profit generated within that particular market. The stronger the leadership the bigger the profit earning differential between the leader and the other competing brands.

This does, of course, refer to a brand leadership established through brand strength and effective business management, and not to a short-term leadership held as the result of a period of very heavy advertising and promotional investment, or from an extensive short-term price reduction.

To have one, and preferably more than one, dominant brand market leader within his portfolio of brands should be the aim of any manufacturer who wishes to enjoy real success in the branded goods business.

The brand leader's strength

The reasons for the brand leader's strength, in terms of profit making, are not difficult to appreciate. They are, in the main linked to the superior volume the brand generates:

1. Lower unit cost of production. Higher production volume provides for the use of large scale, effective capital equipment. The fixed costs of this equipment are spread over a larger

number of units, and so the unit cost of production should be lower.

(Where a competitor has a higher total level of production from a market, but does not have the brand leader, his unit costs may be lower than the leader's. However, even in these circumstances the brand leader will tend to have fewer machine changes, and other additional costs of this kind.)

2. The higher volumes should provide the leader with greater purchasing power, so the equivalent raw material and packaging for the leader should be purchased at a lower cost per unit than they will be for any competing brand. The leader can often be in the privileged position of having a brand formula containing higher quality ingredients and packaging but, because of his buying power, he can obtain them at a lower price per unit than his competitors have to pay for an inferior quality. The benefit of the market leader's purchasing power is likely to extend well beyond raw and package materials—it can also include such factors as media advertising and promotion.

3. What are often termed the 'general overhead costs' of running the business—the Accounting Department, the Marketing Department, General Management etc—should not be any higher for the leader than they are for his competitors. Again, because of his higher volume, the leader should have a lower unit cost.

4. Research and development expenditure will be essential to ensure that the brand advances in terms of performance and presentation. The leader can have a lower R and D expenditure per unit and yet make a larger total investment than his competitors.

5. The leader can, if he wishes, have a lower unit cost for advertising yet at the same time a higher total expenditure than any competing brand. In this way he can maintain a greater impact with the consumer than his competitors, and achieve this at a lower unit cost.

6. The brand leader tends to get stronger support from the wholesale and retail trade. Consumer demand requires that the leading brand should be stocked and priced competitively. In effect, the leader's bargaining power with the trade is usually much stronger than his competitor's.

This can be a major advantage for the leader. First, it means that he is stocked—and sometimes he is the only brand stocked—in the many small stores that are not of consequence individually, but which can be when taken together. Second, the leader frequently gets a superior shelf position, stronger feature, and a price advantage in the bigger stores. In terms of cost differential, the advantage the brand market leader gets through the distributive trade is generally very substantial.

Where a market has become segmented, that is, around the main volume sector a number of specialized sectors have developed, many of the market leader's advantages will also be enjoyed by the segment leaders over *their* competitors. However, the advantages are unlikely to be at anywhere near the same level, as the volumes concerned tend to be appreciably lower.

Can I develop a brand market leader?

It follows that, as the position of dominant brand market leader can be a very profitable one, attaining it should figure prominently in the development of the business strategy.

When he considers his brands and his brand development projects, the strategist should ask himself four leading questions:

1. Have I got a brand that is a dominant brand market leader?

   If the answer is 'Yes', then the follow-up question should be, 'What action should I take to ensure that the brand stays dominant?'

2. Have I got a brand that is a brand market leader?

   If the answer is 'Yes', then the follow-up question should be, 'What action should I take to make the brand a dominant brand market leader?'

   This may mean introducing a new product formulation to provide a better performance. Possibly a new creative presentation in the brand's advertising may be required or a new promotion which markedly increases penetration. It may require the more positive use of price.

   The basic point here is that a brand market leader is normally a very worthwhile asset. A dominant brand market leader is invariably a major profit contributor, and an even better asset.

   Positive thinking as to how a brand leader can be developed to become a dominant leader should be a prominent part of the business strategy formulation process.

3. Do I have a brand that, although not a market leader, could with the right approach and with suitable investment backing become one?

   For instance, a brand that has a high quality position in the market can occasionally come through to leadership. It may be necessary to increase the advertising and promotional support, and to adjust the price and increase consumer penetration. To

provide a sound cost base for the move it may be necessary to
carry out a brand 'value analysis'.
4. Do I have a brand research project which is showing particularly
    encouraging test results—results which could mean that the
    brand would be a strong candidate for market leadership if the
    test results were repeated in the market-place?

    Any project which can produce this level of result in test
    should be a strong candidate for the resources necessary to
    bring it forward to the market-place.

If the organization has a brand, or a new brand project, which shows
signs of having the strength and ability to move forward to market
leadership, then the brand and the proposals backing it should receive
very close attention. Of course the size of the market and the stage of
development it has reached should be important factors within the
proposals—a bid for leadership of a growth market would normally be
more attractive than a bid for leadership of a mature or declining market.

How much is the position of a brand market leader worth?

In considering the above questions, and the investment that may be
required to bring about the desired changes in brand position, it is worthwhile carrying out an exercise to assess how much brand market leadership could be worth to the business.

The calculation is a difficult one to make. Detailed competitive actions
are not easy to forecast with any high degree of confidence. Nevertheless,
a reasonable indication of the worth of leadership should be possible, and
it is important to appreciate that the position is likely to be worth
roughly the same amount to any competitor.

The 'worth of leadership' figures can contribute to business management in a number of ways, two of which are particularly important within
strategy formulation. They can demonstrate the ongoing value of the
'prize' that leadership should bring. They can also give an indication of
how much it could be worth investing to obtain leadership. Sometimes
the very high level of initial expenditure required can be almost frighten-
ing and only when it is viewed in terms of the return that is possible over
the long term can it be appreciated fully. Of course, the returns only come
when market leadership is attained. There is unlikely to be a major prize
for second place.

When a brand is already the market leader, details of the profit contribution it makes will be readily available. The level of contribution should
bring home to the strategist how much it is worth investing to ensure
that the leadership is retained.

When your brand market leader is attacked you must strike back vigorously. The challenger must know that you mean business, and that any attempt to take your market will be a long and very costly operation for him. This is a golden rule. If the attacker moves first into a test market, the strength of the defence may scare him off a move on a national basis. A study of the profit contributions the brand leader makes should help to put the necessary defence expenditures into perspective.

> 'Attaining leadership in a truly competitive market is never easy. When the management of a company makes market leadership one of its key strategic objectives and is prepared to work skilfully, vigorously, and with enthusiasm over a period of time, it can be done.
>
> Market leadership was one of the key strategic objectives of the Lever UK company through the 1970s and into the early 80s. The company made some progress in meeting this objective. At the time Lever competed actively in seven major markets and company leadership was as follows:

Market	1968-69 Leading company	1982-83 Leading company
1. Washing powders	Proctor & Gamble	Lever
2. Washing-up liquids	Proctor & Gamble	Proctor & Gamble
3. Toilet soaps	Proctor & Gamble / Lever	Lever
4. Fabric softeners	*Proctor & Gamble / Lever	Lever
5. Household bleach	Lever	Lever
6. Lavatory cleaners	Reckitt & Colman	Lever
7. Scourers (powder and liquid)	Colgate	Lever

> *In 1968-69 the UK fabric softener market was a very small one in its early development period.
>
> The 'one that got away', the washing-up liquid market, was clearly a most frustrating one for Lever! But in the dishwasher powder market – small in 1982-83 but expected to be a big market in the longer term – never was the leader.
>
> Through the period Lever's strategic objectives were twofold – first, to achieve the appropriate market leaderships with a view to ensuring longer-term profitability and, second, to provide an increasing level of trading profit and cash in the short term. The company was able to meet both objectives.'

There will be occasions when, after detailed study, it may not be good strategy to go for the leadership position, even when a brand with a strong potential is available. A small business may not have the resource available to carry through the total operation necessary. There will be considerable risk involved and this may be too high for the business to carry. It may be wiser to continue to make a 'reasonable' level of profit sitting in the third or fourth position within the main market, or to occupy a more specialist 'niche' which provides some degree of protection from competitive attack. A large business, competing in many markets, may have higher priorities for its limited resources. There may be a case for waiting and making an attack at a more appropriate time. There can be other valid reasons for not taking action.

Nevertheless, the positive reasoning and detailed consideration involved in the evaluation and planning will not be wasted. The competitive market war is not just one battle. It is, in effect, a continuous series of battles. The planning for a brand to make progress in its market should therefore be a continuous effort. New opportunities to make real progress are always available. Sometimes they may appear almost by accident, but in most cases they need to be sought after and developed skilfully.

Finally, it is important to note that many of the recent trends, in consumer markets throughout the world, are strengthening the position of the brand market leader. The highly automated and effective production equipment now available can, when provided with high volume, bring exceptionally low unit production costs — but the high volume is essential if such an investment is to show its real worth. The rapid development of the strong and well managed retail chains means that brand strength with the consumer has become of even greater consequence in trade negotiations; in particular the brand market leader is the one best equipped to withstand the competition of the distributor brands. The rising cost of advertising also tends to benefit the market leader. Developments of this kind all mean that the importance, and the value, of brand market leadership is increasing.

CHAPTER 4

The Market

The market and its development are the key to sales volume. The business gets its revenue from the market through its sales, and without satisfactory revenue it will fail. For success the business must win in the market. An acute appreciation of the market, its potential, and its development is basic to the formulation of a sound business strategy.

The various subjects with which the strategist should be concerned in strategy formulation are discussed in this and the following chapters. The subjects are not necessarily discussed in their order of importance, and yet it is appropriate that 'the market' should be among the first to be considered.

The market, its size, and its movement is a vitally important consideration. While a number of the subjects discussed in this book may not apply to certain businesses, at certain times, the importance of the market must apply to all businesses at all times.

The market—a definition

The dictionary tells us that a market is a place where buying and selling take place, and this is the meaning normally attributed to the term.

In this book 'the market' will be used to describe the volume of business transacted by these buyers and sellers, this volume to be expressed in whatever terms are considered to be most appropriate for the particular occasion. Thus, the market for washing powder in the United Kingdom at a given time may be, for instance, 400,000 tons weight, or £400 million value, or 20 million packets, the measure to vary, depending upon the subject matter and the specific requirement.

The elementary, but very important, basic point is that markets are made up of people who become customers, and the extent and value of a market is determined by the willingness of customers to spend their money on the brands and products in the market.

Within the formulation of the business strategy a number of key questions on the market will need to be asked and answered. The answers will not always be specific and definite. However, it is important to establish a clear indication of probable movements and timings.

What is the size and potential of the market?

After considering the geographical extent, and 'width', the manufacturer should prepare estimates of the size of the market in which he currently competes. This may be a world market, a market covering one continent, or a market covering just one country. It is the market which he views as his, and the one where he actively takes part in the competitive battle. For instance, a major company may have a position to maintain in, say, the European market and develops its strategic planning accordingly. However, the management of its West German subsidiary company would reason in terms of the West German market. In this instance the strategic objectives of the subsidiary would need to be set within the wider objectives of the parent company.

Strategy is concerned with the future, and so the potential, of the market, and within it the potential of the various segments is particularly important. However, knowing where the market is *today*, and how it arrived in that position, is also of significance, and should provide the base from which the various projections of future developments are made.

For the majority of consumer product markets research data is available which provides a clear indication of the size and make-up of the current market. Data giving market shares held by the various brands competing is available, and from this data the manufacturer can build up a picture of the main market, and of the various segments within it.

The absolute level of tonnage, or value, of the current market is most valuable information to have, and in view of the importance of the market potential, much of the data behind the absolute level of market size is of consequence. For instance, details of product penetration, and levels of per home consumption, can often provide important indications of growth potential.

Arriving at an estimate of this market potential, and of the potential of the various segments within the market, is a key judgement decision within the strategy formulation process. It is also most important to be right in judging the timing of any market development.

Getting these estimates right is so important that the strategist should be prepared to use marketing and consumer research in its widest form to provide him with guidance.

Studies of comparable markets in countries with more advanced economies may be helpful, particularly where the climate and the way of life are very similar. Consumer behavioural studies of various sections of the community, and detailed studies of the so-called 'opinion formers' may possibly have a contribution to make.

It is always possible that changes in the law or the environment of a country can have a marked effect on the pace and extent of a market development. Sometimes environmental changes will be discussed and planned within the community well in advance of their implementation. When this happens the strategist should make appropriate allowances in his estimates. At other times the position may be much more fluid and special contingency estimates of the markets may be necessary.

The current size and the potential of the market are particularly important in that they can provide a guide to the profit that should be available to a successful operator today, and into the future. A big company can incur a very high level of opportunity cost if it concentrates its resources on a market which later proves to be very small. Equally, the smaller operator needs to be aware of the resources he will require, and the competition he may encounter, should he move into a very large market. Normally the smaller and more specialized markets, or market segments, are better suited to the smaller operators.

'The UK fabric softener market contains an outstanding example of the importance of getting a judgement decision on market potential 'right'.

The fabric softener markets in the USA, and in parts of Continental Europe, made considerable progress through the mid-1960s. At this time both Procter & Gamble and Lever moved brands (Downy and Comfort respectively) into parts of the UK market.

However, despite the major advertising and promotional support the brands enjoyed during this early period the UK market growth was very disappointing. It is probable that both Downy and Comfort lost considerable sums of money at the time.

In the late 1960s P & G withdrew Downy from the market. Lever considered withdrawing Comfort as well, but decided against it. Lever's reasoning was that the financial losses the brand had incurred were behind it; the important consideration for the company was the market potential and the need to secure a strong brand position within it.

For some four years Comfort was the only major brand in the UK fabric softener market. During this time the market began to show real growth and Comfort was able to secure a dominant lead position within it. In

1973-74 P & G re-entered the market with a brand named Lenor, and Colgate also entered with Softlan.

The UK market continued to grow rapidly through the second half of the 1970s and into the 80s. Despite a number of counter-attacks by P & G, Colgate, and other manufacturers, Comfort remained a dominant market leader throughout the period, outselling its nearest competitor by a margin of over 2 to 1. The UK fabric softener market is likely to become one of the biggest UK grocery markets. It will probably move into maturity in the 1990s and Comfort is well positioned to hold a dominant and what should be a highly profitable position, through this stage and on into the market decline. **'**

What is the geographical extent of the market?

Do we compete in the United Kingdom market, or should we be reasoning in terms of a world market of which the UK is a relatively small part? Or is the EEC the market? Or the United States and Canada? It will be important to establish the geographical extent of the market in which the business is primarily concerned.

It has been claimed that one of the reasons why the Japanese came to dominate the world motor-cycle market is that, from the beginning, they thought in terms of a world market. They equipped themselves with the plant and machinery to meet the volume of a world market, and so had relatively low unit production costs. Their competitors, in the UK for instance, reasoned in terms of the local market only. The UK producers' volume horizons were much lower than the Japanese. They did not regard the extensive investment in plant and equipment as sensible, and so their unit costs were very much higher. Eventually they lost the market to their Japanese competitors.

There is no doubt that other factors contributed to the spectacular achievements of the Japanese motor-cycle manufacturers, but their appreciation of the geographical extent of the market was clearly crucial.

This question of market extent has become of greater importance to European manufacturers over recent years. The development of the European Common Market and the removal of tariff barriers between member countries has meant that, in many instances, their market now extends to the whole of Europe and is not limited to the country where their manufacturing plant is centred.

This does not mean that a manufacturer should no longer reason, for instance, in terms of a market for West Germany, or for France, or for the United Kingdom. It does mean that in his reasoning he must be aware that there is a bigger market available to him and to his competitors, and he must keep this fact very much in his mind when considering both his own and his competitors' current and potential volume.

Where volume is one of the key factors in unit product costs, the extent of the market is vitally important. The major consideration may be to have the highest volume production level for Europe concentrated in one plant, and the sales levels held within each individual country may be of less importance. Much will depend upon the significance of product unit costs, and on how the additional cost of distribution compares with the savings obtainable from the higher production volumes.

What is the width of the market?

Are we right to reason in terms of a butter market? Or should we include the various margarines etc and reason in terms of a total fat or spread market? Where products are interchangeable in the eyes of the consumer then it is important to keep this very much in mind and, as appropriate, to reason in terms of a total market. For instance, where the potential for margarine volume is linked directly with the comparative price for butter, it would clearly be necessary for the margarine manufacturer to keep in mind the effect of higher margarine consumption on the demand, and therefore also the price, of butter.

However, this does not mean that for much of his planning the margarine supplier should not reason in terms of the margarine section of the total market. Within this section there may be considerable potential available to him irrespective of the butter position. It is important that he should use whichever definition and measure of the market that is appropriate for the occasion.

Market trends and the pace of market movement

All markets go through three phases of development. They have a growth period, which is followed by a period of maturity when the market is static, and finally there is the period of decline. It is vitally important that the strategist should be clear about the position of the markets in which he competes.

The classic statement of strategy has much to recommend it: 'Get in early, dominate the growth stage, and then ride through the maturity and the decline—you may have to invest heavily during the growth stage, but if you achieve a dominant lead then, your profits during the two final stages of the market should be most rewarding.'

During the growth stage there are new consumers continually entering the market. New customers to attract, new people sampling for the first time, new minds which are not necessarily already firm or biased in their approach to particular brands. This is normally the most opportune time for the manufacturer to build his market share. Although his total expenditure may need to be high, the cost per new convert is likely to be lower than at any other stage in the market development.

During the growth stage of a market the risk associated with the installation of new capacity is normally lower. There is usually a feeling of buoyancy among traders dealing in it. It is at this stage that the foundations of a brand establishment are more easily laid and developed.

As market maturity takes over, the task of establishing a new entry tends to be much more difficult. Consumers have become 'regular buyers', firmly attached to particular brands, manufacturing plants are established, and the risk associated with erecting a new plant can be extensive.

In a declining market, replacing an established competitor can be an extremely difficult operation. Consumers tend to be older, regular users, whose habits and tastes are firmly based, and they are less likely to change.

Clearly it is very important that the strategist should know what is happening to his markets now, and even more so, what is likely to happen to them in the future. The need is not only to have a clear view of the movement in terms of volume or value, or whatever measure is appropriate, but also of the pace and timing of the movement. Again, this is an area where marketing research, in its widest form and application, has a major role to play in guiding the strategist.

> ❛The UK fabric washing market provides an interesting example of market movement through growth to maturity and then into decline. It also provides evidence that there is no set time period for the growth stage, for maturity, or for decline.
>
> During the early part of the present century for many people a hard soap was the accepted product for washing fabrics. The branded hard soap market was a growth one for a period of some 40 years, before 1890 to about 1930. It was in maturity from, say, 1930 to 1945, and then moved into decline. There was still a UK hard soap market, a small one, in 1983.
>
> The UK high suds washing powder market was in growth through a period of some 40 years from, say, 1920 to 1960. For the next 15 years or so it was in maturity; then around 1975 it started to decline and this will probably continue for some 20 to 25 years.
>
> The UK low suds washing powder market began its growth stage around 1970 and this will probably last for some 25 years. Maturity and decline will follow – just how long each stage will last is an important question for the future.
>
> Fairy hard soap won the battle for leadership of the hard soap market in

the 1930s. The brand was owned by the Thomas Hedley Company which was purchased by Procter & Gamble in 1930. Fairy hard soap has enjoyed over 40 years of what must have been very profitable decline.

Persil was well set to win the high suds market leadership battle. However, in 1969 P & G obtained a breakthrough with Ariel, the enzymatic powder, and so the two brands (Persil and Ariel) are set to share the maturity and decline of the market. It should be very profitable for both.

The UK low suds washing powder market promises to be the biggest of all – it could reach a level as high as 600,000 tons. As the market moves toward maturity Persil Automatic is well placed for a dominant leadership position. Maturity and decline should be very profitable indeed for the dominant leader of a market of this size.

,

Development within the market

Markets can develop of their own accord (often termed 'natural development'). Of course, it is always possible that this natural development may be hastened by promotional and other similar pressures.

There are two ways in which a market can develop: (a) growth in the main market, and (b) by segmentation. It is possible, particularly during the growth stage, for a market to experience growth in both ways.

With the advance of the main market the concern is with progress in the demand for those products which deliver the basic purpose as required by the majority of consumers. This development would normally come during the early stages of market growth. It can often take place when there is natural growth even though the economy of the country concerned is in decline.

From a strategy viewpoint, the development of segmentation within a market is of particular interest. Segmentation may take the form of price or of a series of product or packaging developments which bring the consumer specific performance benefits.

Segmentation frequently comes as a market begins to move towards maturity. A more prosperous consumer society is also often associated with a rise in segmentation – with additional funds available consumers are prepared to pay for the added extras.

As we shall see later, the exploitation of a particular segment of the market can often be one of the more successful and profitable means of market entry where the main market has a dominant leader. Unless a brand has a very significant competitive advantage it is rarely sound strategy to take on the dominant leader in a head-on confrontation. Also, a move towards a particular segment can often help a brand that is struggling as number two or three behind a strong leader.

The strategist needs to anticipate these market developments and opportunities and to make his plans accordingly.

With the development of the main market there is normally a period during the growth stage when a clear downward movement in price will bring a strong market rise in volume.

Reading the progress of the main market with accuracy during its growth stage, and plotting the timing of the progress accurately, is a key requirement. With the volume increases should come cost and price reductions, and these should be followed by further volume rises. Good strategists know when it is most advantageous to lead this process, and when the process is nearing its final stages (ie when the market is moving out of growth). Of course, it will also be important to have the necessary production facilities available to meet the volume increases.

With the development of segmentation the need is to know the direction, the probable strength, and the timing of the movement of the various segments.

With both of these market developments, ie both the main market and segmentation, strategists need to be able to judge with some accuracy the effect on the market movement that varying levels of advertising and promotional investment may bring. In a market with low penetration, the various sampling type promotions can be particularly effective. Strong and persuasive advertising can also stimulate consumer sampling. In the field of segmentation, advertising is normally essential to help spur on a consumer need which has possibly been dormant or underdeveloped.

From a strategy viewpoint it is important that adequate investment is available for testing the market reaction to given levels of advertising and promotional support, and in price adjustments. If a market opportunity exists it must be highlighted and, as appropriate, exploited.

Mature and declining markets

Markets can, of course, pass through maturity and go into decline rapidly. New product developments, possibly bringing outstanding new consumer benefits, may quickly render existing markets out of date.

It can be argued that a market is either a growth market or it is in decline. This is logical, but there is normally a period when a market will move up and down a number of times around a base level before a definite trend can be seen.

The decline of an established market is usually gradual. Hard soaps did not disappear immediately following the launch of the first soap powders. Indeed hard soaps are still sold, over 50 years after the first soap powder introduction. However, fast decline is possible and it has been known for a market to disappear rapidly.

Movements of this kind should affect strategy formulation. Again the requirement is to forecast accurately and well in advance the movement of the market. With the forecast there will need to be a clear indication of the timing of the movement.

The market life

There is a view that all markets have a limited life span, and that the three stages already mentioned—growth, maturity, and decline—are common to all markets.

The record shows this view to be correct. However, when its advocates go on to allocate some predetermined time-scale to both the total life and to the stages within it, then the record would appear to disagree strongly.

It is quite logical that there should be no consistency. The development of new technologies, the rapid economic development of the country, changes in personal and social values, and other similar factors tend to determine the rates of growth and decline. The factors work at different rates in the different markets, with an added variation from country to country. There is clearly no set 'life' for any particular market or type of market.

Judging correctly the time and rate of market movement from growth through maturity to decline, in those markets with which he is concerned, is one of the most important judgements the manufacturer will need to make in the course of his strategy formulation.

It is always possible that a manufacturer may prolong the life of a market. Indeed, one of the skills of a successful operator rests in his ability to prolong the life of a market where he has a dominant position. Normally he would do this by re-staging his brand from time to time, keeping its design and packaging contemporary, and skilfully managing its price.

CHAPTER 5

Economic Climate

The business opportunities which emerge in a buoyant economic climate are normally readily appreciated. Less obvious, but equally important to recognize, are the opportunities which can arise during a period of economic recession.

The current and future economic climate of a country where a company is engaged in business is obviously important in strategy formulation. Economic conditions affect such factors as the number of houses built, the number of motor cars owned, and so forth. Developments of this kind are clearly important to manufacturers in planning their business strategy.

Within the economic scene, the freedom of exchange rates can also provide considerable opportunity. In 1980 the US dollar stood at approximately $2.40 to the pound sterling. In 1984 the rate was nearer $1.20. For the UK business the cost of an acquisition in the USA would have doubled between these years, without any change in the condition of the company to be purchased.

For US companies wishing to buy into the UK, however, the reverse timing would have applied. Quite obviously, the accurate forecasting of exchange rates can be a significant factor within a successful business strategy.

A buoyant economic outlook

Economic forecasts for any particular country or for a group of countries may be developed within the business or be purchased from specialist consultants. They should cover in considerable detail the whole range of government fiscal activity, taxation changes, population trends, consumer spending, housing completions, plant construction activity etc. The forecasts are only as good as they are accurate and, of course, their accuracy can never be guaranteed. In most cases they will provide reliable general indications, rather than specifically accurate data.

For the majority of manufacturers the important requirement is to know when a period of economic buoyancy is coming, to have an indication of its extent, and when it is likely to end.

Within a buoyant economic forecast the need is to give special attention to those factors which can materially affect the business. A rational approach is to concentrate first on the ultimate customer, ie the consumer, and to consider in detail those forecasts which are likely to affect him or her.

The movement of consumer spending power is clearly important: both in quantity and quality. There is a big difference in strategy planning terms between a small number of people becoming wealthy, and a large number of people becoming just a little wealthy. 'How are the more wealthy spending their money?', 'Will this trend move through the whole population in the course of the next one, two or three years?', are the types of questions which are relevant.

It is often important to study countries where the level of consumer prosperity has already developed. There can be no guarantee that the development elsewhere will follow exactly the same pattern, but trends can often be similar particularly if factors such as climate and geography are roughly the same.

The aim should be to use the forecasts to pin-point business opportunities. For instance, as a consumer's spending power grows she may buy a washing machine for the first time. What type of machine is she likely to buy? Do the machines require a special type of washing powder? If the right answers come, then a marketing opportunity for a washing powder which meets the requirements of consumers who own the new machines may be available. Further analysis should indicate the size of the opportunity.

Similar opportunities can apply in other markets. Consumers tend to become a little more adventurous in good times. Higher employment levels bring a higher degree of confidence.

In this form of forecasting, a sound judgement of the timing of the major moves is most important. Markets do not remain buoyant for ever. They tend to have their periods of rapid growth and also slower periods, and judging the timing of the change of pace accurately is generally a key requirement for success. The economics of the country can often give an indication of the likely rate and time of any movement.

Building plants, and erecting production facilities, is usually more expensive during the 'boom' part of an economic development. Demand is high, builders are busy, and so prices rise. Strategists should aim to provide for the plant etc as the market starts its upward swing. Probably the most costly of all positions is to build the plant as the economic cycle is topping out. Land and building costs are high and the plant is likely to run at low capacity as demand levels fall.

The view that a buoyant economic climate provides the ideal time to launch a new brand is normally correct; however, the movement of the market within which the brand is to be launched is probably even more important.

Economic buoyancy will certainly help with traders as well as consumers. During buoyant periods traders are more willing to take a chance with a new brand; in effect, they are prepared to take a slightly higher degree of risk. For similar reasons, a buoyant economic period tends to be an opportune time to launch a premium brand, one aimed above the major market sector.

A depressed economic outlook

As with a buoyant period, it is important for manufacturers to know that a recession is coming and be able to plan accordingly.

In a recession sales volume is more difficult to get, and to hold. Trading profit is more difficult to earn, cash is in short supply and expensive to obtain.

The first move in strategy planning for a recession is to safeguard the position of the business to ensure survival, and that will mean ensuring an adequate supply of cash. This may involve borrowing in advance, or at least arranging the borrowing facility as required.

In the market-place established brands should perform well. They are relatively free of risk for either the trader or the consumer. It is not a time for expensive and high risk ventures which are invariably heavy consumers of cash and other resources.

The whole business should be run on a 'batten down the hatches' basis; all sensible economies in operation should be made. High risk ventures should be shelved, and resources concentrated on existing brands. In particular, cash resources should be harboured.

The opportunities in a recession are likely to come to the manufacturer who has a satisfactory level of cash available. Some companies will find themselves very short of liquid resources and unable to pay the high prices required by the money markets. Such businesses and their brands will be vulnerable.

In the market place the brands will be vulnerable in that they will not have the resources to withstand a heavy competitive attack on their market position. Companies will be vulnerable in that their trading profit will fall, they will have liquidity problems, and they will be a target for a take-over attack.

Analysing the markets, deciding which brands and which companies are vulnerable, which are worthy of attention, and what is the best way to attack, is a most important part of strategy planning for a recession. It will be vital to have a strong base from which to launch the operation. To become over-extended during the course of the attack will invite action from a predator.

The aim should be to come out of the recession as a much stronger business. This may require an ability to survive with a low level of trading profit as investment is made in market share development. An adequate flow of cash will be needed, and in the case of a public company, an ability to hold the quoted share price at a reasonable level.

Many countries have been troubled by high inflation in recent years. Inflation should be a consideration within business strategy. The normal problems encountered by manufacturers during an inflationary period centre on the fact that while their selling prices may be adequate to cover historical brand costs, they are not high enough to recover replacement costs. The result is that the business requires a continuous inflow of new capital to finance its operations. If the business sales volume is increasing, the need for the additional capital will be even more acute.

The answer would appear to be quite simple: increase selling prices more rapidly. The dominant market leader may take the lead in this respect should he wish to do so, but for weaker brands the market really sets the price. They would find it very difficult, and possibly very costly, to make an independent price increase.

It follows that the strong brand leader, if he is an effective and efficient operator, can exert considerable pressure on the other brands in his market by not moving his prices during an inflationary period. In effect, he takes his real prices down.

It cannot be overstated that in a period of recession the ability to generate a satisfactory supply of cash is crucial.

Exchange rates

Earlier in this chapter we mentioned the way exchange rates can markedly affect the investment decisions, and therefore the business strategy, of an international company. With the multi-national companies it is usual for the parent or home business to be a public company, and to be quoted on one of the major stock exchanges. To this parent company, its dividend policy and financial record will be very important, and have a major effect on its share price.

However, the multi-national's operating companies around the world are usually private companies and do not have a stock market quote. For them the dividend is merely a means of passing money home to the parent, and it is unlikely in itself to affect the Stock Exchange price of the parent.

This means that if the multi-national is skilled in forecasting exchange rates it can gain considerable advantage in deciding just when to remit funds back to the parent from a subsidiary, and when to let the subsidiary use the funds for local investment.

This has been very much in evidence between the USA and the UK through the relatively short period from 1979 to 1984, during which time the exchange rate moved from $2.40 to $1.20. Dividends remitted from the UK to the USA by US companies have literally halved in dollar exchange value over the period. On this basis the early period was one for taking dividends home to the USA, and the later years for buying shares in UK markets. For a UK-based parent company the periods for investing in the USA and for withdrawing dividends should be reversed.

CHAPTER 6

Research and Development

'Research is too much of a gamble for us, we don't have a research laboratory. We do have a very good development section which is extremely fast on its feet. We have managed very well.'

This statement, or one very similar to it, will often be heard at conferences or other business gatherings where the subject of research investment is up for discussion.

This approach is often taken by smaller companies, and it can, in certain circumstances, be a sensible policy.

Some research investment is of a high risk nature and in this respect can be considered a form of gamble. A development department which can copy innovations very rapidly as they appear on test or in the market, together with a good operating performance, will often produce good results.

However, for a company that has mastered the management of its research investment, the investment can be one of its main approaches to obtaining a truly significant competitive advantage for its brands in the market. This applies particularly to the large international company, for the results of an effective research investment in its base country can be quickly exported worldwide.

The term 'research' is normally used to denote the original laboratory work involved in developing new products or processes. It usually falls into one of two categories: basic or applied.

Basic research concentrates on the more fundamental issues of scientific discovery. *Applied research* works on the known developments coming from basic research. Many of the universities are deeply involved in basic research. So too are a large number of manufacturers, in particular the major international companies. Applied research is conducted in many universities and also very widely among manufacturing companies. Basic research discovered the synthetic detergent, while applied research has developed its performance with the introduction of new ingredients and more advanced processing.

'Development' is often used to cover what is really an aspect of applied research. 'Development' bridges the gap between research and the consumer. It takes the work of applied research and forms and packages it in a manner which is acceptable to the consumer. Development is concerned with both the product and the packaging, and also with the processing of the product. When a project leaves the research department it may not be suitable for high volume production, and development will be concerned with what is known as the 'scaling up'.

While a business may exist without using research directly, some form of development unit is probably essential for every manufacturing business.

Should we have a research department?

The first question to be asked is: 'Are the markets in which we compete greatly influenced by research developments?' If the answer is 'No' then research investment may not be appropriate. If the answer is 'Yes', then follow-up questions are necessary: 'What is the competitive position?', 'Are there a number of major international companies already strongly established in the research business and competing in the market?', 'Would I be wise to challenge these companies on the main front or is there a specialist sector where I can get research results which will give me a competitive advantage?'

An important question which will be considered later is: 'Would I be better advised to drop the research idea and enlarge my development section?'

If he decides to establish a research department then the manufacturer will need to face certain facts. A very sizeable investment will be necessary. Well qualified personnel will be essential and they will need to be adequately serviced. And if the department is to be concerned with basic research then the investment is likely to be very long term. Basic research projects can often take many years from the researcher's initial germ of an idea to practical use in the market-place. It is also important to face the fact that research projects will not always be successful; in practice the failure rate can be very high.

Of course, it is not essential for a manufacturer to have a series of research projects covering every market in which his brands compete. He can cover just one or two markets and rely on his development effort to keep his brands competitive in others.

It is possible to buy specific research resources and effort from universities and commercial research companies. In this way a manufacturer can overcome a particular problem without incurring the heavy costs of establishing a research unit which could be with him as a fixed cost for a long time.

Managing a research department for results

A high degree of skill is needed to manage a research department which consistently produces good results, that is a department which produces a flow of innovations, a number of which bring either new brands or a significant move forward for existing brands.

The results coming from a research unit are certainly not necessarily linked directly to the level of investment made in it. It is noticeable that some companies are good at research management, while others, including particularly large investors, get relatively poor results.

There are a number of key guidelines which can contribute to success in research management:

1. Getting good people. Good people are important throughout the organization; in research they are just that more important.

    A very high academic standard, while most welcome, is not the only consideration. Really good researchers seem to have an ability which enables them to follow a systematic approach yet also contribute a high degree of creativity.

    It is necessary that the researchers, particularly the very good ones, receive a satisfactory level of resource backing.

    Badly managed, research can become a major consumer of very expensive labour. In certain respects, the research process is highly labour intensive. Computers, high speed measuring devices and equipment of this kind can help, but the pace is set by the researchers.

2. It is of vital importance that the research effort should be skilfully directed. The projects the researchers are engaged on should have market potential and should also have a reasonable probability of success.

    The 'high flyer' project, that is one which is seen to have only an outside chance of success but which, should it come off, will bring a major move forward, should be a contender for a place in every research programme. However, projects of this kind need to be limited in number and in the amount of resource allocated to them—too many, and the research programme will become just a very big gamble.

    Deciding which projects are to be researched is primarily a

marketing/research consideration. Knowledge of the market-place and its future requirements blended with a knowledge of the areas most likely to produce research success is necessary.

However, the direction of the research effort can be such a significant factor within the business strategy that the final decisions should be taken by the Chief Executive. The decision is, in fact, one of the most important within the whole business strategy formulation process.

Concentration of the research effort is an important factor. A thin spread over a large number of projects has limitations— better to concentrate effort over a limited number of carefully selected projects.

3. Providing researchers with the right level of motivation is often difficult but very necessary. Projects can last a number of years and maintaining high level performance requires most skilful management.

   One of the best stimulants is for researchers to have a connection with the market-place battle and to feel a part of it. The danger, however, is that if researchers are involved continually in 'putting out fires' for current market problems they cannot concentrate on meeting the longer-term strategic research objectives.

   Good researchers are like most other good people in business, they want to be associated with a successful operation and they want to feel part of it. Senior management should ensure they are involved in the business, that they feel part of it, and that they are aware that their efforts are appreciated. There is always the danger that a research department which is isolated, and does not experience from time to time the excitement of winning, may lose drive and initiative.

4. It is important to know when to start a research project—it is equally important to know when to close one.

   Research projects should not be allowed to drift on. They should be reviewed periodically and when they are no longer productive, or when it is decided that the particular project is for some reason no longer of real significance, then it should be closed.

5. The majority of research projects which come through to the market-place successfully have invariably been backed by one or two people within the business who 'really believed' in the particular project.

   The enthusiasts are normally either top managers, or they have easy access to top managers, and thus the project rarely lacks backing and resource.

Research is not alone in this respect. Indeed the same remarks probably apply to major developments in other sectors of the business.

A successful research unit can be a most valuable asset to any company, and particularly to a company which has access to a very big market. The products of a successful research unit can move across national frontiers without any payment of duty. They can bring success throughout a world market relatively quickly.

It should always be remembered that the ultimate success of a research unit is recorded in the success of its brands in the market-place, and the return provided by the research investment should be considered and measured accordingly.

> ❛Procter & Gamble may have established a justifiably high reputation for their ability in advertising and salesmanship. However, many of their competitors would consider that over the years they have also demonstrated a particularly high level of skill in managing their research and development, and in bringing the products of this resource to the market-place in a practical form which is attractive to the consumer.
>
> The UK washing powder market provides a good example of this skill. The market has seen three major breakthroughs in the period 1946 to 1983.
>
> The first breakthrough was the introduction of synthetic detergents in the late 1940s/early 50s. P & G were first into the UK national market with an acceptable product, and were generally able to lead the synthetic section of the market through the 1950s and 60s – only Lever's considerable success with its soap powder brand Persil prevented them obtaining overall market leadership.
>
> In 1968-69 P & G were first into the UK national market with an acceptable enzymatic product – the brand was Ariel. For a short time this introduction gave P & G leadership of the UK market. However, Lever's skill in developing Persil, and later Persil Automatic, meant that the leadership was short-lived. Lever went on to enjoy a particularly strong total market position through the 1970s and into the 80s; nevertheless P & G's Ariel has been a most successful brand.
>
> In 1981-82 P & G introduced to the UK the first washing powder to contain a fabric softener. While this innovation has not yet proved itself to be of the same significance as the earlier breakthroughs, it is clearly important.
>
> The fact that in the UK washing powder market Lever has been able to recover market leadership should not detract from the great value to P & G of its technological and innovating abilities. The P & G skill in research and development, and in bringing its innovations to the market-place in a practical form, has clearly been a major problem for Lever. ❜

Research and the size of the market

The cost of running a worthwhile research unit is exactly the same if it serves a company competing in a market with 1 million consumers as it would be if the market had 100 or 1000 million consumers.

This is one of the elementary factors behind much of the growth and market success enjoyed by multi-national companies over recent years. They operate on a world-wide basis. In effect, their market is a world market. This means that it makes very good business sense for them to maintain large research establishments servicing operating companies throughout the world. Their total research investment is large; when expressed as a unit cost on their world turnover, it is very small indeed.

Provided they have fully effective research units which are well directed, the multi-nationals should be able to maintain a lead over local competitors in that their products should have the benefit of the innovations first. Of course, the research units must be successful. They must produce winners.

There are important strategy implications within the research investment considerations. The multi-nationals should have a competitive advantage in those markets and market sectors where the research input is important. Engaging in the smaller local markets where being 'fast on your feet' is of major significance is unlikely to be beneficial to them, and the opportunity cost could be very high.

For the smaller local business, a head-on battle with a multi-national in the major sector of a big market is unlikely, over the long term, to prove beneficial unless research backing can be obtained. For the smaller business, it is normally much better to fight in the more specialized markets or market sectors where the size of the research unit is not necessarily a key factor.

The development contribution

Depending upon the position of the market and its size, and the level of research investment within the market, it would be reasonable to say that a major research-founded innovation may appear about once every 10 years. In some very active markets the introduction of such innovations may be more frequent, in others less so.

However, in a fully competitive market, and particularly one in a growth stage, a continuous flow of new developments for existing brands will be needed. These developments will tend to come under one of three headings:

1.   Improvements in the performance of existing ingredients, eg the adding of a new booster, or the development of a superior mix.

2. Improvements in the processing of the product which enhance performance, eg the ability to produce a smoother liquid which is more effective in application.
3. Improvements in either the product formulation, or in its processing, which bring about a reduction in cost.

In some instances these developments may follow consumer research which indicates an additional need or requirement, and in other cases they may follow experimental work in the laboratory. The production of such improvements is one of the primary tasks of the development section.

Periodically every brand needs to be brought up to date, have its performance sharpened, and improve its value to the consumer. If a major research-backed innovation is to be available, say, once every 10 years, then a development-backed innovation should be available every three years or so between the major moves. With this form of support the brand can go back to the consumer for retrial from time to time and combat competitive attacks.

Many of the development improvements will come in the form of 'spin-offs' from the main research programme. A further development task is to refine and polish for the local market the new products and product developments coming through from research. The strength of certain ingredients may need review, local requirements can necessitate special formula changes, and so on.

In particular, the development section will have a key role to play when a brand comes under strong competitive attack on a performance basis. Meeting this challenge, and meeting it quickly and before the consumer changes her brand allegiance, can make a major difference to a brand's market position.

Value analysis has become one of management's most powerful tools. It aims to maintain current performance at a lower cost, or to improve performance at the same cost. In a highly competitive market-place where it is necessary to improve continually the value of a brand to consumers if market share is to be maintained, and possibly improved, every brand will need to be subjected to a value analysis review. The review needs to be made regularly and it must produce results. The development laboratory is invariably at the centre of the brand value analysis review.

Keeping research and development activity confidential

The good marketing man, given adequate resources, should be able to get a major brand value change (eg a major product performance improvement) home to the consumer within six months of its entering the market. These six months before competitors are able to make any major reply can be of vital importance.

Clearly if a lead of this kind is to apply it is essential that the work of the research and development units should be kept strictly confidential. Equally, however, the manufacturer is entirely justified in taking all legal and ethical steps to discover competitive R and D developments. If the competitor's lead can be reduced to less than six months, or preferably if his innovation can be beaten to the market, then a major gain has been made.

The position is very straightforward. The manufacturer should take all necessary action to ensure that his developments are kept strictly confidential, and equally he should take all appropriate steps to find out what his competitors are doing.

There are many ways in which this can be done. In the main it requires a systematic collection and recording of all information, from any creditable source, which is picked up by personnel during the normal course of business. This can include remarks made by suppliers, information coming from advertising and media agencies, data gleaned from consumer tests, and so forth. All those places where the manufacturer looks for information on competitive brands he should block from receiving data on his own efforts.

Research and development in strategy formulation

Clearly research and development can play a major part in providing a business with a series of brand competitive advantages, and these in turn can provide market success.

How far should the possible (or probable) performances of research and development units be allowed for in strategy formulation? The question applies to both the manufacturer's own efforts and those of his competitors.

In practice, research breakthroughs are extremely difficult to obtain. A strategy based on a breakthrough which is considered possible but which has not advanced beyond early research work, must certainly be rated as speculative and a high risk.

Nevertheless, if the project shows real potential, preliminary thinking and planning should be carried out, even at this early stage, with regard to the financing and resourcing of its exploitation. When once the project has come through its tests successfully, it will be necessary to get it to the market as rapidly as possible. Unnecessary delay in the exploitation could prove very costly.

Where a research project is more advanced and is making good progress the company should certainly have a strategy for its development, with a provisional plan to cover its exploitation. The plans should also ensure that the business is covered if the research project does not reach the market-place.

The business strategy review process should provide a good opportunity to consider the performance, the extent, and the direction of the research investment. Are innovations coming from research at a satisfactory rate? If not, why not? Should certain projects receive greater attention and investment? Should certain projects be closed? Is there a need for a change in the direction of the research effort? How does our performance compare with our competitors? These are some of the questions which should be asked and answered, and every effort should be made to ensure that the answers are as realistic as possible. It is very easy to build exaggerated optimism into research forecasts. The area is a difficult one and a sensible balance is vital.

The great danger in strategy formulation is to use research projects which are in a very early stage of development as the answer, and the only answer, to a difficult competitive market-place position. The risk that they will fail to reach the market-place, or will be unduly delayed, is always particularly high.

Similarly, when a competitor has achieved a worthwhile research breakthrough it should be recognized and competitive plans made accordingly. To ignore it and wake up later with a drastic fall in brand market share and volume is likely to be both costly and deeply damaging.

CHAPTER 7

Opportunities in the Market

A business can make progress for a period by putting right its problems. Cost reductions and changes in organization are good examples of this. But if a business is to make real progress over the longer term, it will need to develop and exploit opportunities in the market.

In previous chapters the market, the significance of brand market leadership, the economic climate, and the contribution of research and development have been discussed. These subjects have attempted to set the scene for what is one of the most important parts of the strategic planning process — the search for, and the development and exploitation of, marketing opportunities.

A marketing opportunity is defined here as a consumer need or requirement which is not adequately met by the brands already in the market. A marketing opportunity, once it has been discovered, can be met by either the further development of an existing brand or by the launch of a new brand.

The normal internal approach to developing and exploiting a marketing opportunity starts with marketing research highlighting the opportunity after discussions and product testing with consumers. Research and development works to formulate a product which meets the consumers' requirements, and preferably meets them more effectively than any competitor. From here the business moves forward to the exploitation of the opportunity.

There are, however, other ways open to the company to exploit a marketing opportunity. Acquisition is one. The company could buy a business and its brands and use them to meet an opportunity. This chapter is concerned primarily with ways of meeting the opportunity from internal sources.

What is a brand?

Marketing opportunities should be met by brands. Before considering the brands already in the market-place it may be helpful to describe how a brand is viewed in this book, what it is, and how it is formed. As we are primarily concerned with strategy formulation in the branded goods business this is a subject of significance.

Brands really first began to emerge during the late nineteenth century. At that time wholesalers held a particularly strong position in the distributive chain, and to a considerable extent dictated what manufacturers should make.

Manufactured products gradually became more complex in their make-up, and manufacturers developed special skills in product formulation and processing. They were able to gain some protection for their skill by the use of patents, hence early names took a form such as 'Scotts Patent Polish'. Later, brand names spread to non-patented goods. Then came the development of advertising which provided a direct link between the manufacturer and the public, and so on to the widespread and highly developed branding which applies today.

A brand is first a name. Over time this name will come to represent the delivery of a particular benefit. In effect, the brand name will come to represent the fulfilment of a specific purpose. The name will also come to denote a standard of performance in delivering the benefit. Finally, the name will come to represent a personality, something that is often referred to as a 'brand image'. This personality is the picture, or impression, and feeling for a brand, which has developed in the consumer's mind.

If a manufacturer has done a good branding job, then in time, the mention of his brand name will immediately bring to mind, in words and pictures, the purpose the brand meets, its performance standard, and a feeling about the name which reflects the brand personality.

The establishment of a brand name is normally a long-term operation. The strength of the brand tends to develop over time as consumers come to appreciate its qualities. Once a brand name has been established, making any significant change in its purpose or personality can be both a difficult and a high risk operation. A performance improvement should not be difficult, but with purpose and personality there is always the possibility that the consumer may be confused.

> Proposals to meet marketing opportunities by making radical changes to the purpose and/or personality of established brands should be scrutinised most carefully. They rarely work.
>
> Within Lever, through a period of over 20 years from 1960, many proposals were tabled to re-launch established brands with extensive changes

in brand purpose and/or personality. A number were allowed to go forward for test marketing. Only two of the operations can be rated as successful.

In the late 1950s and early 60s a number of consumer bodies in the UK were strongly opposed to the marketing methods used by the major soap companies. In particular they were concerned with the advertising and promotional techniques used to support washing powder brands.

Surf was originally launched in the UK washing powder market in 1952-53 as a main sector synthetic detergent. It had limited success.

In the early 1960s Lever decided to re-launch Surf with a 'Square Deal' approach. Essentially, this meant that the brand stopped using the promotional techniques which were common in the UK market at this time. The consumer was initially offered a pack with 'extra powder'. This was later changed; the quantity of powder packed by Square Deal Surf became the same as that of competing brands, and a permanent price reduction was introduced.

During its early period Square Deal Surf struggled. In 1967-68, following further public comment on detergent marketing, the brand strengthened. It has progressed through the years and in 1982 Surf and Surf Automatic held around 10 per cent of the total UK washing powder market. The dramatic change made to the Surf personality was successful. But it received exceptional help.

A more modest success involving a brand personality change concerned the Lever toilet soap Knight's Castile. Through the 1950s the brand held a leading position in the UK market as a beauty soap. In the mid 1960s it went into decline and its withdrawal from the market was considered. In the late 1960s/early 70s Knight's Castile was re-launched to meet a marketing opportunity for a 'pure and simple' family toilet soap.

The re-launch enjoyed modest success. The decline in market share was halted and the brand later staged a recovery. Knight's Castile held around 5 per cent of the UK toilet soap market in 1982. With very limited resource backing it has made a useful contribution over a number of years. 9

The purpose of a business organization is to create and satisfy customers. Its objective is to make profit. In a branded goods business both the purpose and the objective can only be achieved through the brands. The success of its brands is vitally important to everyone concerned with the business. The strength of its brands is ultimately the strength of the business.

Marketing opportunities

A marketing opportunity discovered ahead of the competitors and then developed and exploited, can become a significant competitive advantage. All competitive advantages are worth having. Those derived from marketing opportunities are particularly significant in that they are directly related to brands.

The aim is to find opportunities in the market-place ahead of competitors, to use them for the further development of existing brands, and for the introduction of new brands. Where are the opportunities to come from? How are they to be discovered? They can come from the hunch of one person who has a well tuned 'feel' for the market. It is not unknown for a major new brand to originate in the home, or workshop, of a successful entrepreneur. He may have made the original himself. He liked it; he put it on the market, and found that other people, many other people, agreed with him. He had an outstanding success.

This has happened, and it certainly will happen again. However, it is very much a long-shot and not an approach to be relied on to sustain a developing and progressive business in a competitive market.

A more systematic approach and one which, provided it is taken up in a positive manner, can produce a flow of marketing opportunities, considers:

1. The market, its future development and movement. This should cover both the main market and the various segments within it.
2. The consumers' view on the deficiencies of the brands currently in the market, and their future requirements.
3. The product innovations and developments coming from the research and development department.
4. The brands currently competing in the market.

Items 1 to 3 have been covered in previous pages and so these notes will concentrate on item 4.

The brands competing in the market

The strategist needs answers to a number of questions, in particular:

(a) What are the current strengths and weaknesses of my brands?
(b) What are the current strengths and weaknesses of competitive brands?

This review of the brands in the market should be in terms of the various market sectors and should commence with the main market.

The review of each brand should start with the product formulation and also cover packaging, advertising, promotion and pricing. The sales volume held by the brand, its market share, its cost structure, and its profit contribution should also be included.

In particular, the review should cover each brand's purpose, its standard of performance, its pricing, and its personality. Wherever possible consumers' view of the brand should be included in the review. In the case of performance, this should be accompanied by the laboratory analysis showing the measured performance standard.

The aim is to get an objective review of every brand competing in either the main market or in any one of the various market segments. The requirement is to be sure, as far as possible, which are the strong brands capable of further progress, and which are the weak brands that are struggling and could be more easily attacked and overtaken.

It is important that the brand strengths and weaknesses should be covered in detail. Where a brand has a competitive advantage this should be analysed and its vulnerability considered. Can the advantage be matched or overtaken, or is it completely firm? Are any weaknesses inherent in the brand, or are they of a nature that could be corrected rapidly? For instance, if the problem is consumer penetration, it is possible that a series of well directed promotions could correct this quickly. However, if the problem is in the product formulation, then correction may be much more difficult.

Marketing opportunities for exploitation

With the four reviews before him, the strategist can begin his search for marketing opportunities.

He will know how the total market is expected to move, and within this he will have detailed forecasts of the movement of the various segments. In effect, he will know where growth is expected and at what rate. He will also know where there is expected to be maturity and decline.

His analysis of the current brands in the market will show him where he has strong entries capable of progress, and also where he is weak. He will have a similar analysis of competitive brands.

His researches of the consumer will provide details of his/her views of the weaknesses of existing brands and his/her requirements into the future. He will know the position of the various projects within his research laboratory, and have forecasts of the extent and rate of their progress. In addition he will have full details of the work going on within his development unit. When he brings these various analyses together, the strategist should know:

(a) Where the marketing opportunities are likely to be over the periods ahead.

(b) Which of his competitors is best equipped to exploit the opportunities, given the current situation within the market.

It is necessary to list the marketing opportunities which are thought to exist in the market, and also to attempt to attach a value to each. The valuation is a difficult task, but it is necessary to get at least a rough indication of the quality of each opportunity. The effort and resource invested in the development of an opportunity should be related to its eventual worth.

An objective view of who is currently best positioned in the market to exploit the opportunities which are likely to develop is also vital at this stage. It is really an analysis of who currently has a competitive advantage, and who has the ability and is likely to be concerned to change the status quo.

The aim of this exercise is to reach a conclusion as to which marketing opportunities provide the best fit for the abilities and resources of the business: in effect, to decide where the business can expect to develop a significant competitive advantage over its competitors which should provide for the successful exploitation of the opportunity.

In considering the opportunities available it is important that the evaluation of the effort and resource which may be necessary to exploit them is realistic. It is particularly important to be realistic about the probable level of competitive retaliation if an attack is made on an established position. One of the most frequent mistakes made in strategy planning is underestimating the strength and the extent of a competitor's response to an attack on one of his well established brands.

A progress report on the various R and D projects, and their prospects for a satisfactory conclusion, will make a major contribution at this stage.

If the strategy formulation process is established on a continuous basis very few of the marketing opportunities will be completely new to the business. A limited number of new opportunities may be added at each review, but the bulk of the list will have been built up over a number of reviews. Research and development projects will have been started to meet those opportunities chosen as well suited for exploitation by the business.

Measuring the progress made in R and D on the various projects, considering the resource devoted to each one, trying to assess with accuracy the chances of a successful conclusion, and how long it will take, is a very difficult but necessary exercise at this time.

Where the business already has a strong brand, or a number of strong brands, their maintenance and development should come first. They are the base of the business and they are already in existence. When they are in growth markets, or growth segments, the investment resources may need to be extensive. If the market has progressed to a mature or declining stage, then the investment necessary should be of a more limited nature.

While the search for new marketing opportunities should concentrate in the growth markets, the mature markets should certainly not be ignored. New opportunities in mature markets are normally more difficult to develop—there are fewer entirely new consumers available and the leading brands within the markets are often firmly established. Nevertheless they can, if exploited skilfully, provide valuable additional profit contributions.

> The UK toilet soap market during the late 1970s/early 1980s provides an excellent example of the development and exploitation of marketing opportunities in a mature market.
>
> The market was a growth one through the period 1900 to 1970, then it moved into a mature stage. In the early 1970s the market was dominated by a limited number of well established brands. Lux toilet soap, Palm-olive, and Lifebuoy toilet soap had all been in existence for over 40 years. Camay had been introduced to the market in the 1950s; the launch was backed by a particularly heavy advertising support and for a short period the brand was market leader. Fairy toilet soap had been introduced in the mid-1960s, and it also held market leadership for a short time. These five brands filled the leading position in the market through the period 1960-75.
>
> Imperial Leather was also a very well established brand. It was positioned as a luxury brand selling at a premium price and it had a well developed and favourable personality. The brand tended to hold a market share position below the leading group.
>
> Through the early 1970s the leading manufacturers were all actively engaged in developing and testing possible new brand entrants to the market. As the market was moving into its mature stage they were understandably concentrating their efforts on possible 'speciality' segmented entrants that would sell at premium price levels.
>
> During 1972-75 Lever was working on a new brand to be aimed at meeting a marketing opportunity for a deodorant soap. The reasoning was that the proposed brand would sell at a premium price and claim a limited market share. It was not expected to be a contender for market leadership.
>
> In its consumer test programme the proposed new brand surprised Lever. It received a remarkably enthusiastic reception from consumers. The consumers particularly liked the colour, the fragrance, the lather, and the feel of the product – the deodorant effect was considered to be an added extra and not the main benefit.
>
> Following this consumer reception Lever decided to make certain changes in the brand – the deodorancy was presented in a more feminine manner, bringing a benefit of 'confidence', the perfume level was raised, the price lowered, and the whole presentation lightened.
>
> The brand, originally named Protect and later renamed Shield, was placed into a test market with advertising and support aimed at moving it into the No 1 position in the market.

The test market was a great success, and when Shield moved into the national market it rapidly became the clear leader of the UK toilet soap market. Lever had certainly developed and taken an opportunity.

In 1975 the owners of Imperial Leather sold their business to Paterson Zochonis. The new owners quickly saw a marketing opportunity for their leading toilet soap brand within the UK market.

Imperial Leather was given much stronger advertising and promotional backing; it engaged in trade dealing and in this way its price premium was reduced, and it received stronger in-store merchandising support.

The brand reacted very favourably to this new approach and soon became a member of the leading group of brands within the market, and later the holder of the No 1 position.

Shield and Imperial Leather, one an entirely new brand and the other an established brand given a new approach, became the two leading brands in the mature UK toilet soap market through the second half of the 1970s and into the 80s.

There should always be a greater demand for R and D resource than there is resource available. If there is ever a surplus, this means there is either an over-investment in the area, or a lack of a creative and positive approach to market and business development.

Concentration of effort is certainly one of the requirements for a successful business. In considering the marketing opportunities which are to receive investment resource, concentration is essential. No business can expect, or would necessarily want, to cover every opportunity — better it concentrate on those which offer real prospects of success. It is not the number of opportunities worked on which is important, it is the number and value of those brought through to a successful conclusion that really matter.

With the research and development data available, the conclusions reached from the study of the market and its development, and the position of the existing brands, the strategist should be able to short list the marketing opportunities in which his business may be prepared to invest.

So far, we have considered markets in which the business already has an interest. It is suggested that the basic procedure should be the same for possible new markets. Considerable care will be necessary because lack of familiarity with the new market may result in misinterpretation of its behaviour. It may be wise to consider the case for an acquisition which buys market learning experience.

When considering entry to a new market, it is vital that the evaluation of the probable cost of entry is realistic. The management ability, the financial strength, and the brand strength of the companies already established in the market should be examined carefully. A common error in strategy formulation which concerns a new market is to underestimate how much an established leader is prepared to pay to defend his position. To move into a new market and then to discover that the cost of entry is so high that it weakens the whole business can be disastrous.

With a continuous strategy review in operation, the business will be developing, at any one time, a series of marketing opportunities, supported as appropriate by research and development projects. They will be at various stages of evolution and there may be a need at the periodical reviews to rearrange priorities as the requirements and potentials in the market-place change.

This book has concentrated on the product formula development, but in practice there is also a need for marketing development. The rapid exploitation of an opportunity may be greatly enhanced if the marketing approach to the consumer is right. For instance, the right expression and presentation of the consumer benefit provided by the product is vitally important. Considerable consumer research and experimentation can be necessary to clarify issues of this kind. Frequently it will be advisable to prepare exploratory advertisements and test alternative packages.

Marketing opportunities can be based on the discovery of new consumer needs which do not require any extensive research or development effort. The product formula required may be very simple and easily prepared, the real discovery is the new purpose. Here marketing development is likely to be the key consideration in meeting the opportunity.

At the periodic reviews the opportunity should also be taken to drop those projects which are not registering satisfactory progress or where the potential has weakened. The number of projects which will eventually reach the market is limited. Concentration of effort means that the weak should be discarded, and the temptation to stay with an interesting project which is failing, and where the potential is in doubt, resisted.

One of the most important requirements to emerge from this process of searching for market opportunities is that the company should be ahead of its competitors with new developments, and should not allow itself to be trapped into chasing after the opposition. Once a business falls behind it requires a very conscious effort to change the position. It may be that one stage in the competitive product development process must be leap-frogged so that the initiative is regained.

It is worth repeating the very basic and vitally important point that the making and taking of marketing opportunities will be essential if the business is to record real progress over the longer term. Profits may be improved by the use of more effective and efficient operations within the current business, but cost effectiveness of this kind has limitations. Progress in the long term will require that the business make and take marketing opportunities to expand its base.

PART 3

CHAPTER 8

Product Costs

You ignore product costs at your peril for they are basic to your brand, its competitive position, and its development into the future.

In the bigger consumer goods markets product costs invariably represent a major part of the manufacturer's final selling price for his brand; in many instances they will exceed 50 per cent of the final price.

Product costs, their current level, and that to which they may be expected to move in the foreseeable future, with varying production volumes, are crucial to the formulation of business strategy.

As he considers his product costs in detail the strategist should be looking for opportunities to develop competitive advantages. He should be concerned to develop approaches which will enable his business to get better value from its investment in this area—better value, for instance, in terms of an improved performance with the same or lower costs, or in terms of a maintained performance at reduced cost. This chapter examines the following approaches he may consider:

● Raw materials.
● Packaging.
● Processing.
● Production overheads.

Towards the end of the chapter the experience curve is considered. This subject has featured prominently in strategy considerations over recent years, and is concerned with the behaviour of product costs as production experience accumulates.

The product cost area is one where it is especially important to ally the right strategy with fully effective operation if truly satisfactory results are to be obtained.

Raw materials

Raw material costs start with the brand formulation specification. Detailed consumer research should play a major role in highlighting the particular brand product formulation which, in the consumers' view, provides the most satisfactory delivery of the benefits (both the main benefit and the appropriate subsidiary benefits) specified in the brand marketing requirement.

The aim should be to obtain this most favoured formulation at an acceptable cost. Even if the first costing of the formula appears acceptable, a continuous search for savings should be maintained. It is necessary to examine every formula ingredient and its cost, together with an analysis of the benefits it contributes both in its own right and in synergy with other ingredients.

Skill in the laboratory is at a premium in formula compilation and in the adjustments which may be necessary. Frequently a given result can be obtained by various blends of particular ingredients; optimising the blend for performance at a given cost level can be both a highly skilled and rewarding operation. Setting up suitable consumer product testing research, and reading the results with skill and sensitivity, can also be important.

When there is pressure to reduce ingredient costs it is necessary to assess the effect of the withdrawal of small amounts of particular items. Judged individually, withdrawals may have no effect on the consumers' response to product performance. When a number of withdrawals are grouped together, however, the effect of performance can be most marked. This is one reason why many companies refuse to make small formula adjustments one at a time, but insist on bringing them together and making any change only after wider product testing.

When new ingredients are to be added to a formula it is also necessary to ensure that they deliver in terms of performance to the consumer. Assessing with any high degree of accuracy the level of their contribution can be extremely difficult, but the manufacturer should have an indication, even a rough one, of just what he is getting for his money.

It is also necessary to keep a check on competitive brand formula developments. Information should be available on two fronts: the consumers' reaction to competitive formula changes, or at least a laboratory check on the changes, and a check on probable competitive formula costs.

Looking ahead and judging the probable future cost of existing and new ingredients can be of significance in strategy. Suppliers should be subject to the economics of larger scale production—the experience curve should work for them and their costs should come down. Patents may run out or may be overcome. Competitive action may have a material effect on the pricing of a supplier who has previously held a monopoly position. Judging the effect of developments of this kind on the price of an important ingredient can be very important.

'When the price of a commodity rises sharply there is an added incentive to review its use and to consider its replacement with a less costly alternative. Synthetic detergents are partly based on mineral oil, so the sharp rise in the price of this commodity in the mid-1970s prompted many manufacturers to review their product formulations, and beyond this their energy consumption in general.

In a relatively short period new formulations were available which maintained, and in certain instances improved, product performance with a lower cost of active (ie oil) ingredients. Much of the economy came from the skilled blending of the various grades of active. Similarly, it was found that blowing towers (an important part of the detergent manufacturing process) could, with skilled handling, be run effectively with a lower fuel consumption.

It can be argued, of course, that the really effective operator would not need an oil price rise to prompt a review of his formulas and production processes – the savings available were of substance even before the oil price changes. '

Another source of competitive gain can be the control of material waste. This is really a case of good management and housekeeping. When the raw materials expenditure for a year runs into millions of pounds, even relatively small savings are of consequence.

Many manufacturers prefer not to speculate in the supply and pricing of the commodities they use. Others take a different view; they believe they should have an intimate knowledge of their particular commodities and that they are well placed to judge market price movements.

This is a matter for each individual management to decide for itself. It is primarily a question of having confidence in the skill and negotiating ability of the buyer. Skilful speculation of this type can be very beneficial and can provide a competitive advantage. There is invariably a risk involved—one of the important issues is likely to be the degree of risk and its substance within the business concerned.

‘Sometimes the experts can be wrong! There is a particularly interesting example of a raw material price forecast which, had it been accepted and acted upon, would have had a major effect on the Lever brand, Persil.

In the 1960s it was forecast that prices of the basic raw materials of soap powders, ie vegetable and animal oils and fats, were likely to rise through the 1970s and into the 80s. Against this it was also forecast that the basic raw material of synthetic detergents, ie mineral oil, would fall in price.

This could have brought about a difficult position for Lever, as its leading washing powder brand in the 1960s, and the UK market leader, was Persil, which was a soap powder.

In the late 1960s and the early 70s, as a result of the forecasts, suggestions were made that Lever should change the formulation of Persil and make it either a blend product or a synthetic.

Fortunately the suggestions were rejected. In the mid-1970s there was an explosion in the price of mineral oil and so, in terms of raw material costs, soap powder Persil found itself with a major competitive advantage.’

Packaging

Many of the remarks about raw materials apply equally to packaging materials. Costs in packaging also start with the brand specification. There will similarly be considerable skill involved in obtaining the optimum balance between quality and cost. A wide range of packaging materials is available and it is important to experiment and test the options to reach the optimum position. The need to control waste applies very strongly to packaging, and the maintenance of a close watch on competitive developments and costs is also very necessary.

From time to time there are technical breakthroughs in packaging materials. The move from a metal container to the more pliable plastic for liquids, such as those used for washing-up, was a major breakthrough. The competitive advantage they bring is certainly very well worth having, but it will normally be short term.

There is one particular respect in which packaging materials differ from raw materials and the difference can be of consequence. Packing materials are very much part of presentation—raw materials may be concerned in presentation but normally their contribution is less important. This can mean, for instance, that the carton is of a special gloss finish, or a special make of board. To get a particular effect in presentation six colours of printing ink may be used on the carton in place of the normal four, and so on. The additional expenditures may well be worthwhile but it is important that management should know how much it is paying for presentation. A reasonable indication of the cost of presentation is the difference between the actual price paid and the price which would apply for a serviceable package without the gloss.

The value analysis approach can also be applied to packaging. The packaging field is one where the question of whether to make or to buy is frequently raised. This subject is outside the scope of this book but it is most important that the opportunity cost of proposals to invest in such areas as printing, carton making, and bottle blowing *always* receive full management attention.

It is perhaps worth noting that the cost of package design, already mentioned in Chapter 2 on competitive advantage, is normally a relatively small consideration in terms of unit cost, and yet it can play such a major part in the brand presentation. It can also frequently have a material effect on the cost of other items within the brand packaging.

> If you have a major brand in a market such as fabric softeners, or washing-up liquids, you are likely to be a very big buyer of plastic. The bottles in which such products are now sold to the consumer are invariably made of some form of plastic. During the mid-1970s the price of plastic rose sharply and many manufacturers became acutely aware of the costs involved in their packaging.
>
> The quantity of plastic used by a manufacturer will depend primarily on two factors: (a) the number of bottles sold, and (b) the design and size of the bottle concerned. A factor of considerable importance is the thickness of the walls and other sectors of the bottle. In turn, this thickness is greatly influenced by the bottle design as this affects the stress and strain placed on the various parts of the bottle when it is filled with liquid.
>
> Designing a bottle which is attractive to the consumer, fully effective in use, and which limits the amount of plastic used for each bottle, is a highly skilled and painstaking operation. When you are selling many millions of bottles each year cost-effective packaging can be very rewarding.

Processing

Here we are concerned with the costs incurred in the process of production, and with the behaviour of costs as production volumes fluctuate.

Production unit costs are influenced primarily by three factors: (a) effectiveness and efficiency in operation, (b) capital investment, and (c) volume.

The factors are not entirely separate in their effect. The volume passing through a given plant, for instance, can most certainly affect the efficiency of the operation within the plant. If a plant can have, say, five days of straightforward throughput, it is likely to run more efficiently than if it has, say, 25 changes in the five days.

The most effective and efficient operation is unlikely to produce competitive unit costs if it is working with worn out and unsuitable equipment.

The standard of effectiveness and efficiency reached in the operation of the production process is essentially dependent upon good management, with a skilled and positive contribution from the personnel concerned. Accepting that 'there is always a better way' should mean a continuous drive to improve efficiency.

The condition of the plant is clearly important. When should the plant be scrapped and replaced by new and more effective equipment? The textbook answer is that plant should be replaced as soon as it can be shown that the cost of new plant will bring savings which represent a satisfactory return on the new investment involved. The calculations in the new plant proposal will be considerably influenced by the production volumes involved, and by the rate of return required on the investment.

While it is accepted that proposals for new production plant should compete with other investment proposals for the limited resources of the business, most manufacturers tend to be unduly slow to scrap and replace plant that is becoming out-dated.

In considering the return an investment of this kind brings, it is important to note that it is usually a relatively low risk investment.

In terms of unit cost the difference between a really efficient production unit, and one which is running at about an average level, may not seem material. In terms of the total sum involved (unit $\times$ volume), the amount can be substantial.

The standard of efficiency achieved within the running of a plant can have a material effect on its capacity, on the total amount of investment made in plant, and beyond this on the profit return on investment made by the business. 'Is my plant the industry leader in terms of effectiveness and efficiency?' 'And if not, why not?' are very pertinent questions for the Chief Executive to ask.

Checking on the efficiency levels of competing businesses is a difficult task. Naturally, figures of this kind are jealously guarded and rarely ever published. Rough indications may be gained by comparing the number of people employed and the total plant output.

Businessmen have always appreciated that volume can have a marked effect on unit costs. Over recent years, with the introduction of more advanced electronic and mechanical equipment, and more advanced technology within plant construction, volume has become even more important.

A typical approach to considering the influence of volume is to analyse the costs to be incurred in a particular plant as either fixed, or variable, with output. The fixed costs remain the same whether the output is 100 or 1000 units. To arrive at the total cost per unit the figures for fixed and variable costs are added together. The importance of volume will be quickly appreciated when the difference between the 100 and the 1000 output levels of unit cost is calculated.

In a much more sophisticated form, the approach set out above is often employed within business accounting presentations, usually for the calendar or budget year. For certain short-term considerations the figures coming from the fixed/variable cost analysis may be quite satisfactory. They will almost certainly have value for an executive required to hit specific short-term profit targets. Similarly, information of this kind may be helpful if, for instance, a short-term price battle should develop, or where indications of the volume necessary to cover particular advertising and promotional outlays are required.

Normally, these occasions really require the use of a marginal cost, ie the difference in total cost occasioned by the change in volume of one more or less unit. In practice it is impossible to calculate marginal cost accurately; an approach which uses an analysis of costs as either fixed, or semi-variable and variable with volume output, often goes some way to meeting the requirement. The great significance of volume in the determination of unit costs is discussed below in the section on the experience curve.

Production overhead

Within the cost analysis by volume a large proportion of the fixed costs will probably be production overhead. These costs include such items as depreciation on plant and buildings, factory management costs, general maintenance costs, and the plant lunch room facilities.

If the plant is a one-product facility, it can be said that all the various items included under production overhead are part of the production of the one product. In practice one-product facilities are very rare—the majority of plants make a series of products.

This means that in arriving at a production cost for each product a series of arbitrary cost allocations will be necessary. It is important to appreciate this and to allow for it when making cost comparisons with other manufacturers, and also when considering the total level of a brand's contribution to overhead and profit.

The trend is for plants to become more automated in their operation, more capital intensive, and this will normally result in a higher level of production overhead. This development means that a larger proportion of production costs are likely to be classified as fixed, certainly over the short/medium term, and also the amount of allocated cost contained within a total product manufacturing cost is likely to increase. It also means that volume, and its influence on unit costs, will become of even greater significance into the future.

The 'experience curve'

The whole question of volume and its effect on unit cost has received considerable attention over recent years following the research work of the Boston Consulting Group, and its introduction of the experience curve concept which relates to overall cost behaviour. The initial study of the curve was carried out by the Boston Group in 1965-66. The extensive study included a large number of cases over a lengthy period.

The experience curve has certain similarities with the longer established learning curve approach. It is, however, wider in concept and includes costs beyond those of direct labour. In fact, the Boston Group would claim that the experience curve can be concerned with all costs of every kind required to make and deliver the product to the ultimate consumer. Sales expenses, marketing costs and other overheads can all be included.

The Boston Consulting Group has summed up the effect of the experience curve as follows:

> Costs appear to go down on value added at about 20 to 30 per cent every time total product experience doubles for the industry as a whole, as well as for individual producers.

It should be added that the costs do not just go down of their own accord— they have to be pushed. The downward movement can be explained by a number of factors such as people becoming better at their jobs over time, an increase in specialization, and additional investment in more highly developed plant. In effect, the costs go down primarily under the pressure of good management, investment, scale, and competition.

Businessmen may argue with some of the detail of the experience curve concept, but its general acceptance is widespread.

If the concept is accepted then it can clearly play a valuable part in helping to forecast the movement of product costs, with given market size developments, and over specific periods of time.

In practice, using the experience curve for forecasting can pose problems. When considering production processing costs, and other costs directly related to volume, the year-by-year figures may fit the curve line. When costs such as marketing are included, the year-by-year figures can diverge from the curve line. The very heavy advertising and promotional expenditures associated with new brand launches and other similar 'once only' activities can cause short-term variations. Of course, the curve may still apply over the long term.

It should be noted that the experience curve is concerned with accumulated product experience. A newcomer to an industry does not have to start at the beginning of the industry curve. If he is skilled, in particular with the plant he purchases and the personnel he recruits, he may join the curve at its current industry position, although if he is completely new to the industry, some short-term start-up difficulties are probably inevitable. Much depends on the complexity of the operation.

According to the experience curve concept product costs should always trend downwards, even in periods when the market size may have fallen, as the accumulated experience will still be increasing.

During a period of rapid market expansion, unit costs should fall still more rapidly. The faster the climb in total market volume the more rapid should be the fall in unit cost.

The forecast cost levels coming from the experience curve for a given market development will be estimates subject to 'a reasonable degree of error'. The Boston Group statement says '... at about 20 to 30 per cent every time total product experience doubles for the industry as a whole'.

Despite the possible problems the experience curve concept, and the wider reasoning which can follow from it on pricing etc, has been an important factor in the strategy development of many businesses over recent years.

A management which accepts experience curve reasoning should continually ask itself certain important questions:

1. Are my product costs moving down?
In effect, the experience curve states that added value costs for the same product should never stop going down. This may be a difficult proposition to get accepted within the business, but it should certainly be the aim. There are a number of natural follow-up questions: for example, 'If our costs are going down, are they moving down fast enough?' 'If our costs are not moving down, what action must we take to get them on the right track?'

2. What is happening to the volume of the market? Who within the market has gained in share and volume? How are my competitors' costs moving on the experience curve approach?'
There may be a good reason why volume has been lost in a given market; it could be a part of the business strategy that such losses be incurred. However, whenever one competitor loses market share another one is bound to gain. If the experience curve is operating the competitor who has made the gain should have a superior rate of downward movement in cost, if he has an effective management. A gain in volume should result in a more competitive position.

'Getting production managers to accept the experience curve concept and, on added value, the downward movement of unit costs it forecasts can be very difficult – to many production managers this may appear to be an unreasonable requirement.

Lever Bros was always very proud of its Warrington plant. For its size, and of its kind and form, it was thought to be one of the most efficient plants in Europe, and possibly in the world.

The plant specialized in the production of Persil Automatic and through the late 1970s and early 80s was responsible for producing an ever-increasing quantity of the brand.

The General Works Manager and his staff at Warrington took the Boston Consulting Group experience curve effect statement as a target. Their proud claim was that 'year on year they beat it'.

The effect of brand volume on unit cost, and the experience curve concept, reappears in the next chapter.

Finally, it is worth repeating the very important basic point: unit costs do not go down the experience curve automatically, they have to be pushed down by management action.

CHAPTER 9

Pricing

The skilful management of price can secure the longer-term profitability of a brand, and it can be a key factor in turning a promising growth brand into a dominant market leader. Used carelessly, price can provide a competitor with the opportunity to displace a leading brand and establish a new leader.

Price is an important part of the brand value equation. It is equally an important factor within long-term strategy. A brand's ability to contribute to the costs of its production and distribution, to the general costs of running the business, to the trading profit, and to the eventual payment of dividends, depends on the amount of 'margin' it is able to generate. This margin is the difference between the brand's direct cost of production and its selling price. The total margin (brand unit margin × sales volume) is the figure of real consequence.

Price is one of the factors in setting the level of the brand unit margin. Price is also a key factor in determining brand volume. It follows that price is a major factor in determining brand profitability.

Often thought of as merely a shorter-term tactical 'tool', price should be one of the most important considerations within the longer-term strategic plan. Here it is proposed to consider price in the formulation of strategy in four different situations:

1. Where a brand is a dominant market leader.
2. Where a brand is one of two or three brands which share market leadership.
3. Where a brand is at a lower level in the market.
4. Where a brand is a segment leader.

Pricing policy for a dominant market leader

A dominant market leader should have all the advantages over its competitors that much higher volume can bring, and it is important that the manufacturer makes quite sure that he is in fact getting them.

Given that the various volume advantages are working for him, then the dominant brand market leader should have the privilege of setting the price structure for the market. He can have a great influence on the brand margin levels which apply through the whole market.

In terms of performance value to the consumer, the dominant leader should be able to provide the greatest consumer benefit for the least cost. At whatever performance level he chooses for his brand the dominant leader, given that he is an effective and efficient operator, should be able to produce that performance level at a lower cost per unit than *any* competitor.

He will also have all the advantages of lower unit distribution costs, and this is particularly important with regard to the retailer's mark-up costs.

Should the dominant brand market leader decide to take a low unit margin, then all his competitors are likely to have low unit margins. His volume can still allow him a very big total margin. This will not apply to competitors who do not enjoy the same high volume.

In fact, his competitors will have higher unit costs, higher retail trade margins and, if they are to have similar selling prices to consumers, lower selling prices to the trade. The effect of this pressure on their brand unit margins can be well appreciated—life will not be easy for them.

6 Persil Automatic is probably the most successful brand introduced into the UK grocery markets since 1945.

The brand was actually launched into the UK national low suds washing powder market in 1969 after a period in a regional test market. At the time of the national launch the low suds market was relatively small. The market development was clearly linked directly with the growth in ownership of fully automatic washing machines. While there was little doubt that the automatic would ultimately become the predominant washing machine in UK households, there was considerable variation in the estimates of how rapidly the conversion would take place.

A very general estimate formed at the time of the national launch of Persil Automatic was that the UK low suds market might eventually grow to some 600,000 tons and that it might take some 20 to 25 years to do this.

Persil Automatic was the first major brand to compete in the low suds market. Following its move national the brand quickly became market leader.

The Lever plan for the brand was very simple and straightforward. Persil Automatic was to dominate the market right through the growth stage and on into maturity. The aim was to hold the market share at over 40 per cent and so build a brand which in the longer term could hold a volume of over 200,000 tons.

Lever was very conscious of the 'best value' concept in planning the Persil Automatic development. The company was confident that the brand's purpose was the correct one for a brand aimed at dominant leadership of the market.

Every effort was made to keep the brand's overall performance at a very high level, although in certain particular areas, such as protein stain removal, some competing brands may have been superior.

Detailed attention was given to the presentation of Persil Automatic. The tone and style of the presentation was always directed to the development of the very favourable Persil personality. While the advertising investment was maintained at a high level, the brand was not necessarily the highest advertising spender within the market in terms of either expenditure per unit of sales or total investment.

In 1974, as the total UK low suds market grew to over 50,000 tons, a strategic price decision was taken on Persil Automatic. Henceforth the brand was to run with a relatively low unit margin, in effect, with a relatively low unit price. Brand profit development was to come from volume.

The pricing decision had three main aims — first to encourage the rapid development of the market, second to restrict the funds available to competitive brands to attack Persil Automatic, and third to ensure that it was extremely difficult for the distributor brands to market a powder with a reasonable level of performance and at a price which could show a major difference from Persil Automatic.

The use of this pricing policy could possibly have meant that Lever was forgoing some short-term profit with a view to ensuring a strong brand position for the future. Against this, however, the policy brought volume gains which were valuable to brand revenue and contribution. The strategy for Persil Automatic enjoyed outstanding success.

In 1973 Procter & Gamble launched Bold Automatic, a low suds enzymatic washing powder, and gave it extensive advertising and promotional backing both during the launch period and through the following years.

In 1979 P & G launched Daz Automatic and Lever launched Surf Automatic into the market. Both launches were strongly supported.

In 1981 P & G launched Ariel Automatic into the market. This brand had an enzymatic formula and it received a most extensive advertising and promotional backing.

In 1982 P & G launched a re-staged Bold Automatic with a fabric softener contained within the product. Again this operation was backed by extensive advertising and promotion.

Through the 1970s and into the 80s the retail multiple chains were developing rapidly and almost all of them were active with distributor brands in the low suds market.

Despite all this activity Persil Automatic held over 40 per cent of the UK low suds market in 1983. The brand was a dominant leader of the market and outsold any competitive brand by over 2 to 1.

Distributor low suds brands held less than 10 per cent of the market in 1983. This compares with the 30 per cent plus they were able to claim in many of the major UK grocery markets.

In 1983 the low suds market totalled approximately 330,000 tons – roughly on target for 600,000 tons in the 1990s – with Persil Automatic well positioned to dominate the market as it develops, to move forward to a sales tonnage of over 200,000 tons, and become a very substantial profit contributor. **'**

Should the dominant brand market leader decide to take a high unit margin, he will provide the whole market with a form of price umbrella. For a period the market leader's total margin will be at a higher level, but so also will be the total margins of his competitors. This high margin will be available to the competitors to improve their formulas, to invest in stronger presentation, and to develop their brands generally.

Clearly, the decision of the brand market leader on the level of unit margin he proposes to take will be of major consequence to everyone operating in the market.

The stage of development reached by the market should be of major significance to the market leader in making his pricing decision. If the market is in its growth stage then additional volume is available. The leader will presumably want to get the major share of the new business and so will need to limit the activities of his competitors and dissuade new competitors from entering the market. A low level of unit margin for the brand market leader should go some considerable way to achieving these objectives.

For the potential new competitor, the level of return which he can foresee from his investment should be such that he will not be tempted to invest. In particular, he will not be tempted to build production capacity.

Existing competitors will have their returns so restricted that they will have limited resource available for the development of the competitive advantage which will be necessary if they are to affect the market leadership.

As the volume of a growth market rises, so brand unit costs should come down. If the arguments of the experience curve concept are accepted, costs should come down even if the size of the market does not increase.

A question facing the brand market leader in such circumstances is, 'Should I lead prices down?', and if so, 'How rapidly?'

Much will depend on the particular circumstances which apply for the given brand leader. Should he wish to dominate the market into its mature stage, he would be advised to ensure that his prices move downward as the volume moves forward, and his unit costs decrease. He will not want any major new competitor to build plant, or any existing competitor to increase capacity. Lowering his price is one way of making sure this is less likely to happen.

As to the leader's own position, the additional volume can mean that his total margin will increase despite the lower selling prices.

‘During 1968-69 price had a particularly important influence on the strategic development of the UK washing powder market.

Procter & Gamble launched a washing powder named Ariel into test market in the UK in 1968. Ariel was an enzymatic washing powder with the ability to remove certain difficult stains from fabrics; at the time this ability represented a significant competitive advantage for the brand. The powder was the first of its kind to be widely available in the UK. It was supported by a very effective brand advertising presentation. Ariel sold at a price which represented a substantial premium over the general price level applying in the market at this time.

Ariel was a great success in its test market, it became a clear leader, and P & G moved it rapidly into the national market. The product was basically unchanged, there was a door-to-door sampling, a strong advertising presentation, and the premium price was maintained.

Ariel was also very successful in its national launch and for a period moved into clear leadership of the total UK washing powder market.

Lever was not prepared for the Ariel operation or for its success. The company did not have an enzymatic powder ready for the market at the time of the Ariel launch, nor did it have adequate production capacity available to produce a similar product in quantity. In financial terms, Lever believed that the Ariel brand margin was most reasonable and that after its initial launch expenditures it would be able to show a very worthwhile level of profit contribution.

In 1969, after a 'crash' operation in plant construction, Lever launched an enzymatic washing powder brand named Radiant. The product was very similar in formulation and performance to Ariel. Lever believed it had a good advertising presentation for the brand, but had to accept that P & G had already mounted a particularly effective presentation for Ariel. Lever knew that if Radiant was to represent best value to a satisfactory number of consumers, and stop the progress of Ariel, it had to reach those consumers at a lower unit price. Lever also accepted that for a period the Radiant price differential would need to be more than just marginal.

During the Radiant launch period, a major worry for Lever was that P & G would drop the Ariel unit price to, or below, the Radiant level. This could have enabled Ariel to increase its market lead and brand volume, and take from Radiant its one brand advantage – a lower price. For Lever to have met an Ariel price reduction with a further reduction for Radiant would have been extremely expensive. The brand was heavily committed to extensive launch expenditures, and beyond this it would have been necessary to drop the prices of other brands in the market.

Fortunately for Lever, P & G maintained the Ariel unit price. Radiant was able to enter the national market with a reasonable degree of success; it carried out its main job of stopping Ariel's progress, and gave Lever valuable time in which to re-stage its other brands in the market. In fact, Ariel began to lose market share following the Radiant launch and never fully recovered; Persil was able to reclaim its market leadership, and Lever regained company leadership of the market. From the Lever viewpoint, the threat of Ariel becoming a dominant market leader, with all the advantages this could bring P & G, had been overcome.

If Ariel had reduced its unit price at the time of the Radiant launch would it have 'killed off' the Radiant brand at birth? Further, would the lower unit price have so increased Ariel's market share and volume that it would have moved forward to become a dominant market leader? Beyond this, could Ariel have taken this dominance into a highly profitable period of market maturity and decline? These are very interesting hypothetical questions.

Should the market have reached the mature stage and be more or less static in size, or have moved into decline, then the pricing position of the dominant brand leader can be very different.

The probability of a new competitor entering the market is much lower, although during the early part of the mature stage of the market the position may need careful study. Consumers will have become firmly attached to the established brands, and moving them (the consumers) to a new brand will be that much more difficult. In these circumstances the leader should be able, if he wishes, to take higher margins without running undue risk. His competitors will in all probability be delighted to follow him. When the market goes into decline the higher unit margins should most certainly be available.

How should the leader react if the smaller brands do not follow his price moves? If they do not move down with him he will expect them to lose volume, and so he is unlikely to be concerned. It is when they do not move up with him that strong action may be necessary. He may be advised to 'teach them a lesson' by reducing his own price, possibly to a level below that applying before his increase. Over the short term the move may be costly to him in lost revenue, but if he wants to bring about a discipline within the market, and to ensure that his competitors know he means business, he will be wise to act strongly.

A failure to act could mean that the competitive move will be repeated, his dominant position will gradually be eroded, and with the erosion will go his volume and his unit cost competitive advantage.

What if the dominant brand market leader opts to go for a high unit margin? If all his competitors are relatively small operators then he may be able to hold position without any challenge. The smaller men may 'know their place' and take the higher returns which the leader's umbrella will allow. The mere threat by the leader that he is prepared to use short-term price action if necessary may keep the smaller competitors quiet. However, there is always the possibility that the higher level of return accruing to the leader will attract new competition, and also the smaller men may become ambitious. If the dominant brand leader ever lets it be known that the short-term returns are essential to him, this may be seen as an opportunity by a competitor.

Pricing policy for brands sharing market leadership

In this situation it is likely that the brands at the top of the market will have settled to a value relationship position, in price and performance, which means that they hold their regular consumers, and lose and gain 'switchers' from time to time.

Each competitor will keep a very close watch on the others. In particular they will be concerned to react to and counter any shorter-term trade price adjustments. Over a period they can be expected to balance one another in this respect.

Much of the competition in the market-place is likely to be in the form of sales promotion and advertising presentation, as the brands try to make the best use of the limited product changes which come through from their respective development laboratories. Each competitor will be working to develop a breakthrough competitive advantage. Such an advantage will need to be of real significance, a significance which, if exploited to the full, will be able to bring about a major change in brand shares and volumes within the market.

During the period of peace in the market, the brand unit margins are likely to be at a level which provides reasonable profitability for all the major competitors; this assumes that the level of operating efficiency for all of them is roughly the same. If any one competitor believes he has any form of competitive advantage in such factors as product innovation, advertising presentation, or promotional development and application, then he is likely to attempt to keep the brand margins on the high side to allow him funds to practise his advantage.

Once a competitor believes he has developed a competitive advantage significant enough to warrant an attempt at a major leap forward for his brand, then the pricing position is likely to change.

If the competitive advantage breakthrough is in the form of a major product performance improvement, the brand concerned may introduce it without a price increase even though an extra product cost is incurred. In this way the value of the brand to the consumers will be enhanced, and the aim will be to maintain price stability in the market. The various indirect price incentives (coupons, free gifts etc) may be used to encourage the consumer to try the brand. In effect, the brand will be saying to its competitors, 'Why engage in a price battle from which none of us can gain?'

Other brands in the market can either accept this position or move for a price adjustment. If the product improvement is really significant, and particularly if it is costly, they may move for a direct price reduction. In this way they will attempt to adjust their brand's value in the light of the new performance standard in the market. They may also engage in various indirect price adjustments.

If the product improvement is of lesser significance and relatively inexpensive, then the price adjustments are more likely to be of the indirect kind.

In these price developments the degree of price elasticity which applies for each particular brand competing in the market is always important. This is a question of the level of brand loyalty held by each brand. Clearly, brand personality is a significant factor.

This question of the degree of a brand's price elasticity is one that affects, to some extent, all of the various pricing situations discussed in this chapter. The brand's record through previous price moves, well structured consumer research, and price testing, can provide valuable guidance on this issue. Before he engages in price activities the manufacturer would be well advised to equip himself with reliable information on price elasticity covering both his own and competitive brands.

The duration of the price activity in the market is likely to depend upon the significance to the consumer of the competitive advantage held by the aggressor brand, and the success of the brand in getting this advantage home to the consumer. If the move is fully successful, the brand should make a major gain in market share which in turn should mean a marked increase in volume.

The increase in volume should bring lower unit costs. In fact, the advantages of a strong brand leader should begin to show.

In a truly successful operation the advantages brought by the increase in volume will offset the cost of the product improvement.

It should be noted that when a brand gains say, 6 per cent of a market, the other brands in the market are bound to lose, in total, 6 per cent. In big markets where only a limited number of brands compete, the movement in brand volume generated by brand share gains of relatively small levels can have an important effect on the total unit costs of competing brands.

This last point is very simple, but in markets which have been highly competitive, and where only two or three brands have survived, it is crucial. If Brand A holds 45 per cent of a market with Brand B on 38 per cent, and A is able to make a gain of 5 percentage points and B loses 5 points, A will have changed his relationship with B quite dramatically—his volume will have moved from being some 18 per cent more than B's to a position where it is approximately 50 per cent more.

What if one of the two or three leaders makes a price move without a competitive advantage? This can take the form of a direct price reduction, or of not following an increase of the other leaders. In practice, moves of this kind can be made via special dealer discounts or allowances of other kinds.

The important consideration is whether or not the brand is allowed by the other leaders to make a move of this kind unchallenged. If they are under heavy pressure for short-term profit or cash they may feel that they cannot take action. The danger in not taking action can be that the aggressor brand gains market share and increases volume and is then able to make a reduction in his unit costs. The brands which lose share will increase unit costs. If the position is allowed to become more permanent, a new competitive relationship will be in operation.

In practice, competitive brands are more likely to reply with price adjustments, and no one brand will benefit. Clearly, before making a price move of this sort it is important to know the position and probable reaction of your competitors: it could be a valuable opportunity, or it could be extremely costly.

Pricing policy for brands holding a lower level share in the market

For a brand in this position the general advice would be to 'follow the leader'. This assumes that the brand does not want to engage the leader in direct price competition—he reasons he cannot afford such a move and feels that he is sure to lose as the result of a competitive action. His direct and indirect unit costs of production are probably higher than the leader's. His price to the trade is probably lower than the leader's (it would need to be to get an equivalent price to the consumer, as the trader would normally tend to take a lower margin on the leader). He is in no fit condition to fight. Better that he shows his respect, and follows the leader when he moves.

This would probably be good commercial advice, and normally the small brand would follow it. There are occasions when the small brand may decide not to follow the leader. If the squeeze becomes so tight that he feels he must risk a move of his own, then he may take it. The period which follows is likely to be extremely worrying for him.

The small brand can avoid direct confrontation with the leader by the use of differential pricing. This is illegal in some countries, but in many it remains an approach which can be employed by any company. It simply means charging different prices to different customers. Thus, Chain A may pay 100 per unit, Chain B 110, and so on.

Such a policy can bring customer relations problems. However, the fact that the brand is small may mean that it will pass without widespread notice—it does not have to be announced publicly. Often the various 'overrider' schemes employed by small brands are forms of differential pricing.

Where the small brand is owned by a major operator and is used by him as a form of counter or control on a competitor's strong leader, then a very different position exists.

Here the owner of the small brand may be attempting to stop his competitor (the leader) from raising margins as the market matures. His aim would be to restrict the profit flow to the leading brand. If the leader is to discipline the small brand the short-term cost could be very high indeed.

A small brand operation of this kind can be made to work, but it requires extremely fine judgement. It is probably a case of annoying the leader, but not too much! The small brand owner needs to be sure he isn't vulnerable to such a move himself in another market.

Pricing policy for a brand that is a segment leader

Segmented brands are, in fact, part of the total market and as such are part of the total market price structure. However, in view of their special value to their particular group of consumers, they would normally expect to have a greater degree of price flexibility than a similar sized brand competing in the main market sector. Much will depend on the strength of the segment, and the strength of the particular brand.

Brands segmented on a performance basis normally carry a premium over the main sector brands. Experience will have shown the level of the premium possible in line with a given volume position. Normally, segmented brands would find it commercially advantageous to follow the leader, and in this way they would maintain the established differential.

Entering a market with a brand in a segment which is growing much faster than the main market, and eventually turning the segmented brand into a main market brand, is one way of challenging a dominant leader. For a move of this kind good judgement is necessary to ensure that price movements are used to obtain the maximum help for the segmented brand. The aim would be to narrow the gap with the main maket brands just prior to the period of challenge on the leader.

Price war

When there is widespread price cutting within a market, and this continues for a lengthy period, it is often referred to as a 'price war'. Price wars can be started by accident, or deliberately.

Accidental price wars are usually the result of rumour and misunderstanding. For instance, a rumour of a competitive price move is picked up by a salesman and reported to senior management. A second and a third rumour follow and so action is taken. The rumour was in fact a mistake, but the action taken as the result of it causes other counter actions and the whole price-cutting movement begins to snowball.

A price war started deliberately is a very different matter. Here one competitor within the market sets out to use price aggressively to attain a particular objective, other competitors meet his attack, and price activity gathers momentum.

With the majority of price wars nobody seems to win. The old adage, 'Never start a price war unless you are sure you are going to win it' has much to recommend it. To win would mean you achieve your objective at a cost which is considered to be reasonable.

To be sure of winning the manufacturer will need to have resources which provide for under-cutting of the competitors' prices to the necessary extent, and for the necessary length of time. In effect, this means having a proportionately greater reserve of funds available for the price activity than that available to competitors. He who is forced to concede first will probably be the loser.

The aggressor must always be prepared for a counter-attack in any other market where he trades and is vulnerable.

In the right circumstances a price war can work effectively for an aggressor. It needs careful and studied preparation, and skilled judgement in operation. It is a weapon which should be used with deference and in a controlled manner.

It is clearly a great advantage in a price war to have lower unit costs for the equivalent product than your competitors — in effect, to have a significant competitive advantage in unit cost. Given that you have this position, the funds which you may need to fight the battle will be reduced accordingly.

It is always important to know just how hard your opponents in the price war are likely to fight. How important is the market to them? How strong is their total company? And how are the senior managers (or owners) likely to react?

If the move is to 'teach a lesson', then it may be selectively aimed rather than a broad sweep at the market. Similarly, if the aim is to remove, or greatly reduce, a segmented brand, then again it may be possible to be selective.

Ideally aggressor brands should plan to achieve their objectives from the price war in a short period. Sharp, decisive action is to be preferred to a long drawn out and grinding encounter.

What if your brand becomes locked into a price war, how should you respond? You must be sure of the extent of the funds available to fight the battle, and you also need an estimate of the total cost of fighting over given periods of time. With these estimates available you can decide whether or not you wish to engage in battle. There could be circumstances in which the business would be better served if a decision is taken not to go to war. Indeed, it could possibly be advantageous to sell the brand, or company, to the aggressor or another competitor in the market.

It is necessary to look ahead and consider the market, and its make-up, when the battle is over. How big will the market be? How many brands will be left? What is the price structure likely to be? What are the surviving brand profit levels likely to be? These are important questions which need to be answered.

Having taken a decision to fight, you need a plan to hold position at the lowest outlay. A small brand does have some advantages going for it, and it is important that these should be played to the full.

Will special packs help? Normally the small brand has a higher degree of flexibility in manufacture. Will differential pricing help? The timing of special offers may be significant and the retail trade can be encouraged to 'help the small man'. A very high level of effectiveness and efficiency in manufacture is vitally important. A big brand will have the advantage of its volume, but it may find aggressive local actions difficult to handle. Large organisations can become bureaucratic and slow—the smaller business will need to be fast on its feet.

Skilled management judgement is always a major factor in winning price battles. Judging correctly just when to attack and counter attack, which of the various price approaches to use and how much to give, these and other judgement decisions are very important.

If the manufacturer of a small brand knows that at some time in the future he is likely to be drawn into a price battle, and it is one he is unlikely to win, then he could be well advised to consider selling his brand, or possibly his company. The price he will be able to obtain before the battle is likely to be much higher than after the attack.

Price and quality

It is often argued that the price level of a brand will act to convey a given level of quality to the consumer.

In some markets this may be correct. There is a distrust of the lowest priced brand—'It can't be good at that price.' This is more likely to apply in markets where the purchase decision is emotional. In markets where the consumer purchases frequently and is encouraged to put the brands available to her personal performance test regularly, the price level is unlikely to be a major factor in her judgement of the brand's quality. Nevertheless, a manufacturer would probably be wrong to sell a high performance brand too cheaply, unless there is a good strategic reason. Price is part of the total personality of any brand and if placed unduly low may pose a credibility problem with some consumers.

CHAPTER 10

Advertising

Of all the factors involved in business strategy formulation there can be little doubt that the one which tends to be discussed, criticised, praised, and generally argued about more than any other is advertising.

This is in part understandable. Everyone sees and is conscious of advertising, particularly the advertising for their own brands. Everyone knows the kind of advertising that works with them personally.

Many of the factors concerned in strategy formulation can be measured with some accuracy, for example the ingredients contained in a particular formula, or the speed of a processing machine. Advertising, and its effect, is much more difficult to measure. Indeed, an exact measure is just not possible, and skilled judgement will be an important factor in its evaluation.

Branded goods manufacturers do not have to use advertising. There are a number, a very limited number, of prominent brands which have achieved market-place success without advertising. However, for by far the majority of consumer brand successes, advertising has played a significant part in the brand's market progress.

In this book we are concerned primarily with the part that advertising can contribute to the formulation of a successful business strategy. In particular, we are concerned with the return an investment in brand advertising can bring, at given levels of expenditure, over specified periods, and in varying competitive circumstances.

In formulating a business strategy, estimates of the level of advertising investment necessary to achieve certain agreed objectives, will be required. Getting these estimates right may well open up valuable business opportunities. This chapter reviews a number of the considerations involved in the advertising investment decisions.

The advertising job

Before discussing the advertising investment it is necessary to consider the job brand advertising is expected to do. Advertising is an important part of brand presentation, and so, to a certain extent, the job of advertising has already been covered. The subject is particularly important because the investments involved are likely to be extensive, so a restatement of the purpose of advertising is probably justified.

The job of advertising is to help build and maintain sales volume. It does this by encouraging consumers to try the brand advertised, and by giving those consumers who are already users assurance, confidence, and encouragement to continue buying.

Advertising presents information about the brand or product in a persuasive manner. In the course of this presentation advertising should play its part in building the desired personality for the brand.

The task of brand advertising is thus threefold:

1. To persuade consumers to try the brand.
2. To provide existing users of the brand with assurance and confidence, and encouragement to continue buying.
3. To play its part in developing the desired brand personality.

It is important to note that, while these brand advertising tasks are always present, they are not necessarily present at the same level of intensity for each one at any given time. The requirement will vary depending on the position of the brand, and the position of the market. Thus, at the initial launch of the brand, the need to persuade consumers to try is paramount. At a later stage, when the brand has settled and the market is mature, there will be a greater need to provide assurance for regular buyers.

During its growth stage there will be a high proportion of new consumers joining the market. Even during the mature stage there will be some movement in its consumer make-up: some new users will enter the market and others will leave. However, the proportion of new users will tend to be lower. When the market moves into decline the number of new consumers is likely to be very limited.

Once this reasoning as to the tasks that advertising is required to perform is accepted, and if it is also accepted that the emphasis between the various tasks will need to vary depending upon the position of the market and of the brand, then it can have a very major influence on the level of a manufacturer's brand advertising investment.

The quality of advertising

There are two key factors concerned with the effectiveness of any advertising campaign—the amount of money invested in the campaign, and the quality of the advertising. It is an elementary fact that media space, whether it be television time or a newspaper or magazine page, costs the same amount of money for a bad advertisement as it does for a good one.

It is important to judge brand advertising against its (ie brand advertising) objectives, and not against the objectives of the total brand. The highest level of creativity in advertising is unlikely to bring the all-important repeat purchases if the basic factors in the brand's value equation (purpose, performance and price) are wrongly directed or incorrectly balanced. An effective level of creativity in the advertising can play a major part in securing the consumer's initial trial purchase, but for the repeat purchase the brand itself must play the major role.

It is necessary to have fully effective advertising working on a well constructed brand value proposition. If the brand, for instance, brings a new and significant benefit to the consumer, or has a performance which is markedly ahead of rival brands, and this can be demonstrated, then the advertising has something basic to work on and with good creativity should be able to make a full contribution. There is certainly some truth in the old adage, 'advertising works best for good brands'.

Successful specialists in advertising seem to agree that there are a number of basic rules or guidelines which should be observed in the forming of an effective advertisement. When these are followed, and highly skilled creativity is added, the prospect of producing an advertisement which will be effective is very high.

Of course, it is accepted that from time to time an advertisement will appear which performs brilliantly and yet does not seem to conform to the basic guidelines. In fields such as advertising where creativity has a very special contribution to make, this can happen. However, there would be a high degree of risk in a major strategy if it depended for success on the production of a brilliantly creative advertisement.

The brand personality

The brand personality, or brand image as it is sometimes called, has already been mentioned. While it will be formed by a whole series of contributory factors including the name and the pack design, probably the most important contribution will come from the brand advertising.

This is the so-termed 'added value' contribution of brand advertising. It has been the subject of considerable adverse comment from consumer associations and similar bodies who believe it can mislead consumers and is involved in providing false values.

The brand presentation will always form some kind of an impression of the brand in the consumers' mind. It cannot avoid doing so. Clearly, the manufacturer is justified in taking active steps to ensure, as far as he can, that the impression is favourable.

Should he overplay the brand personality building in his presentations he is likely to end up with advertisements which fall short in terms of effective selling. Further, the record shows that if the brand fails to deliver to the consumer in terms of performance and price, the added value of the personality will have only a limited effect.

In markets such as those for household cleaning products the truly successful brands have invariably provided a best value position for their consumers in terms of purpose, performance and price, and to this they have added an acceptable brand personality.

This is how David Ogilvy, doyen of advertising, writes of brand image in *Ogilvy on Advertising*:

> You now have to decide what 'image' you want for your brand. Image means *personality*. Products, like people, have personalities, and they can make or break them in the market-place. The personality of a product is an amalgam of many things—its name, its packaging, its price, the style of its advertising, and, above all, the nature of the product itself.

In its March/April 1955 issue, the *Harvard Business Review* published an article by Burleigh B Gardner and Sidney J Levy entitled, 'The Product and the Brand'. It contained what remains one of the best simple statements explaining the brand personality factor:

> The image of a product associated with the brand may be clear-cut or relatively vague; it may be varied or simple; it may be intense or innocuous. Sometimes the notions people have about a brand do not even seem very sensible or relevant to those who know what the product is 'really' like. But they all contribute to the customer deciding whether or not the brand is the one 'for me'.
>
> These sets of ideas, feelings, and attitudes that consumers have about brands are crucial to them in picking and sticking to ones that seem most appropriate. How else can they decide whether to smoke Camels or Lucky Strike; to use Nescafé or Borden's instant coffee; to drive a Ford or a Chevrolet or a Plymouth?
>
> Justifying choice is easier with the cars; there at least the products have clearly visible differences. But the reasons people give for choosing a brand of cigarettes (and soap and bread and laxatives) are pretty much the same. Thus you find drinkers of any brand of beer justifying their preference in identical terms: 'Schlitz is better because it's dry.' 'I like dry beer, so I prefer Bud to Schlitz.'
>
> Something must make a great difference: the conceptions of the different brands must be compounded of subtle variations in feelings about them, not necessarily in product qualities. A big problem in this area then, is what kind of symbol a given brand is to consumers.

There is a strong argument that the Gardner and Levy comment over-plays the brand 'personality' contribution to consumer buying behaviour, and underplays the ability of consumers to notice the performance differences between brands. It also underplays the importance of price to the consumer. The record shows that consumers are frequently able to recognize relatively small performance changes. The record also shows that some of them are very price conscious. Nevertheless, the comment does sum up succinctly the brand personality case.

How much to invest in brand advertising

This question has been examined many times over the years by economists, advertising specialists, businessmen, and others. They have tended to differ in their answers and clearly there is no one correct approach or formula to decide how much to invest in brand advertising.

The question is important to strategy formulation. The sums of money involved may be very large, and the profit at risk if the answer is badly wrong can be substantial. Beyond this there are very real opportunities for those who invest heavily at the right time, and save their money for other investments when the time is wrong.

The normal approach is to consider the various methods said to be used in operating companies to arrive at brand advertising appropriations. They vary from a calculation based on a percentage of sales, a sales case rate, an advertising 'job to be done' calculation, through to the provision of a fixed annual investment.

The subject is a difficult one to cover with any certainty. Even when the case rate approach is said to apply, further examination shows that the actual rate is allowed to change from period to period, and then exceptions are made for major re-launches and particular competitive actions. Frequently, the more mechanical type approaches are used as a form of control or discipline for more junior brand managers, with senior executives reserving the right to make adjustments as they consider appropriate.

The problem is further complicated in that if brand advertising is viewed within a co-ordinated marketing plan, there may be other brand investments, eg promotions or price, which may be used to supplement, or replace, brand advertising at specific periods.

In this chapter it is proposed to consider the question of brand advertising investment in terms of the brand's present position in the market-place, and its possible position in the future. Naturally, the remarks must be general as in real life so much would depend on the broader strategy aims, and the competitive pressures, of the particular business concerned. The size and profit potential of the market, and of the brand within this market, would also be major practical influences.

The discussion here is ordered as follows:

1. A new brand launch.
2. A brand re-launch.
3. An established brand.

A new brand launch

If the market which the new brand is entering is small and relatively undeveloped, and the market development is expected to be slow and gradual, the total brand marketing approach may need to be a patient one. In markets of this kind the earlier battles are frequently concerned with obtaining store distribution. Without it any form of brand promotion is unlikely to succeed.

An example of this type of market and brand operation is the UK market for automatic dishwashing powders. The major influence on the size and development of the market is clearly the ownership of automatic dishwashing machines. In the UK for a number of years this ownership was at a very low level of between 1 and 3 per cent of households. At this time many stores did not consider it worthwhile to stock any of the brands available, and rarely would stores consider stocking more than one.

Clearly, in circumstances of this kind an investment in large scale advertising, on television for instance, would not have made good business sense. A more modest approach with careful media selection, was more likely to succeed.

A new brand attempting to move into an established market of considerable size and value faces very different issues. There will be a need to move volume up rapidly to obtain lower unit costs of production. Early sampling of the brand will be necessary, and use of the various promotional 'tools' will be essential.

During its opening period a brand's purpose should be established with the consumer. This means that the benefit the brand brings should be defined and registered in the consumer's mind. Its performance ability should also be established, and its personality in part formed.

It is during its opening period that the brand's foundation is built—a secure foundation is essential for a successful longer-term position. There is a great deal of truth in the argument that 'You only get one big opportunity to establish the brand, and that is at the initial launch.' It is extremely difficult and costly to attempt to change a brand's purpose at a later stage in its life. If a new performance level can be developed for an established brand it should be possible to register it with the consumer, but it is invariably much better and cheaper to get it right at the initial launch. Changing a brand's personality can be particularly troublesome. It is probably one of the most difficult changes to accomplish successfully.

It is a fact that the number of brands which have been able to recover from an unsuccessful opening, and move forward to real success, is remarkably low. The usual procedure is for an unsuccessful launch to be followed by a number of attempts to reposition the brand, each one requiring considerable investment backing, and each one ending in failure. On rare occasions brands have been rescued after unsuccessful openings. Usually the rescue has been brought about by a major change in brand performance, a change significant enough to provide the brand with a fresh start, and for the consumer to recognize and appreciate it rapidly.

The lesson for a new brand launch is very clear. The manufacturer should take every reasonable action to ensure that his new brand is right— right for those consumers to whom it is directed in terms of the benefit it promises, right in terms of its performance in delivering the benefit, right in terms of its price, and right in terms of its presentation, style and approach. And as a fundamental consideration, he should be sure that his brand's competitive advantage is strong enough to support a new brand.

Given this desirable situation the brand advertising investment during the opening period should be the strongest, within a sensible business plan, that the company position can support.

It is certainly desirable that the investment at this time should be at a level which exceeds the expenditure of the leading brands in the market, or market sector, in which the brand intends to compete. At its launch the brand is fighting for consumer recognition. This could mean that its message will need to be put over strongly enough to be recognized above the general level of brand advertising in the market-place.

Failure to get the brand, its name, its purpose and performance, through to those consumers to whom it is primarily directed at this time could prove fatal. At the initial launch of a brand the claim that 'it will be cheaper to overspend rather than to underspend' has considerable credibility, provided any overspending is kept to a reasonable level.

A brand re-launch

Brand re-launches are necessary from time to time. Established brands need to be kept up to date, their formulas may need revision, their packaging may need design changes and so on.

When a brand re-launch is based on a significant improvement in performance, or the development of some other worthwhile competitive advantage, it is clearly a good time to go back to the consumer, looking for trial or re-trial. This is a time when good advertising can be most effective: it is a time when a major investment in the brand advertising should bring very good results. The brand has something to say and should take all reasonable steps to ensure the appropriate consumers hear its message.

However, it is important to distinguish between the really worthwhile re-launch and one that is of limited significance. Thus, a re-launch which is merely a new advertising presentation, or a change in pack design, is likely to have limited effect. The danger is that a limited brand re-launch will be seen as a significant move by those close to it within the business, and both the level of investment and the result expectations placed unduly high. The outcome is likely to be disappointment and a financial problem.

An established brand

It is in the context of established brands that the strongest debate on the topic of advertising investment takes place. Views fall into two broad groups:

1. An established brand should have a consistently high level of advertising support.
2. The level of advertising support can vary considerably, with high levels at specific times, eg major re-launches, and with much lower levels at other times.

The advertising support level of an established brand can have a crucial effect on strategy planning. The profit, and cash, flowing from an established brand during a period of low level advertising can be substantial and provide a most valuable additional source of funds. The question to be asked is 'What is the risk to the brand's position?'

The case for the consistently high level of investment gets its main support from the fact that many leading and successful companies appear to follow it. This is a strong recommendation.

The late Mr J O Peckham who before becoming an international marketing consultant, was a senior executive with the highly respected marketing research company of A C Nielsen in the USA, has been active in research of the advertising investment issue. In a well regarded paper published in 1976,* Mr Peckham looked at the 15-year performance of 34 brand leaders in non-durable consumer goods markets. Of these brands, 65 per cent maintained leadership over the 15-year period. All made consistent product and packaging improvements over the period. Almost 80 per cent of the successful brand leaders maintained a 15-year share of advertising expenditures consistent with the brand's share of consumer purchases. This is factual market evidence and is again a very strong recommendation for maintaining a consistently high level of advertising support.

If the brands were all in strong growth markets through the period then the need to attract new triers would always have been present. This

* 'Why Advertise Established Brands?', *The Nielsen Researcher*, Number 3, 1976.

is hardly likely but there would have been the normal movement of consumers in and out of the markets.

It is interesting to note that out of a total of 34 brand leaders examined, 22 kept their lead. Of the 22, 17 had advertising expenditures consistent with their share of consumer purchases, five had a share of advertising well below their share of consumer purchases.

Given that in a specific market the leading brands all have the same purpose, all have the same price level, and all the same performance ability, then it is understandable that presentation, its quality and quantity, takes on unique significance in brand progress. It would be the one key value area left in which to differentiate. However, this would be a highly unusual market and would demonstrate a dismal lack of initiative on the part of the competing businesses.

The case for the view that the level of advertising placed behind an established brand can safely be varied from time to time, is also backed by research. The highly detailed and most thorough research carried out by Dr R Ackoff for Anheuser-Busch on beer in the USA in the 1960s* demonstrated that reductions could be made in the advertising expenditure for the Budweiser brand which need not mean a reduction in sales volume.

Budweiser was the brand leader, it was advertised continually and at a consistently high level. Dr Ackoff arranged tests whereby in certain regions of the USA the advertising levels were reduced by varying amounts of up to 50 per cent. Sales volumes did not suffer adversely and the experiment was gradually widened to other regions of the country. Dr Ackoff was able to state:

> From then on, more and more areas were similarly treated, and the reductions were gradually increased until the advertising expenditure per barrel was $0.80 in contrast to $1.89 when research was initiated. During this period (1962-68) sales of Budweiser increased from approximately 7.5 million to 14.5 million barrels, and its market share increased from 8.14 to 12.94 per cent.

Dr Ackoff also experimented with what he terms 'pulse' advertising. This was using a pattern of off-and-on rather than continuous advertising. Two types of pulsing were considered. In one, advertising expenditures in all media were off or on together. In the other, only one medium was used at any time, but the media were alternated. An experiment was designed to test the first of these types of pulse. It involved four treatments, and the level of expenditure in each was varied.

One of the pulsing patterns was found to be significantly better than the others, and slightly better than normal advertising when accompanied

*The Art of Problem Solving by R L Ackoff (John Wiley and Sons Ltd, 1978).

by a high level of expenditure. Another pattern was found to be best when accompanied by a low level of expenditure.

Summarizing his experiments with Budweiser, Dr Ackoff states:

> It would be foolish, of course, to claim that the improvement in company performance was due entirely to changes in advertising. Other types of changes, some based on research and some not, were also made during this period. One thing is clear: the changes induced by the research described here did not hurt Anheuser-Busch.

Another academic who has been very concerned with this subject is Prof A S C Ehrenberg. Together with G J Goodhardt he published a paper entitled, 'How Advertising Works'* in 1980. This is what the paper says on advertising to established buyers:

> Much mass-media advertising reaches established buyers. The need here is to have satisfied customers. With *frequently bought* goods they provide the repeat-buying on which continuing sales crucially depend.
>
> With *infrequently bought* goods the effect is indirect: satisfied customers provide good word-of-mouth recommendations and a confident retail trade or technical sales force.
>
> Accounts of persuasive advertising usually do not greatly discuss its influence on the established buyer as such. Many of the models have a 'feed back loop' or the like, but say little.
>
> Each purchase is usually still treated like a new one, as if converting a largely ignorant consumer each time. As Boulding wrote in his *Economic Analysis*: 'Most advertising, unfortunately, is devoted to an attempt to build up in the mind of the consumer *irrational preferences for certain brands or goods*. All the arts of psychology—particularly that of association—are used to persuade consumers that they should buy Bingo rather than Bango.'
>
> Persuasive advertising could play a role if there were a continuing drain of established buyers who had to be replaced with new customers, just to keep sales steady. But we saw in earlier essays that there generally is no 'leaky bucket'. (Exceptions, such as baby products, are rare.)
>
> Persuasive advertising could also have a role if it were to increase the brand's sales. But the sales-effectiveness of advertising for established brands has never been demonstrated, despite almost innumerable attempts to do so. There are hardly even any unsubstantiated *claims* to that effect. Marketing companies know full well that advertising their established brands does not usually pay for

Understanding Buyer Behaviour, paper No 16. 'How Advertising Works' by A S C Ehrenberg and G J Goodhardt.

itself directly in increased sales since their sales do not normally go up.

There are then two possibilities. Either advertising for established brands is pointless or it is defensive. We believe that it is defensive; advertising helps to keep one's satisfied customers by reinforcing their existing habits and attitudes. It is a price to pay for staying in the market.

Suppose Brand X were to cut its advertising while its competitors continued theirs. On the strongly persuasive theory each purchase is positively influenced by the advertising and sales should drop quickly.

But this seldom happens. Most marketing men would, however, fear a *slow* decline in sales. This is what the weak reinforcement theory would also lead one to expect. The existing customers of Brand X would no longer receive reinforcement from its advertising, and be more open to the advertising of the competitive brands. But the effects would be slow, partly because the reinforcing effects of *using* Brand X would still persist.

Many manufacturers have conducted detailed research on brand advertising levels and their effect on brand sales. Naturally, they keep the detail of their research and the results confidential. If they have clear indications as to how to save on brand advertising expenditures without losing sales volume, they have developed a competitive advantage.

How much to invest in established brand advertising remains one of the most debated subjects in the whole field of manufacturing and marketing branded goods.

In this book it is accepted that the principal task of advertising changes depending upon the position the brand has reached in its development, the position of the market in which the brand competes, and the specific competitive pressures which apply.

At the initial launch the brand is intent on obtaining consumer trial. Similarly, when the brand receives a major re-launch which is of consequence, it requires trial and re-trial. At other times the brand is primarily concerned to provide assurance and confidence to existing users.

The two tasks differ in their nature and so brand advertising, its content, its frequency, and the investment placed behind it, can differ.

However, the style, the tone, and the environment of both the 'trial' and the 'assurance' advertisements should be appropriate for the desired brand personality.

In markets where there is a rapid growth and therefore a continuous flow of new consumers to the market, the approach outlined above may need revision. A much stronger emphasis on consumer trial would apply throughout. Similarly, in markets such as baby foods, where the consumers are changing continually, the 'trial' approach would need to be followed on a more regular basis.

Viewing the advertising investment for an established brand as an investment which can vary in its intensity, and size, depending upon the requirement of the brand, and of the movement of the market in which the brand competes, can bring substantial rewards. It can be argued, of course, that there will always be a degree of risk.

Advertising and the barrier theory

There is a view which sees advertising as a barrier to entry to a market.

The reasoning is as follows: if the brands already established in a market advertise very heavily, any new entry will have to advertise at a level at least equivalent to the established brand, or it will not be able to break into the market. The view is occasionally quoted as a reason for small manufacturers being unable to break into a market dominated by two or three large companies.

The small manufacturer faces the same basic problems as all others who attempt to change an established market. First, he must put together a brand which can represent best value to a satisfactory number of consumers. Having done this, he must persuade consumers to try the brand.

There are many ways to encourage consumers to try a brand. Advertising is merely one way, and it is not necessarily always the most effective. It is possible to force trial by other approaches such as sampling door-to-door or by generous trade offers. Nevertheless, it is accepted that brand advertising would normally be very helpful in obtaining trial for a new brand competing in one of the major consumer markets.

The advertising does not necessarily have to be at the investment level of the established brands in the market, but if it is to make any impression on the consumer there will probably be a necessary minimum level of investment.

However, the smaller manufacturer attempting to invade a major market currently held by one or two established brands is likely to have problems wider in their form and context than just advertising. If he plans for his brand to take a major market share in a big market then he will need to get the consumer trial already mentioned. He must also have available sufficient brand stocks to meet the consumer demand following the trial, and a satisfactory quantity of these stocks will need to be in the retail stores. If the brand is to be produced at a reasonable unit cost he must also have appropriate production facilities.

In effect, the small manufacturer will need an adequate supply of capital to finance the operation, production facilities to produce at the required volume, and an organization able to compete at the new level of business he is proposing to achieve.

A particular problem is the speed with which his competitors are able to copy any major product innovation he may have, and include it in their own brands. With their established brands, effective production facilities, and skilled marketing they may be able to exploit the competitive advantage more rapidly than he can. The major plus he has had in his limited test marketing may no longer be exclusive when he is able to engage in a national operation.

In fact, the small manufacturer's main problem will be the very high degree of risk that his proposition carries. He can expect to experience considerable difficulty in arranging the necessary financial backing for his operation because of this. If his competitive advantage is significant and he is able to protect its exclusivity, then the risk will be markedly reduced and he will find the problem of raising the necessary capital greatly eased.

It is understandable that the small man is usually well advised to make his attack on a major market in more than one step. Initially he would be well advised to attack a specific market segment; when he has had success and established a business confidence, he can if he wishes begin to take the next step towards an attack on the main market.

The issue of the barrier theory of advertising has often been raised, but it is very difficult to find a market where it has actually been the key factor in delaying, or preventing, a competitive entry.

CHAPTER 11

Promotions

Used skilfully promotion can be very effective in raising the demand for a brand rapidly, and then holding it at the higher level so that the economies of high volume manufacture and distribution can be exploited. Equally, skilful use of promotions can greatly reduce the impact and effect of a competitive brand attack.

Promotions are a positive tool within the marketing approach of a consumer brand company. Often viewed merely as a shorter-term tactical influence, promotion can in fact play a major part in the development of a longer-term brand strategy.

Two types of promotion are considered here:

1. *Strategic promotions.* These normally require substantial investment and resource backing, and are used to attain objectives which are of major significance in the longer-term progress of the brand.
2. *Tactical promotions.* These are used from time to time to attain certain specific brand tactical objectives. The improvement of brand distribution through a particular class of trade, or the introduction of a new pack size, are examples where tactical promotions are normally applied. They usually receive only a limited level of investment and resource backing.

This chapter is concerned primarily with *strategic* promotions which can in turn be either aggressive or defensive.

Aggressive strategic promotions normally have one basic objective: to encourage consumer trial for the brand concerned. They give the consumer the opportunity to submit the brand to her own best value test, the opportunity to try the brand for herself, and to appreciate the benefits it provides.

Defensive strategic promotions are designed to protect the brand from competitive attack. In particular, defensive promotions are directed to stop competitive brands gaining access to their brand's regular users.

Aggressive strategic promotions

One of the outstanding examples of an aggressive strategic promotion is free sampling, particularly when it takes the form of a door-to-door household distribution. When he carries out this operation the manufacturer is ensuring that the consumer has the opportunity to try his brand; he is actually giving her a packet in her home.

Sampling by the door-to-door approach can involve major up front investment. The sample must be produced and distributed, and it will need to be of an adequate size to ensure the user can appreciate the brand performance. The physical distribution in itself can be an involved and costly operation. All the outlay will need to be made before any payback is received. Can such an operation be worthwhile? Everything will depend on the specific circumstances; a straightforward answer is not possible. A number of pertinent questions will need to be answered:

- How big is the market, or market segment, in which the brand competes?
- How many consumers are likely to be interested in the brand?
  If the market is a small one then a house-to-house sampling operation is unlikely to be justified. If only a limited number of consumers are expected to be interested in the brand then a 'closely directed' sampling approach may be more appropriate.
- Does the brand have a significant performance competitive advantage over the other brands competing in the market?
- When the consumer uses the brand will she be very impressed/ impressed/or will she merely 'just notice'?
  A significant advance in performance would normally be necessary if it is to register clearly with the consumer, and to justify the heavy sampling cost.
  To get the consumer to change from a long-standing brand attachment it may be necessary to ensure that she is 'very impressed'.
- What is the cost of manufacturing and distributing the sample?
  For a door-to-door sample the cost of production would need to be relatively low. Would the plant be idle but for the sample production? If so, it may be reasonable to cost the manufacture at marginal, or variable, cost only.

● How long will the sample last the consumer? Will she be back in the market in one week, two weeks, or three months?

    If the consumer is to be taken out of the market for a long time this must be given full consideration within the various cost estimates and operating plans.

● Will the sampling effort be part of a totally co-ordinated brand marketing operation, and will this include a satisfactory level of consumer advertising and store distribution?

    The advertising should help to build consumer confidence and explain the brand. It would be very wasteful to get the consumer enthusiastic for a brand which she is unable to buy in her regular store.

● When the consumer goes to make her first purchase will she consider the brand price reasonable?

    The superior performance may have a value to the consumer; the key question is 'How much value?' If she considers the price to be unduly high when she goes to make her first purchase then the enhanced performance may not ensure that the brand represents best value to her. The performance/price relationship will need to be correctly balanced to obtain the consumer's vital first purchase.

To these questions others may be added. From an analysis of the answers it should be possible to build a statement showing the costs and revenues likely to result over suitable time periods. From this statement it should be possible to arrive at a view as to whether or not a promotion as aggressive as a door-to-door sample is right for the particular brand concerned.

A successful promotion of this kind, well timed and used in favourable circumstances, can have a dramatic effect on the progress of a brand, and on the competitive positions within the market concerned. The brand could move to immediate leadership of the market. With this position should come all the economies of high volume production and distribution. The heavy investment in plant and machinery will be working, and in a relatively short time the brand will have become a valuable asset with profit-earning potential.

Of course, it would be wrong to suggest that results of this kind can come from the strategic promotion alone; they would come from a co-ordinated marketing operation with the strategic promotion as a major element.

❛Two excellent examples of strategic promotion, working within co-ordinated marketing operations, and producing outstanding results, occurred during the late 1960s and mid-1970s in the UK washing powder market.

In 1968 Lever held a 51 per cent share of the market and Procter & Gamble was 6 points behind with 45 per cent. In terms of sales volume, Lever held a 20,000 ton lead over P & G.

P & G attacked vigorously through 1969 with a new brand, heavy advertising, door-to-door sampling and other strategic promotions. The attacks were successful, and for 1969 P & G moved to a 52 per cent market share with a 7 point lead over Lever who now had 45 per cent. P & G had completely reversed the sales volume position and now held a lead of approximately 24,000 tons.

During the years which followed Lever was able to make a steady recovery and by 1973 both companies held 46 per cent market shares.

In 1974 and 1975 Lever moved on to the attack. Lever had a new brand, established brand re-launches, heavy advertising, and very strong strategic promotions. Included in the attack were sampling, couponing, and introductory price packs. It was a successful operation and in 1975 Lever increased its market share to 52 per cent. P & G's share dropped back to 40 per cent. Lever now had a 40,000 ton lead in sales volume.

This marked the beginning of a particularly good period for Lever in this market. By 1980 Lever, with a share of over 52 per cent, held a 15 point lead over its rival. As the total market had grown the Lever lead in sales volume was now 60,000 tons.

The following market estimates show the position:

UK washing powder market

	Market share %	Sales volume 000 tons	Market share %	Sales volume 000 tons
		1968		*1969*
Lever	51	173	45	153
P & G	45	153	52	177
Lever volume lead on P & G		+20		−24
		1973		*1975*
Lever	46	156	52	176
P & G	46	156	40	136
Lever volume lead on P & G		−		+40

In a market where the fixed costs of production and distribution are very high, a volume lead of 20,000 tons is most valuable. If the lead is extended to 60,000 tons the effect on profitability can be dramatic. ,

There are many ways of obtaining brand sampling other than a sample distribution door-to-door. Coupons may be distributed, established brands can carry coupons for the new brand, magazines can carry special introductory offers etc. However, the door-to-door sample operation is an outstanding example of aggressive strategic promotion; it almost guarantees that the consumer will try the brand irrespective of competitive action. In the big consumer markets, where the competitors are invariably strong effective companies well able to mount an extensive defence of their position, this can be particularly important.

For many manufacturers operating in specialized markets, a door-to-door approach may be far too random, and therefore too expensive, as a means of obtaining trial. A specifically directed approach would be more appropriate.

The need, when considering the various alternatives for gaining brand trial, is to have guidance as to the depth of brand penetration each one is likely to obtain, and the cost that will be incurred both in total and per household or per person penetrated. It is also necessary to consider the number of households (or people) who 'repeat purchase'—it is from the repeaters that the vitally important regular buyers come.

Marketing research should help with guidance as to the level of effectiveness likely to be achieved by the various sampling approaches.

Price can be used as a 'tool' to gain consumer trial. Special packs can provide the consumer with a particularly attractive unit price. This approach is unlikely to be as wide in its penetration as, for instance, a door-to-door sample. The investment required, however, will almost certainly be much lower.

The need to consider strategic promotions within the broader view of a co-ordinated brand marketing plan will be evident. There is considerable synergy between the various marketing tools during the initial launch, or re-launch, period for a brand. Advertising helps the sample, the sample will help to get trade distribution, the effect on the consumers of the sample will stimulate trade feature, keen pricing, and so forth.

The opportunity for a manufacturer to make a real impression with a brand comes rarely, in many cases only once during its life-time. The opportunity comes whenever the brand gets a significant competitive advantage, in particular one that is readily appreciated by the consumer. It will mean that the brand has, for instance, developed a new additional purpose of substance, has obtained a significant performance advance, or is able to provide a major price reduction. It is unlikely to come from a change in presentation alone. Significant advantages are invariably very difficult to develop. They are hard to come by; when they do arise it is vitally important they be exploited to the full.

The manufacturer's aim is for the purchase of his brand to become a form of habit with the consumer. Well entrenched habits are hard to break. The initial 'trial getting' promotion may have performed well, but there will almost certainly be strong defensive promotions from competitors, and so it may be necessary to follow the launch, or re-launch, attack with another particularly strong promotion. The objective may be, for instance, a reinforcement and widening of penetration, or the countering of a competitive increase in value.

One major strategic launch promotion is unlikely to be enough to win the battle, and the manufacturer needs to be aware of this in forming his strategic plans.

Defensive strategic promotions

Preventing a competitive brand from obtaining consumer trial, and possibly building a repeat buying habit, is the job of the strategic defensive promotion.

Here the defending manufacturer will be taking positive action to persuade the consumer, and in particular consumers who are his regular buyers, not to try the new or re-launched competitive brand.

In planning a defensive action the first question to be asked should be, 'Is my brand worthy of defence?' The actual process of defending a brand can involve the use of considerable resource and effort. This should only be expended if it is worthwhile. If the brand, after the attack, is expected to be able to move forward and make good profit returns or if, by merely holding ground, it can expect to make good returns, then the defence could well be the right move.

If the brand already has a low position and is on a downward trend, then an expensive defence action may be the wrong move. Defence of a brand purely on the basis of 'company pride' is rarely a wise move.

A useful calculation to attempt at this time is this: How much is 1 per cent of market share worth to me? How can I avoid losing 1 per cent market share, and how much will it cost?

Defensive promotions are normally about improving the brand's value to the consumer in the shorter term. They give the consumer a good reason to 'stock up' with the brand so that she has no need to try the competitor's new brand. In particular, the aim should be to get regular users to stock up, working on the basis that 'they are our customers and what we have we intend to hold'.

Promotions which provide a quantity of extra product free can be effective defensive promotions. They can achieve the double aim of keeping regular users buying, and also ensure that they buy more than usual. On-pack coupons can also be effective in tempting the consumer to buy and then bringing her back for another purchase.

These various moves are all disguised forms of price reduction. As the man in possession, the defending brand should have the lower unit costs, so why should he not have a straight price cut? If he wishes to cut price then he can. There are probably two main reasons why he may prefer to compete more indirectly on price:

1. His competitor will probably follow his price move; indeed he may succeed in bringing all prices in the market down.
2. Moving his prices back up may prove extremely difficult.

However, a straight price adjustment can, in certain circumstances, be a very effective defensive move. A short-term deep price reduction can be mounted rapidly, and if the attacker follows the move he could be involved in a relatively high level of expenditure. The reduction will need to be handled with care if a price war is to be avoided.

The time available to the defender to mount his first defence will be very short. The attacker's initial offer to the consumer is likely to come within four or five weeks of the public announcement of his brand launch. This emphasizes the importance to the attacker of maintaining a strict control of information on his new brand moves—for him, a leak of his plans could prove very expensive. For the defender, advance knowledge of his competitor's impending attack can indeed be most valuable.

The defending brand may also be interested in mounting what is known as a 'strike back' promotion. The reasoning is that the defender will have lost some ground from his competitor's initial attack. At the time of his brand launch or re-launch, the new development in the product will have given him (the attacker) the initiative. His promotions, his new pack, and the big advertising backing behind the brand will all have been working for him. The defender's initial reply will have been short term—a 'free product' pack or something similar.

However, before consumers settle, before buying the competitive brand becomes a habit, the defending brand will need to go back to them in earnest. He will have studied the competitive product and packaging in detail, he will know its presentation and pricing. There may be a weakness in the position, and he may, for instance, have a product development of his own which his laboratory can rush through.

The strike back promotion is the one where he goes back to the consumer with his brand's 'added values'. It is the promotion which attempts to bring back the waiverers to his brand. It unsettles those consumers who have been attracted by the new competitive brand before they have formed a buying habit.

Just how much effort and investment should go into the strike back promotion will depend on the circumstances. The strength of the brand proposition to the consumer will be particularly significant.

In considering the various strategic promotions and how they may be used in the market-place battle, it is important to consider which of the competitors in the market have the ability to use them. They will normally require considerable financial backing, adequate stocks of the brand, available production capacity, suitable flexibility in operation, and also administrative ability.

Tactical promotions

In practice, the difference between a strong and well planned tactical promotion, and a lighter weight strategic promotion, is difficult to appreciate. Brand developments worthy of the backing of a strategic promotion will not appear frequently, but there will be a need from time to time to remind consumers of a brand's performance ability, or to go into the market and attempt to convert waiverers into regular users. Tactical promotions can help in tasks of this kind. They need adroit planning, and the level of investment placed behind them also needs careful control. They are often concerned with the marginal sales volume and the marginal revenue it brings, so they can be significant in terms of periodic results.

When one competitor in a market is shown to have a clear superiority over others in his ability to devise and exploit shorter-term promotions, then they can have an important longer-term effect. A consumer who buys a brand continually over a period of time, as a result of skilfully devised promotions, can develop a regular buying habit for the brand.

> In the UK in the early 1960s both Lever and Procter & Gamble used 'plastic flower' promotions on a wide scale. With every packet of the particular brand of detergent purchased the consumer received a plastic flower free. Daffodils and roses were two of the popular flowers used.
>
> This form of promotion was often criticized by consumer bodies at the time. The flowers were, in fact, welcomed by a very large number of consumers and for a period were a most effective promotion.
>
> For many consumers the plastic flowers were an attractive free gift, often attractive enough to encourage them to change from their regular brands. This applied particularly in the winter months when garden flowers were not available.
>
> Millions of the plastic flowers were purchased and so the unit cost to the manufacturers for each one was very low.
>
> The majority of consumers were not content with just one flower. They wanted to collect a bunch and so they were encouraged to buy the brand for a number of weeks. The promotion provided a great incentive to try the brand over an extended period, to form an attachment to it, and to become a regular user.

Promotions and the brand personality

The manner, form and style of a brand promotion are bound to make their contributions to the total personality of the brand. They cannot help but do this. It follows that all promotions, whether aggressive or defensive, should be designed and presented in a manner which accomplishes the double requirement — they should be successful in achieving their object-ive, and they should help the brand to develop its chosen brand person-ality.

Promotions and advertising

Within a co-ordinated marketing investment plan for a brand, advertis-ing and promotions are complementary. Each has its part to play, and the brand investment must be balanced so that each one can contribute at an optimum level within the total plan.

In Chapter 10 on advertising one of the most important questions to emerge was 'how much should be invested in advertising an established brand?' The point was made that, to a considerable extent, advertising an established brand serves to remind the consumer of the brand and the benefits it offers, and provide reassurance and confidence.

In presenting a brand promotion, the brand, its package, and its basic promise of performance are invariably featured. The promotion will fre-quently encourage the consumer to think about the brand and its per-formance. The leaflet which is distributed to consumer homes in support of the promotion, the magazine advertisement, the store display mater-ial, the coupons — *all* will carry a brand presentation.

There would seem to be no good reason why this promotional activity should not both meet the planned promotion object, and also play a part in the presentation of the brand. In effect, the promotional investment would be helping to remind the consumer of the brand, and also building the brand personality. Viewed and used in this manner the promotional investment can play a major part in helping brand advertising. In certain respects it will be doing the job of brand advertising. The financial advantage gained by viewing and using the promotional investment in this way can be substantial.

CHAPTER 12

New Brands

Successful new brands are important to a business. They can change a company's market share position dramatically. After the introduction period they can make major contributions to profitability, and they can have a remarkable effect on the morale and attitude of personnel. The important requirement is that the new brands must be successful.

Through the 1960s and into the early 70s, it sometimes seemed that a company was judged by the number of new brands it was testing or about to test. The tougher economic climate of the last decade brought a new approach. Progressive companies continue to be very interested in new brands, but they now appreciate that they must produce *successful* new brands. Test market brands which fail waste resources. Beyond this, a 'failed' test market means a loss of operating time, and this can be particularly expensive if it allows a competitor to move in and take over the opportunity.

The fact is that by far the majority of the new brands which were tested, and often launched into the market, during the 1960s and 70s, were failures. They were failures in terms of sales volume, market share, and profitability. Indeed, the real cost to their companies was often much higher than the figures shown in the accounts. The opportunity cost, particularly in terms of management time and effort, was often particularly high.

Why do so many new brands fail?

The simple answer to this question is that the new brand failures do not represent best value to a satisfactory number of customers.

New brand problems normally centre on performance and price. Research has shown that, given the brand has the right purpose, to succeed against established brands it must have either a significantly better performance, or a better performance with a lower price. Some new brands *may* be successful without meeting these requirements—they are very few. This position fits well with the 'best value' approach.

If the aim is to dislodge an established brand on a performance basis then the probability is that a significant performance advantage will be needed, one that the consumer can recognize readily. A marginal performance advantage is unlikely to be sufficient unless it is accompanied by a worthwhile price advantage.

Too many new brands appear to rely on their presentation to carry them through. They expect their advertising both to encourage trial and bring considerable added value. In most cases this is asking too much of advertising.

For new brands which compete in markets where consumer buying behaviour is more emotional, advertising may make a bigger contribution, but even in these markets placing undue reliance on advertising presentation to bring added value is a high risk.

New brands can fail for operational reasons. Failure to get an adequate level of consumer trial can restrict the number of repeat purchases which, in turn, will restrict sales volume. Failure to get a satisfactory level of store distribution can mean that the advertising and promotional investments are ineffective. There can be problems with production and the earlier product coming from the plant may not perform at a satisfactory standard.

However, the real problems are more likely to be of a policy rather than operational nature. Mistakes in operation can limit progress, but they can usually be overcome. Mistakes in policy stop progress altogether and are much more difficult to correct.

Where do new brands come from?

There are three main avenues for the birth of a new brand proposition:

1. Consumer observations and research.
2. Laboratory research and development.
3. Development work based on a brand already in the market.

The classic approach is for the marketing researchers to have discussion sessions with consumers and from these and other researches, come to conclusions about the strengths and weaknesses of existing brands, and how the consumer would like to have the products improved. These conclusions are worked on and gradually a new consumer need, one not already met in the market, becomes clear. A marketing opportunity has been discovered, and the research and development department then needs to get to work and build a product to meet it.

It can happen that a new brand concept may begin in research and development. A new ingredient may be offered by a supplier which, when blended with others, gives a particularly good result. Marketing research shows this result to be very attractive to the consumer, and so the basis for a new development is available.

The thought that a major new brand can come from development work based on a brand already in the market would normally be dismissed as most unlikely. 'Me too' brands are rarely fully successful, yet there are often small brands already in the market that are based on a purpose which is very appealing to the consumer. They may not have been successful because of poor design, or lack of marketing support, or the manufacturer does not have the necessary resources and organization to exploit the brand to the full. Given the product development, marketing, and sales force backing of a stronger organization, the brand could succeed. A number of leading brands have been based on developments of this kind. They are certainly not typical 'me too' brands.

As an alternative to launching a new brand it is possible to purchase the small brand or the company owning it, but this may not always be feasible or necessarily desirable.

Shrewd manufacturers are always examining brands operating in the markets in which they have an interest, and they are always looking for opportunities of this kind.

> ❝Successful new brand development and market introduction require skill, energy, and probably most important of all, a full management commitment with a positive attitude.
>
> In this activity much depends on the approach of the people who search for the new marketing opportunities and produce the new products. The right blend of skill and enthusiasm is essential for real success. The active support of senior management is also an important requirement.

Lever in the UK realized that if it was to achieve its longer-term profit and market share objectives a series of successful new brands would be necessary.

Between 1968 and early 1984 Lever introduced 11 new brands to UK national markets. Five of these introductions became brand market leaders, and two others became sectional leaders.

An article published in February 1979 in the *Financial Times* commented on the Lever position at that time: 'The company has adopted a policy of conducting the most meticulous evaluation of new opportunities, and in those cases where a real opportunity is discovered, every possible resource is put behind it both in terms of the launch and subsequent development.

'Real commitment to development has been built up within every department. Very few projects finally reach the market-place, but those that do benefit from a level of commitment which few other companies in packaged goods can match.

'Half the current sales volume is accounted for by brands launched since 1968, an impressive achievement in difficult and very competitive markets.

'A powerful machine has been developed to find and launch new products. The chairman is personally involved and runs the development brand review to decide where the company is to put its resources on a priority basis. Great importance is attached to evaluation and market research expenditures are large. The development of advertising and its evaluation plays an important role, and the sales force is well drilled to handle few but large operations.'

New brand test marketing

Is it wise to test market a new brand proposition? There are arguments for and against test marketing. The eventual investment in launching the brand will frequently be extensive, and it is clearly important to take every reasonable precaution to ensure that this investment is used profitably. While all the various consumer research activities may have been carried out, the argument for a test in the real world, where the consumer pays real money, has obvious merit. A move of this kind will also provide the production departments with the opportunity to be sure they are completely on top of the processing, for example.

When the test market has been running for a reasonable period of time a detailed reading can be made of it. If it is basically a successful operation then the plans can be 'fine tuned' and the brand move confidently into national distribution.

This was at one time the accepted approach for a new brand. It was usually necessary for the test to spread over a full year to allow for gaining initial consumer penetration, as well as reading the very important repeat buying rate.

The approach has a number of major drawbacks, however. It makes public the details of the new brand's purpose, performance, presentation etc, to all competitors. A lengthy test market will give them time to copy many of the innovations and build them into their established brands. They can also prepare their counter-attack plans and be ready for action as soon as the new brand indicates that it is to go national.

Test marketing can involve a high level of opportunity cost and this applies particularly if, after a year or more in the test market, the brand is considered to be unsuccessful and plans for a move national are dropped. A great deal of valuable time will have been wasted.

Against all of this the manufacturer should have learnt much in the test market. His move national should be one in which he can have full confidence. The 'bugs' in the brand mix will have been removed, he will have clear guidance on his price/volume position, and he can organize his production accordingly.

The high costs of test marketing pose a challenge to the marketing research profession: surely it should be possible to test a new brand objectively and thoroughly without having to place it on public view in a large sector of the country for a lengthy period of time.

Considerable progress has been made over recent years in meeting this challenge. There are now a number of approaches available to the manufacturer which it is claimed provide, from a series of special tests and researches carried out in private or semi-private, a very clear guide as to just how a new brand will behave if it is launched nationally with certain given levels of price and advertising/promotional support.

> Sometimes a test market can provide information and experience which would be difficult to obtain by any other research method.
>
> In the late 1960s Lever launched a brand named Blast into a regional test within the UK oven cleaner market. The brand had performed well in consumer testing, and Lever believed it could become the leader of an expanding market.
>
> After a year in its test Blast became the regional market leader. Despite this success Blast was never taken national as Lever decided to withdraw from the market.
>
> There were two main reasons for Lever's withdrawal. Firstly, the market failed to show any signs of real growth. After heavy advertising and promotional activity it remained a relatively small market. Secondly, the brands already in the market put up a particularly strong defensive action, most of it concentrated in 'below the line' expenditures.
>
> Lever had to devote a major part of its local sales and marketing effort to get Blast to market leadership. The opportunity cost of such an effort on a national scale could have been very high indeed.
>
> Blast had demonstrated an ability to become a market leader, but in view of the small market and limited profit potential, Lever decided the effort required was just not worthwhile.

Many manufacturers have for long been very much aware of this new brand test marketing problem. They have been working to provide themselves with an acceptable solution. Naturally, they consider their methods and the results they provide as strictly confidential. If they have succeeded in developing an approach in which they have full confidence, and which avoids test marketing, they have developed a competitive advantage.

New brands—how much to invest

You make or break a new brand in its first 18 months in the market! There may be a small number of brands which have failed badly in their opening period but have later gone forward to become very successful, but very few.

A new brand introduction may fall into one of two broad categories: one which is spread over a number of years or one intended to move to high volume quickly.

A brand entering a relatively undeveloped market which is growing slowly could well plan for its introduction to be spread over a long period. Unduly heavy support expenditure during the initial launch period would be wasteful—the number of consumers interested in the brand is limited, store distribution may be slow opening up, and it may be unwise to use the mass media for advertising or promotions during the early period.

For new brands attempting to enter one of the major markets a slow introduction is unlikely to be the best approach. A slow introduction would enable competitors to copy any competitive advantage the new brand may have. It would also mean a low level of volume for a lengthy period, which would incur the penalty costs accompanying this lower volume.

A new brand entering a major market would normally be interested in moving its volume as high as possible, as rapidly as possible. In this way it will get all the advantages which high volume can bring, and get them quickly. This means that it will be interested in getting consumer trial as rapidly as possible, and also widespread store distribution to ensure that repeat purchases are covered.

To achieve the desired results for his new brand when entering a major market the manufacturer will need to invest heavily during the early period of the brand's life. The important question is, how heavily? You cannot answer this question with specific figures. So much depends on the market, its size, the competition and so forth.

The advertising investment would, of course, need to be viewed within a totally co-ordinated marketing plan, a plan which provides for the use of the various promotional 'tools' as well as advertising.

While it would be wrong to attempt a specific answer, it is possible to make a number of broader points which should help to put the investment in perspective:

1. For by far the majority of brands the initial launch period is the most significant period in the brand's life. It is most important that at this time all those consumers to whom the brand is directed (ie all the potential users) get the opportunity to know of the brand, to appreciate the benefits it brings, and to submit it to their own personal best value test.

   This means that the new brand advertising should be strong enough to register with these consumers irrespective of the other advertising messages they may receive through the period. For the new brand to be the strongest advertiser within its category may not be enough, it will need to ensure that its message is heard by consumers within the general marketplace.

   The promotional investment must be strong enough to ensure the consumer trial requirements are met.

2. At the initial launch, provided the business proposition is a good one for them, many sectors of the retail and wholesale trade will be prepared to 'give the new brand a go'. If it fails they will never greet it with the same enthusiasm again. Getting store feature the second time around for a new brand which has failed in its first attempt will be more than just difficult, it will be almost impossible.

3. The initial launch period is so important to the new brand that at this time it is better to over-invest in the advertising and promotion rather than risk an underinvestment. It is a period when it is better to be 'safe rather than sorry'.

   During the opening period the new brand is 'news' to the consumer and to the retail trade. At this time it has its big opportunity to make an impression and to get its message across—it will never get a similar opportunity again.

At its launch, it is vitally important that the brand's 'value equation' is 'right', and its presentation completely satisfactory. In particular, its advertising should be satisfactory in both quality and quantity. There is unlikely to be a second chance—the opening launch period will set the brand's position and standing for its life.

Making a new brand entry into a market in which the company already holds a major share

Is it wise for a company which already has a major share of a market, with possibly the leading brand, to launch a new brand into the market knowing that it will take a large part of its business from the existing brands? This is a very real question for many companies. Similar considerations apply when the proposed new brand is in a different form, for instance a liquid that has the same basic purpose as a powder.

In the definition of a brand given earlier in this book it was stated that every brand should be directed to meet a specific consumer need. Over time the mention of the brand name should immediately bring to mind, in words and pictures, the need the brand meets, its performance standard, and a feeling which reflects the brand's personality. A marketing opportunity for a new brand is a consumer need or benefit not adequately met by existing brands.

There would not seem to be a business case for a manufacturer having two brands both aimed at meeting exactly the same marketing opportunity. There may be exceptions — if, for instance, the first brand launched to exploit the opportunity has for some reason failed, or if the new brand is in a different form, and it is known that for some consumers this new form offers advantages.

However, we know that as consumers become more prosperous and more sophisticated in their tastes, and as markets grow, no one purpose is likely to be right for every consumer in the market. It is necessary to define any new purpose, and to quantify it. The requirement is to be sure that the new marketing opportunity warrants a new brand in its own right rather than become an additional, secondary purpose, for an existing brand. If a new brand is warranted then the business should give it every consideration irrespective of the existing brand shares it may hold.

The new brand will, in all probability, get a large part of its business from existing brands and the company's entrants will suffer. However, if there is a marketing opportunity available for a new brand it will eventually be known to others competing in the market. If a competitor should launch a new brand to meet the opportunity then the established brands are equally likely to lose share and volume. With a competitive brand launch there will be no compensatory volume for the manufacturer of the established leading brand.

Beyond this, there is the added factor that it will be possible for the manufacturer to direct, position, and pace a brand if he owns it. If the brand is owned by a competitor then he (the competitor) will have the privilege of positioning and directing it, and he is likely to do this in a manner calculated to cause the established leader as much trouble as possible.

‘ During the early 1970s Lever was actively engaged in the development of a deodorant toilet soap. The brand concerned was Shield and it was eventually launched into the UK national market in 1976.

At the time, Lever already had a strong brand entrant in the toilet soap market which provided a form of deodorant benefit — Lifebuoy Toilet

> soap had for long been well established as a soap which 'prevented BO'.
>
> There was a view in Lever that if Shield entered the market it would take most of its volume from Lifebuoy Toilet and that Lever would end up with two deodorant brands instead of one and with very little extra business.
>
> However, the view that Shield was more 'feminine' in its approach, that it would have a distinctive fragrance and form, and be able to command a position of its own in the market, prevailed. The brand was consumer tested and eventually launched into the national market.
>
> It was accepted that Shield would get a part of its volume from Lifebuoy Toilet, however, there was clearly an opportunity in the market and if Lever did not take it then one of its competitors was likely to do so.
>
> In fact, when Shield entered the market it became a clear market leader. It took some business from almost every other brand in the market, and Lifebuoy Toilet soap did not suffer unduly.

In a very big market a strategy frequently followed by the company market leader is to surround his lead brand, the one meeting the main purpose in the market, with a series of segmented brands. In this way he is both meeting the consumers' additional requirements and providing the leader with a form of protection. A way for a competitor to attack a strong leader is to launch a brand which first becomes a segment leader and then later, when it is well established, moves on to attack the main position. If the leader has filled the segmented positions they will not be available to his competitors.

> In the late 1970s Persil Automatic held a share of over 50 per cent of the UK low suds market. The brand provided a very high level of performance at a competitive price.
>
> At this time it was reasoned within Lever that there was an opportunity in the market for a brand which offered a very good standard of performance (below that of Persil Automatic) and one which would sell at a lower price level (again below that of Persil Automatic).
>
> Lever accepted that such a brand would take some of its volume from its established leading brand; it equally accepted that a marketing opportunity existed and if Lever did not meet it then others (in particular the distributors) would probably do so.
>
> Surf Automatic was launched in late 1979 to meet this marketing opportunity. It did, in fact, take certain of its volume from Persil Automatic. However, Lever was convinced that with the two brands its position and volume in the market was much stronger than it would have been had it

failed to meet the opportunity. For Lever, Surf Automatic fulfilled a double requirement: it became a very worthwhile brand in its own right, and it also provided a degree of protection for Persil Automatic. **,**

Launch a new brand or re-launch an established one?

The laboratory has produced a new ingredient which provides a move forward in product performance. Should this development be used on an existing brand, or should a new brand be launched to carry it? There can be no set answer to this question, but the answers to certain follow-up questions will provide some guidance:

- What is the market condition of the established brand? Is it struggling and in deep decline? Or is it in good shape with a healthy market share position and a well established, very favourable, personality?
- Just how significant is the new product development? Is it a relatively minor one and unlikely to be noticed by the consumer? Or is it of real significance and readily appreciated by the consumer?

A minor product development is most unlikely to warrant a new brand. There may be a case for a new brand for some particular competitive reason; however, the case would need to be very special.

A major product development could represent a 'significant competitive advantage' and there is always the possibility that it would be wasted on an established brand which is struggling. Pulling a brand back from deep trouble is always both difficult and highly risky. If the established brand is in good shape the new development could possibly allow it to challenge for market leadership or at least for a better position in the market. If the brand is already the leader, it could be taken forward into a dominant position.

As a very general rule, a significant product performance development can support a new brand; a minor development would be better used on an existing brand.

New brand—the name

Should a new brand have a name of its own, or should it be placed under the umbrella of an existing brand name? The use of an established name is often referred to as a line extension.

This is an important consideration in strategy formulation in that the line extension approach is claimed to be a very much cheaper way of launching a new brand. The important questions are, 'Does the use of a line extension approach bring a less expensive introduction but a greater chance of failure? Does the use of a line extension name inhibit the new brand's development? Can the use of a line extension name harm the established brand from which the name is taken?'

There are strong and widely conflicting views on this subject. The case for the line extension is basically straightforward. The manufacturer is saved the trouble and expense of establishing a new brand name. The strength and standing of the established name will reflect on the new line extension. The additional advertising expenditure which will concentrate on the line extension at its launch will also be helpful to the established brand. It may also be claimed that there will be a more willing acceptance of the extension by the retail trade, and this will be based on the success of the established brand.

The argument against the line extension really goes back to the fundamental use of the brand name. It has already been stated that if a manufacturer has done a competent branding job then his brand name will automatically bring to the consumers' mind the delivery of a particular benefit, a level of performance, and a type or form of personality.

If this is accepted, then clearly there can be a considerable risk involved in a line extension. In particular there is the risk that the extension will never have the opportunity to develop a brand position for itself—the established brand will always be too strong. From the other side, there is the risk that the line extension may act to confuse the position of the established brand.

There have been many line extensions which have become outstanding successes; there have also been many failures. There are a number of general rules for the successful use of the line extension approach:

1. If a line extension is to be used, then within its product category the new entry should have the same performance standard as the established brand has in its category.
2. The price positioning of the extension in its market should be the same as for the established brand in its market. For instance, the line extension should not engage in a high level of price dealing, unless a dealing approach is used by the parent brand. If the parent is premium priced so also should be the line extension.
3. The brand personality proposed for the extension should be basically the same as the personality of the established brand.
4. The established brand and the extension should not compete. For instance, if the line extension meets the same consumer need as the established brand, but has a superior performance, and therefore needs to talk in its advertising of 'outperforming' or 'outclassing' other brands, there is obviously the risk that it

will be downgrading the performance and position of the parent.

There can be an important exception to this general rule: when the manufacturer believes that the form of the new brand will become, in a relatively short time, bigger in the market than the form of the parent. In these circumstances the approach should be to avoid direct competition by emphasizing the form and performance of the extension in its category. For instance, a washing powder manufacturer may believe that washing liquids will rapidly become bigger than washing powders; in such circumstances he may be fully prepared for his liquid to take business from his powder. However, in promoting his liquid's performance he would take care to compare it with other liquids and not with powders.

5.   A new brand with a 'breakthrough' new purpose will almost certainly need a separate brand identity.

6.   In very broad terms, if the new opportunity in the market is potentially very big, the brand is likely to be worthy of its own name. If the opportunity is a relatively small one, a line extension may be satisfactory.

These are very much general guidelines and there will most certainly be line extensions which break them and go on to be highly successful.

> ❛One of the most interesting studies of the use of the line extension approach can be seen in the UK low suds washing powder market.
>
> In the 1960s the predominant washing machine used in UK homes was known as the 'twin tub'. This type of machine allowed for the use of high sudsing washing powders. The user could observe the lather level given by the washing powder as it worked in the machine – there was a marked consumer preference for a high and relatively thick level of lather. Both Lever (Persil) and Procter & Gamble (Ariel) had strong leading brands in the high sudsing washing powder market.
>
> In a number of countries on the continent of Europe the leading type of washing machine in use was known as the 'automatic'. This type of machine requires a low sudsing powder – a high sudsing powder is likely to cause the machine to flood. The automatic type of machine has certain features which make it more attractive to many consumers than the twin tub.
>
> Observers of the UK washing machine market were strongly of the view that buyers would move to automatic machines during the 1970s and beyond. However, the movement promised to be a slow process and to some considerable extent it would be controlled by the speed at which twin tub owners replaced their machines.
>
> Washing powder manufacturers within the UK were following the posi-

tion with very close attention and in the mid 1960s Lever test marketed a low suds powder under the name of Skip.

The basic problem in launching an entirely new brand was that during this early period the market was a very small one, the launch expenditures very high, and even if the brand was successful, the resulting revenue very low.

Skip was not a success. It was known that P & G were also carrying out tests with low suds powders at this time, and they were thought to be meeting similar problems to those troubling Lever.

In 1968 Lever entered a test market with a low suds brand named Persil Automatic. The reasoning behind this selection of name centred on two key points: (1) that the use of the Persil name would bring to the low suds brand the very favourable connotations and personality of high suds Persil, and (2) the need for a very heavy investment in advertising during the early years would be avoided as the parent brand advertising would act to support the line extension.

Within the limited market Persil Automatic was successful. During its earlier periods it held relatively low volumes; however, its advertising and promotional backing was very restricted, and so it was able to make a limited but worthwhile financial contribution.

By 1973 Persil Automatic was firmly established as a strong growth brand in the UK market. In that year P & G launched a new low suds brand named Bold. This new brand was given very heavy advertising and promotional support, but it enjoyed only limited success and ran at roughly half the volume and market share of Persil Automatic.

It was not until 1981 that P & G recorded any real success in the UK low suds market when they launched their own line extension named Ariel Automatic. However, Persil Automatic continued to progress and established itself as an outstanding leader of the total UK washing powder market.

Both Persil Automatic and Ariel Automatic followed the guidelines for successful line extensions set out in this book. Their performance standards within the low suds market were similar to their parent brands' standards in the high suds sector, their price positioning was similar, the personalities of the new brands were also similar to their established parents, and the new brands did not compete with their parents.

From their earlier actions, it would seem that both Lever and P & G would have preferred to have had independent brands in this market, and yet both ended with their leading low suds brand as a line extension.

*

The UK scourer market also provides a study in the use of line extensions.

Within this market the leader for many years was the Colgate brand Ajax. Vim, the Lever entry in the powdered scourer market, challenged Ajax

> closely through the early 1970s but was never able to take over the clear leadership for any lengthy period.
>
> It was known at this time ie in the early 1970s, that consumers were very interested in having a cleaner that performed as well as the powdered scourers and in addition avoided any form of surface scratching.
>
> In 1974 Lever launched into the UK market a liquid scourer named Jif. The use of the name Vim for this product was considered and rejected. Jif was a non-scratch cleaner and was presented as superior to powdered scourers in this respect; in effect it competed strongly against the powdered scourers. In 1975 Colgate launched a liquid non-scratch scourer named Ajax Cream into the UK market.
>
> Jif was a very successful brand and by 1982 had become the leader of the total UK scourer market (ie powders and liquids) outselling Ajax cream by over 2 to 1.

It is important to distinguish between a line extension and a new variety. The line extension reasoning applies to a new form of product. With a new variety the basic product and the main benefit are unchanged and there is merely a change in, for instance, the flavour or the perfume; the established name would normally be used.

When a manufacturer decides to give a proposed new brand its own name he should accept in his strategy planning that it will probably be necessary to invest extensively to get it established, and that a really firm establishment of the name will take time, possibly a number of years.

These remarks have been primarily concerned with the use of a line extension associated with a strong and successful established brand. If a line extension is proposed for a new development, and the established brand is weak, then it is likely that the extension will also be a weak contender in its market unless it has a particularly significant and valuable competitive advantage to offer the consumer.

New brand pricing

The pricing of a brand is always a key decision, with a new brand it is of particular significance.

When the new brand is entering an established market then the manufacturer has the existing value structure to guide him. He will have full information on the comparative performance of the brand from his laboratory testing, and also detail from research as to how the consumer rates its performance. However, irrespective of the performance rating, the decision as to where to set the new brand price remains with the manufacturer. He can, if he wishes, deliberately set a low price during the early period and in this way give the brand a higher value to the consumer. He can, if he wishes, price the brand above the level as shown by the value equation, and if he does this he should know that he may be limiting his chances of success.

If the brand performance is of the kind that opens up a new segment in the market, then the manufacturer may reason that he should take a premium price position. Price testing can help guide him on the extent of the premium he should take.

Of course, the price should not be set in isolation. The brand costs are an important factor, as are the advertising and promotional investments planned, and also the profit/loss returns the manufacturer considers appropriate over the early years. Much will depend on the manufacturer's competitive position. His capacity situation will also be a factor: if his plant has vacant capacity his aim may be to fill it rapidly. The pricing decision should be a part of the long-term co-ordinated marketing plan for the brand.

When a new brand is meeting an entirely new purpose then a different set of circumstances applies. The competitive performance analysis will not exist for there are no brands meeting exactly the same consumer requirement. There may be brands meeting needs of a somewhat similar nature and this should be helpful; skilful consumer research should also be of assistance. However, the pricing of an entirely new brand is a most difficult issue and one where a clear policy approach is necessary.

A number of questions concerning the new brand will need answering:

- How big is the market for the new brand likely to be?
- What is the 'top-side' volume potential for the brand?
- Where will the new brand get its business?
- Will the business be additional or replacement business?
- What protection has the brand got? (Protection, for instance, in terms of patents, or protection in the form of a manufacturing process which cannot be easily copied and which requires considerable time to commission.)
- How easy is it to copy the brand?
- Do competitors already have capacity to make a copy of the brand?
- Can they get capacity rapidly?
- How much investment is required to provide for given levels of capacity?

With an entirely new brand the manufacturer has a choice of taking one of two broad strategy approaches. He can employ either skim pricing or he can use penetration pricing. The two approaches tend to cover a wide span, but there are many intermediate positions he can take up. If the extremes are considered, however, the strategy considerations are more easily appreciated.

Skim pricing is an approach which would launch the new brand at a high price and with a high contributory margin, the aim being to skim the cream from the market during the early period. The price may be moved down to a lower level at a later date.

One of the arguments claimed in favour of skim pricing is that it allows a manufacturer to 'feel his way' with a brand. In many cases the first consumers who have a need for a particular benefit tend to come from the more affluent sections of the community. With this group, price is not necessarily so important a factor in the buying decision as it may be with the majority of consumers. The skim approach is often thought to be a safer policy as it can avoid a heavy up-front loss on the launching of the brand.

With a penetration pricing approach the manufacturer would launch the brand with a relatively low unit price and a low unit contributory margin, the aim being to get a high level of penetration right from the start, and from this should come a high level of sales volume.

There are two great advantages claimed for the penetration approach. Firstly, the high level of sales volume should enable the manufacturer to use his plant and other production machinery effectively and at a reasonable capacity immediately. Secondly, the low level of unit margin should discourage competitors from investing in plant and trying to enter the market.

> ❛The UK lavatory cleaner market in 1980 was a relatively small one – in terms of volume totalling roughly 10,000 tons.
>
> Lever was considering the launch of a new brand named Frish into the market. Frish had obtained very favourable response in its consumer researches. The brand was based on a marketing development rather than a technological breakthrough. The Frish formula was considered to be a relatively easy one for an appropriately skilled competitor to copy, and it was not possible to obtain any patent protection.
>
> There was considerable debate within the Lever company as to the unit price at which Frish should be launched into the market-place. The small size of the lavatory cleaner market was one of the arguments used to support a 'skim price' of 46p per unit. Against this it was considered that the lack of protection would mean the brand would be copied quickly after its entry and that a 'penetration' price of 37p per unit should be used.
>
> Frish was launched into the national market at a price of 37p per unit. The launch was highly successful and the UK lavatory cleaner market doubled in size to over 20,000 tons. Frish claimed over 50 per cent of this greatly enlarged market.

> Many 'copy' brands of Frish appeared in the market during the next two years. They were invariably priced below Frish, but the price differential was a small one. The Frish market share remained around 50 per cent and the brand continued as a dominant leader. **'**

The answers to the questions posed above should provide guidance to the best pricing approach for a particular new brand. Given very strong and tight patent protection, a higher unit margin during the early periods may be justified. If the market is seen to be relatively small and so unlikely to interest the bigger operators, then again a high unit margin may be appropriate.

However, if the market is thought to have a large potential and the brand is relatively simple to copy, then penetration pricing would most probably be the right move.

There really is no simple formula to provide an easy solution to the pricing problems posed by the launch of an entirely new brand. Skill, sound judgement, and courage, are required of management.

New brand to stop a competitor

Is it worth launching a new brand merely to stop a competitor? There can be no one simple answer, as so much will depend upon the particular circumstances, the strength of the brand to be launched, and the strength of the competition. Launching a new brand is invariably a major operation involving considerable investment and a high level of opportunity cost. It should only be undertaken after very careful consideration.

However, there can be occasions when it is vitally important that the progress of a competitor should be stopped, and a new brand can have an essential role to play in the operation. When it is known that a competitor is to enter a major market with a new brand, one which has the ability to become market leader if it is not challenged, then exceptional action will be necessary. Of course, the initial move should be to review the ability of existing brands to meet the challenge. If the required ability is not present then launching a new brand may be the right move.

To play a worthwhile part the proposed new brand must have the ability to represent best value to a satisfactory number of consumers. The prime aim of a new brand launched in these circumstances would be to stop the competitor from obtaining both market share and volume, in particular to stop him obtaining the benefits which the higher volume levels of market leadership can bring. If the market is a growth market, then the aim will be to stop the competitor getting into a commanding position and growing with the market. He may be difficult to stop during the early growth stage, but stopping him will be even more difficult if he is allowed to continue his leadership into the later stages of market growth and maturity.

A new brand launched primarily to stop the progress of a competitive brand is, in effect, 'buying time'. If successful, it should give the manufacturer time to marshal his resources and developments either for use on his existing brands, or on a further new brand to be launched into the future.

The chances of success for a new brand launched in this context will hinge very much on the skill and judgement of the people forming it. Brands of this kind are frequently formed under great time pressures. The aim should be to create a brand which will both stop the competitor and go forward to be a successful brand in its own right. It is a time when concentration on the basics will be essential.

Clearly, the risk, and the cost, involved in the launch of a new brand to stop a competitor is likely to be very high. However, if a competitor is allowed to have a lengthy run at a major market without real challenge, he may obtain a commanding position within the market which could stretch over many years. The real cost of allowing a competitor to occupy a position of this kind can be substantial. With the funds generated from a commanding position he could become an active competitor in other markets. Given these prospects, the cost of launching a new brand to 'buy time' may not necessarily be excessive.

> ‘When Lever launched Radiant into the national UK high suds washing powder market in 1969 the aim was that the brand should be successful in its own right. However, within this aim Lever had as a first priority that Radiant should stop the progress of Ariel and provide a time period during which the company could re-stage its other brands in the market.
>
> The threat posed by Ariel was indeed a major one for Lever. The brand had raced to the No 1 position in the market and was showing every ability to move into a dominant leadership. From this position Ariel would have generated a high level of profit which Procter & Gamble could have used to restrict Lever in the washing powder market, and to have launched further attacks in other household cleaning markets.
>
> Radiant achieved its main aim. After its launch Ariel began to decline and never recovered the commanding position it had previously held.
>
> In the early 1980s Lever withdrew Radiant from the market. It was originally an enzymatic powder and when, for industrial relations reasons, the company removed the enzymes from the brand formulation, its position weakened.
>
> Radiant had made a financial contribution during its relatively short life, but its main success had been in stopping the progress of Ariel and in 'buying time'. The threat of a competitive brand becoming a dominant leader had been removed. For Lever the Radiant operation was most certainly very worthwhile. ’

New brands and the trade

A new brand may have performed remarkably well in its consumer testing, it may have an outstanding advertising presentation, and it may have plans for strong consumer promotions, but it is unlikely that the brand will succeed unless it gains at least *adequate* store distribution. Without it the number of consumers who will be able to purchase the brand will be strictly limited. The heavy consumer advertising and promotion will be in part wasted.

Clearly it is important to get a satisfactory level of store distribution for a new brand, and to get it quickly so that the initial advertising and sampling investment may work to the full. In most developed countries gaining adequate store distribution for a new brand involves persuading a limited number of key buyers that the new brand will represent a good business proposition for them, and that it is worthy of a suitable allocation of their limited shelf and display space.

'From the late 1960s into the early 80s Lever embarked on a strategy which planned for a most aggressive approach to new brand introduction. Obtaining and holding the confidence of the key buyers was a most important consideration within the Lever strategy.

The table below, which shows how grocery trade buyers in the UK rated the top manufacturers in terms of new product development performance, confirms that Lever had considerable success in obtaining and holding the confidence of the key grocery buyers in the UK.

New product development
Top ten companies

	1984	1982	1980	1978	1976
Lever Brothers	1	1	2	4	2
Pedigree Petfoods	2	5 =	3	1	4
Kelloggs	2	8	13	10	8
Procter & Gamble	4	7	7	6	5
Birds Eye	5	5 =	4	3	6
United Biscuits	6	2	1	2	1
General Foods	7 =	23	14	19	9
Mars	7 =	9	5	7	11
Rowntree Mackintosh	9	15 =	6	8	14
Heinz	10	27	10	5	3

Source: *New Products in Grocers 1984*, Kraushar and Eassie. '

They will be impressed by the consumer testing results the new brand is able to present, they will be concerned to know of the advertising and promotional investment which is backing it, and they will certainly wish to know the amount of profit contribution they can expect the brand to make to their business. They will also be influenced by the track record of the company concerned in launching new brands.

It is understandable that the key buyers should examine any new brand proposition with great care. New brand failures can be very expensive for them—they tie up capital and store space, and they invariably cause costly administration.

In their evaluation of a company and its track record in new brand activity the key buyers will consider many points, but the success rate of the company is likely to be the dominant factor. The key buyers need to be tough in their business approach and understandably they have a great respect for success.

When a company embarks on a strategy that plans for extensive new brand activity it would be well advised to appreciate fully the significance of store distribution, and the importance of developing and holding the confidence of the key buyers. It is an area where the old adage, 'Nothing succeeds like success', holds true.

CHAPTER 13

Distributor Brands

How do distributor brands (brands sold under a store's own name — sometimes known as retailer brands, dobs, or own label) differ from other competitive brands? Surely they are just another form of brand competition? Why should they be considered separately?

These are reasonable questions since distributor brands are, in many respects, the same as any other competing brand. However, there are certain major differences:

1. The distributor who owns the brand is unlikely to have any production facilities of his own. He will buy the complete brand either from a specialist producer or a normal manufacturer who has brands of his own competing in the market.
2. The distributor is unlikely to have any research or development resources employed on the brand.
3. The distributor is unlikely to engage in any advertising for a specific brand, although he may have advertising for his store name which will be a form of indirect advertising for the brand.
4. Within his store the distributor has the privilege of deciding which competing brands he will stock. He can if he wishes limit the competition for his brand. Beyond this, the distributor will decide the selling prices of all the brands within his store. He will be subject to competition from other stores and this will act as a control on his pricing freedom. Nevertheless, he can, if he wishes, give his own brand a price advantage.
5. The distributor will clearly have no difficulty getting store distribution for his brand. He decides its shelf positioning within

his store, and also the shelf space to be allowed to the various competing brands. He also decides which brands are featured.

Over recent periods distributor brands have made considerable progress in many of the consumer markets in developed countries. The levels reached by these brands varies depending upon the stage of development reached by the particular retail trade, and the attitude of the traders toward the own label business.

UK distributor brands are probably slightly ahead of the general level for Europe. In the USA, possibly because of the size and extent of the markets, and also because legislation acts to limit the buying power of the major chains, no one or two retailers have yet built dominant positions within the national retail trade. Own label brands in the USA appear to be, in general, as prominent as those of the more developed markets of Europe.

The UK has a limited number of strong and progressive chains which have worked hard to develop their own label brands. In many of these stores it is quite common for distributor brands to hold over 30 per cent of a market; frequently the distributor brand will be the category leader.

The strong growth of the distributor brands has been encouraged by a number of factors, including:

1. The growth of the retail chains. As the chains have extended their business by opening new stores and increasing trade through their existing outlets, so the volume of their distributor brands has grown.
2. The managements of the retail chains have become more professional in their approach to distributive brand marketing. At one time the chains considered the distributor brands as a way of picking up higher margin business at the 'cheaper' end of the market.

    Over recent years they have come to appreciate that the distributor brand represents the store. Its standard is regarded as the standard of the store. They have a need to ensure that it is of appropriate quality and well presented. Many chain managements have put this reasoning into operation.
3. The retail chains appreciate that a strong distributor brand position can considerably strengthen their bargaining position with manufacturers.
4. In certain instances the chains have come to the view that it is in their longer-term interest to build their house name so that consumers see it as a quality alternative to manufacturers' brands.

Distributor brands are of real significance in many of the consumer markets in the United Kingdom. They are taking major market shares and the volume that goes with these shares—the market shares were previously held by manufacturer brands. The UK experience is not an isolated one, many other developed countries have a similar experience. Manufacturers should beware! The major chains are growing and the indications are that their growth will accelerate into the future. Are the distributor brands also to be allowed to accelerate into the future? In many markets they are moving from what has been their traditional position in the lower price sector, and are now beginning to use better formulations and to move to middle market positions.

The distributor brands are getting their market share, and volume, because many consumers consider them to be best value. This is a fact which manufacturers must face.

❛The UK dishwashing liquid market contains an interesting study in distributor brand development.

In 1962 the market was reckoned to be around 55,000 tons in total volume. The three main soaps and detergent companies (Lever, Procter & Gamble and Colgate) held approximately 75 per cent of this market, and the rest was held by a large number of 'other' small brands most of which were owned by distributors. The clear market leader with a share of approximately 25 per cent was Fairy Liquid. This brand had a high performance level and was premium priced.

By 1972 the market had grown to some 120,000 tons in total. The three large companies now held a share of approximately 50 per cent, of which Fairy Liquid held almost half, ie a 25 per cent market share.

The other brands in the market had now grown to a 50 per cent market share. It is probable that one of the manufacturers of these 'other' brands was now enjoying production volume levels higher than those of the major soap companies.

Between 1962 and 1972 the major companies had concentrated their efforts on attempts to bring into the market high performance brands selling at premium prices. The 'other' brands were almost all of a lower level performance with lower prices.

By the early 1980s the total market had reached approximately 160,000 tons and was moving toward maturity. Fairy Liquid continued to hold approximately 25 per cent, but no other premium brand had been able to build a sustaining share – Sunlight Lemon Liquid (Lever) had performed well for a period but later had difficulty in holding share. The 'other' brands held about 50 per cent of the 1980 market.

It is in part understandable that the major companies were anxious to build brands in the premium sector of the market – they reasoned that in

> this sector they could utilize their skills in product development and in brand presentation.
>
> However, in retrospect, it can be argued that in the early 1960s a major opportunity was missed to build a really big brand in the main sector of the market. There was clearly a strong consumer requirement for a brand which offered a reasonable level of performance at a lower price level. The major companies appear to have misjudged the consumers' requirements during the important growth period of the market – the distributor brands were able to move in and meet the need. The prospect now is that as this very big market moves into maturity and later into decline, only one manufacturer brand of any substance (Fairy Liquid) will exist.

Can the distributor brands be beaten?

It is sometimes argued that manufacturer and distributor brands do not really compete as they trade in separate market sectors.

This is a highly questionable argument. It is dangerous to think in terms of a market having sectors which are completely water-tight – there are many examples which prove this is not so. All brands in a market are in competition with each other, and the position of the brands, and the consumers' rating of their value, is changing continually. Of course, there will be brands which establish a strong position as a result of giving a high performance, and there will be consumers who want this and will become loyal to such a brand. However, if this performance lead is weakened, or the price differential widened, experience shows that over time the position of the brand will change.

It is in part understandable that manufacturers prefer to compete with high performance products which have been produced following a lengthy research and development effort. However, if such products become so expensive to produce that their price is considered unduly high by a large number of consumers, then a major market sector will be available to the distributor brands.

Distributor brands have to be beaten as all other competitive brands must. Because they have certain privileges which do not apply to manufacturers' brands they pose a special form of competition.

The manufacturers' brands must give the consumer 'better value' than the distributor brands. There are guidelines which may be helpful to a major manufacturer in coping with the threat posed by distributor brands:

1. The manufacturer should make every effort to have his brand dominate the major volume sector of the market. (This is not necessarily the highest performance sector.) If this domination is achieved all the economies of greater volume should accrue to the manufacturer.

This does not preclude the manufacturer, should the market's size warrant it, from also entering brands in other sectors of the market. Thus, he may well have a brand that delivers a high level performance. In particular, if there is a lower price sector of any substance then he should give detailed consideration to making a brand entry. In all cases his aim should be to ensure that his brand is the clear leader of the particular sector concerned. However, the major effort should focus on dominating the main volume sector of the market. This will not only provide all the advantages of higher volume to the manufacturer, it will deny this volume to the distributor.

2. The manufacturer should work to ensure that his product formula is 'cost effectively' superior. He should ensure that his formulas have a real competitive advantage, that the extra ingredients they contain do, in fact, bring the consumer additional benefits which she values, and that she is prepared to pay for any additional costs which may be incurred.

   An important consideration is that the product formula should not be expected to carry ingredients which are not appreciated by the consumer. Ingredients included primarily for advertising and presentation reasons rarely prove worthwhile over the longer term.

3. The manufacturer should ensure that his operation is both fully effective and efficient. In particular, that he is taking all the advantages which should accrue from his volume. This is a prerequisite for success in any competitive business.

4. The manufacturer should ensure that his brand receives a satisfactory level of advertising and promotional investment support. In this way he maintains direct contact with the consumer, and the consumer is the distributors' customer. One of the manufacturer's most important bargaining counters with the distributor is the consumers' demand for his (the manufacturer's) brand.

5. The manufacturer should take care not to be 'greedy' in the level of the unit contributory margin he takes from his brand. In many markets manufacturers appear to have left a gap into which the distributor brands have been able to move. Many manufacturers place undue reliance on the presentation of their brand adding value. They appear to believe that the consumer should be prepared to pay a higher price for a brand merely because it is advertised.

   It is important that the manufacturer should be aware of the performance difference between his brand and the distributor brand. If the difference is very slight then any price differential should equally be very slight. Blind product testing with consumers can be helpful in showing the real performance difference between the brands. Over the longer term this will be the important consideration in judging the level of price differential to apply.

6. An effective research and development effort, and an innovative marketing approach, should be maintained to bring worthwhile product improvements forward to the market place. Developments may be introduced into premium brands initially, but inclusion in the major volume brand should always be the aim.

If the manufacturer meets these guidelines he will ensure that he holds the highest level of volume in the market. Given that he is effective and efficient in operation, his unit cost for an equivalent product should be lower than that of any other producer. With his unit margin at a lower level it will be difficult for anyone, and in particular the distributor, to attack his position with any real prospect of success. Provided he has chosen his performance/price relationship wisely, it will be extremely difficult for any competitor to offer the consumer better value. Skilful presentation should add further to the value of the manufacturer's brand.

‘ In 1983 the UK low suds washing powder market totalled approximately 330,000 tons. It was a growing market and was expected to reach 600,000 tons in the early 1990s.

The dominant leader of the market in 1983 was Persil Automatic. The brand was taking a relatively low unit margin and this was clearly an important factor in limiting the growth of distributor brands operating in the market.

In 1983 distributor brands held shares of around 30 per cent in many of the major UK grocery markets. In the low suds market distributor brands held only a 10 per cent share.

This market share gave the distributors a volume of approximately 30,000 tons, the proprietary brands 270,000 tons. If the distributor share had been allowed to grow to 30 per cent their volume would have been close to 100,000 tons.

Looking ahead to the 1990s, with a share of only 10 per cent the distributor brands would have a volume of only 60,000 tons. If their share is allowed to grow to 30 per cent their volume will be 180,000 tons. The difference of 120,000 tons must come from proprietary brands.

Beyond this, with a volume of 180,000 tons, the distributors will be much more effective competitors as the market moves into maturity.

> In cases such as this the manufacturer will frequently be under pressure to take a higher level of shorter-term profit. The 1990s are a long way away – the company's stock market rating is more about profit today.
>
> The great danger is that the manufacturer who takes a higher unit margin approach can lose on two counts. Firstly, the higher unit margin can restrict volume in the shorter term and so his absolute margin level will not increase. Secondly, he can forgo the opportunity to make really big profits during market maturity. At this stage (maturity) he should be able to take higher unit margins on his dominant leader volume. If he has sacrificed his dominant share position he is most unlikely ever to recover it. The big 'cash cow' brand, so important for the development of the business, the making of profit, and the payment of dividends, will have been lost.

This chapter has been concerned primarily with the position of a major manufacturer, one who is likely to be interested in the main market sectors. For the specialist manufacturer, interested in specific sectors of the market, the position will be different.

The smaller operator's strength tends to be his speciality. The distributor is unlikely to find it worth his while attempting to copy the speciality brand, although over recent periods a number of major distributors have begun to move into the speciality sectors of some markets. There is a need to exercise skill in fixing the unit margin of the speciality brand. An unduly high unit margin can encourage the entry of a distributor brand even though the volume available may appear to be limited.

It is worth noting that at least one very important aspect of distributor brands is exactly the same as any other competitive brand: *the best time to stop them is before they get started.*

Should a manufacturer make distributor brands?

This question has figured prominently in many strategy discussions over recent periods. The pro argument is as follows: The company has vacant capacity so why not use it to produce distributor brands which will at least make a marginal contribution? Total volume will increase and added benefits should accrue to our own brands. As there is vacant capacity in the industry, if we do not make the distributor brands, someone else will.

The contra arguments reason that if the distributor brand business is to be obtained then the distributor must be given a better deal than he is currently getting. This means either a better product, a better price, or both. The distributor brand will be made that much more competitive in the market-place. Beyond this, it is reasoned that the negotiations are likely to be difficult – the distributors are also very important customers.

The contract will tend to be a short-term one, with no security for the long term. The whole exercise is likely to be much more trouble than it is really worth.

There is no simple resolution of this problem for all manufacturers. So much will depend upon the position of the particular company concerned. If it has no worthwhile brand strength and has considerable vacant capacity, then to make distributor brands may certainly be the right thing to do. For the company with considerable market strength and a reasonable capacity load, a move into making distributor brands could be wrong.

There is another argument: If you manufacture the distributor brands you can at least be sure of the quality and know exactly how it compares with your own. Indeed, you are well placed to ensure that the quality is always positioned suitably below your own. It is not a particularly convincing argument — the aggressive and well managed distributor can be expected to have a view of his own as to the quality of his own label brand.

There is an alternative to making distributor brands open to the major manufacturer who has capacity available. He should ask the question, Is there room in this market for a worthwhile lower priced brand?

Such a brand would need to be a sensible business proposition in its own right for it would require effort and resource to launch into the market. It would have the advantage that it is under the manufacturer's control — he will decide the formula, the presentation, and the market positioning of the brand.

There should be certain volume/cost advantages in manufacturing such a brand compared with making a series of distributor brands, and as the manufacturer's total volume should increase, there could be some benefit for his established brands. A brand of this kind may deter the distributor from entering the market, and should he enter, it could certainly limit his growth.

> Square Deal Surf was launched into the UK washing powder market in the early 1960s to meet a consumer demand for a washing powder that provided a good standard of performance at a price below the market's general level.
>
> Square Deal Surf Automatic (a low suds powder and a Surf line extension) was launched into the UK market in 1979 with a price position in its market similar to that occupied by its parent in the high suds sector.
>
> While the Surf brands have not been close challengers for market leadership they have been successful and have been able to gain a very worthwhile level of market share.

Distributor brands have never been able to command high levels of market share in the UK washing powder market; there are a number of reasons for this, one of them being the existence of brands such as Surf and Surf Automatic.

CHAPTER 14

Brand Portfolio

If all your brands are development brands with very bright longer-term futures then it is probable you will have trouble in the shorter term — you will run out of cash.

If all your brands are well established older brands, then you will have a plentiful supply of cash today, but you will have trouble into the future as your brands lose their volume and cash generating ability.

If you want to have a reasonable life today, and to progress and prosper into the future, then you need a balanced portfolio of brands.

This is the simple reasoning behind the brand portfolio concept.

The brand (or product) portfolio

There can be little doubt that the brand portfolio concept became a factor of considerable consequence within the strategy planning of many companies during the 1970s.

The prominence of the approach owes much to the very colourful presentation on the subject made by the consulting organization, the Boston Consulting Group. They succeeded in making 'cash cows' and 'dogs' (or 'pets') very familiar to everyone in business strategy planning. One of their Perspectives papers (1970) on the Product Portfolio opens:

> To be successful, a company should have a portfolio of products with different growth rates and different market shares. The portfolio composition is a function of the balance between cash flows. High growth products require cash inputs to grow. Low growth products should generate excess cash. Both kinds are needed simultaneously.

The paper closes with the following paragraph:

> Only a diversified company with a balanced portfolio can use its strengths to truly capitalize on its growth opportunities. The balanced portfolio has:
> —stars whose high share and high growth assure the future;
> —cash cows that supply funds for that future growth; and
> —question marks to be converted into stars with the added funds.
> Pets are not necessary. They are evidence of failure either to obtain a leadership position during the growth phrase, or to get out and cut the losses.

Source: *The Product Portfolio*, The Boston Consulting Group, Perspectives 1970.

The brand portfolio in strategy

From a strategy formulation viewpoint a number of important issues concerning the brand portfolio concept require discussion. Firstly, however, it should be stated that businessmen appear to agree with the broad statements made by the Boston Consulting Group in their presentation of the brand portfolio approach. Well established brands in mature markets are normally strong cash contributors; growth brands do tend to consume a relatively high level of investment and effort; most businesses have a number of brands which are in the 'question mark' position; and probably all businesses have their 'pets'.

Of the questions for discussion, the first must be, 'If the portfolio is heavily loaded with growth brands does this really mean trouble?' It will probably mean a shortage of cash. However, cash can normally be raised if the underlying business prospects are good enough. Convincing investors may prove difficult, and the price for the new capital may be high, but nevertheless, cash should be obtainable. It is, of course, possible that part of the price to be paid for the new funds may be the loss of complete control by the present owners and this could be considered a very high price indeed.

The requirement is that management should appreciate the need for funds well in advance of them becoming necessary, and action taken to arrange the financial cover in a manner, and at a time, which is most beneficial.

It may also be necessary to concentrate effort. This will require a rigorous review of the various development projects, the setting of an order of priority, and the arrangement of a timetable for action. Really worthwhile development projects are hard to come by. Normally, a business would be pleased to be embarrassed by an abundant supply of them. The important consideration is that they show genuine potential, and that plans can be made in good time to fund their progress.

A portfolio heavily weighted with established brands in mature markets should mean a very plentiful supply of cash over the short- to medium-term future. A lack of development projects could mean a dismal long-term future.

However, there is no reason why the cash should not be returned to the shareholders via dividends, or by the purchase of the company's own stock where this is allowable and makes business sense.

When a management, trained and skilled in a particular industry, goes out to find a home in a 'development field' for its surplus cash, difficulties can often follow. The basic problem would seem to be that the management believes the guidelines and skills which have worked well for them in their current market will automatically work in others. It does not necessarily follow.

The danger of a portfolio weighted towards established brands is that the development of the strong cash position will not be appreciated early enough, and plans will not have been made to take care of it. One of the problems seems to be the fact that professional managers frequently appear most reluctant to return surplus cash to stockholders.

For the independent company, with owners intent on remaining independent, there is a very real need for a balanced brand portfolio. A bad balance, bringing either too little or too much cash, can well mean the end of their independence. For a competitor to make effective use of the position, he will need to have observed it developing. A cash shortage could mean that either the development projects will need to be curtailed or existing market share allowed to fall through lack of adequate support for established brands. This could provide a competitor, particularly one well aware of the position in advance, with an opportunity either to mount a take-over bid, or to buy share cheaply in the market-place.

Similarly, where a company has a cash surplus developing, and the position can be spotted during its early stages, then the opportunity for a profitable take-over may be available to a predator. This can have an even greater attraction where the established brands have become under-priced or have been badly managed in other ways. A position of this kind can often develop in a business where a number of senior managers are about to retire, and satisfactory follow-up appointments have not been made.

When your competitor is an operating company within a conglomerate or a multi-national, then the important portfolio position is that of the holding company. The parent will have a portfolio of operating companies and if he has cash problems then his subsidiaries may be required to produce cash irrespective of their local position. Indeed, if the multi-national is involved in a particularly difficult market fight in his home market, and this fight is demanding of his resources, he may well have severe cash problems. Such a time could be a good one to attack his subsidiaries.

'During the five years 1978-1982 the trading profit (before tax) of Procter & Gamble UK was in decline. The published figures were:

1978 – £10.6m
1979 – £ 7.9m
1980 – £ 6.4m
1981 – £ 5.8m
1982 – £ 0.8m

If the company had been an independent unit with a local Stock Exchange quotation the period could have been an extremely difficult one for the business.

However, the P & G parent company in the USA was in a sound financial position and this was the important consideration. The portfolio approach reasoning did not apply to the P & G UK subsidiary on this occasion. It is possible that the P & G parent company was maintaining a portfolio of its operating companies and a unit in some other part of the world was acting as a 'cash cow' and providing funds to cover the UK activity. '

'Dogs' or 'Pets'

Most markets contain a number of brands which hold only a low level of market share; in the brand portfolio matrix they would be classified as 'dogs' ('pets'). In fact, it is probable that the majority of brands marketed come under this heading. For some companies almost all of their brands are 'dogs'.

If companies in this position followed the basic advice, they would be planning to remove their 'dogs'. After all, these brands do not make a worthwhile profit; in some instances they may not even make a contribution.

There can be little doubt that established brands which are not able to make a contribution (ie unable to make a gross profit after charging their direct costs against their revenue) should be removed. To keep such brands would require some very special reason.

However, for brands which do make a contribution, and beyond this possibly a small trading profit, the issue can be different. If any one such brand is dropped there is unlikely to be any change in the total fixed costs incurred by the business. In this circumstance should the brand be dropped? And if the company has a number of such brands should they all be dropped? And if they are all dropped what will be the effect on the profitability of the business?

In many cases the company will be faced with a need to find a way of living with the 'dogs'. They must be made at least to contribute. Management should strive to improve the effectiveness and efficiency of the business operation so that the better 'dogs' become small 'cash cows' and make a trading profit, and that all brands make a reasonable contribution. At the same time management should ensure that these problem brands do not occupy an undue amount of its time and resource. A business is unlikely to grow and to prosper if it relies entirely for its future on making 'dogs' contribute to profits. However, for a period they may have a part to play and be worthy of an appropriate level of management attention.

The adoption of the brand portfolio approach forces a rigorous review of all the company's brands and development projects. Such a review will invariably bring two factors to the fore:

1. The 'cash cows' are vitally important. They not only support the 'stars' and the development projects, they also provide the funds for the general running of the business and for the payment of dividends. Protecting the 'cash cows' should be a key priority within the strategic plan.
2. The need to keep a sensible control on the expenditure and resources placed behind any specific development project. Every effort should be made to make the development brands progress reviews realistic. Enthusiasm is important to a development brand, but misplaced enthusiasm can prove very expensive.

The brand portfolio concept may have certain limitations, and a review of the company brands carried out in accordance with the concept will not in itself bring about the formulation of a sound business strategy. However, if it stimulates a realistic appraisal of the brands, their present position, and their potential, it will have made a worthwhile contribution. If a similar exercise is carried out for competitors and their brands, a valuable business opportunity may be highlighted.

> ❛An example of a portfolio approach in operation occurred with Lever Bros through the period 1974-83. The company launched nationally six new brands three of which became national brand market leaders; the company was also able to increase the volume of its two big growth brands – Persil Automatic (low suds) fourfold and Comfort (fabric softeners) threefold. This activity necessitated considerable investment; however, through the period the company was able to increase its trading profit and generate substantial levels of cash.
>
> Of some significance in this whole operation was the fact that Lever had leading brands in a number of mature markets such as Persil (high suds), Domestos (household bleaches), and Lux and Lifebuoy (toilet soaps). It was possible for the company to use these brands as 'cash cows' through the period.❜

CHAPTER 15

Operations and Company Culture

Even the highest level of effectiveness and efficiency in its operations is unlikely to rescue a company which has got its strategy badly wrong.

This is not to say that a high level of effectiveness and efficiency in operation isn't very desirable for a company: indeed, the statement tends to undervalue effective operation. In fact, the most skilfully formulated strategy will fail to produce worthwhile results without the help of an effective operation.

In practice, business strategies are rarely hopelessly wrong or completely right. They are more likely to be partly wrong or partly right. This is one of the great contributions of effective operations—they can turn a partial success into a real success, and steer a near failure into safety. In particular, effective operations can often 'buy' valuable time so that resources may be regrouped and plans prepared for further action.

Operating efficiency can affect strategy formulation and achievement in many ways. It is not the purpose of this book to consider business operations in great detail, however, and discussion centres on the following:

1. Moving into a strategy which would otherwise not be attempted.
2. Countering when under attack.
3. Getting the full potential from a successful introduction.
4. Business operations in general.
5. Operations and company morale.

At the end of this chapter company culture is discussed. A strongly developed culture can be a great asset to a company, it can be most helpful in ensuring effective operation, but it is certainly no substitute for a winning strategy.

Operations

Moving into a strategy which would otherwise not be attempted

A longer-term business strategy comprises a whole series of shorter-term operations. For instance, a strategy to enter a particular market with a new brand will involve a whole series of operations throughout the business from the initial research to the national launch. The success of the strategy will require success in the operations.

Before a strategy is embarked on, a series of estimates will be necessary. They may of necessity be very rough 'back of an envelope' calculations, they may not even have been committed to writing, or they may be highly detailed. The point is that someone will need to have formed an opinion as to 'What we are likely to get in return for a given outlay of money?' or, put in a slightly different form, 'How much will it cost in money and other resource to achieve a given result?'

The estimates which will go to forming the answers to these questions will invariably be based on, or greatly influenced by, the responsible individual's operating experience. The standard of effectiveness and efficiency reached by the organization, or part of the organization, in operation will be a key factor in arriving at the estimates for the particular parts of the proposed strategy.

The good operator will beat the bad in that his costs will be lower and his expectation of achievement higher. There will be many opportunities which the bad operator will feel he cannot attempt, the total cost will be too high. The good operator will find the proposed moves acceptable, for him the total cost is such that he can foresee a worthwhile profit return.

Countering when under attack

A frequently encountered competitive market-place problem for an operator is where one of his major competitors gets a worthwhile product innovation first, and introduces it rapidly to a national market.

The innovation is unlikely to come as a complete surprise to those operating in the market. It may already have appeared in some other country, or it may have been tested in some way, either in the market or in a consumer test, and information on the new development will have been picked up. However, the innovator will have a lead and full details of his new introduction will not be known until it appears in the market.

For the defending company good operation is vitally important in these circumstances. It will need to 'buy time'. Firstly, it will need to take all reasonable action to stop the consumer penetration of the innovation, and secondly to get its own counter attack into shape and into operation as rapidly as possible.

The skill and the speed with which this defending action is carried out will be crucial in the market battle. The difference between the results obtained at this time by a first class operator, and those by one of average ability, will be of real consequence.

Producing new promotional packs with a 'holding' promotion, and getting them into the stores rapidly, developing and producing a new formula product with a 'counter attack' pack, and then selling and distributing it to the right places, will be important to the defensive strategy, and the good operator will make the moves rapidly and skilfully.

Every market point saved is valuable. It is valuable in itself, it is valuable in that it is a point denied to the opposition, and it is valuable in that it provides a better base from which to counter attack.

Getting the full potential from a successful introduction

One of the most pleasant surprises for a manufacturer is when his innovation does much better in the real live market-place than it has in any of his consumer or market tests. This is also a great opportunity — it must not be missed. When something of this kind happens, it is important to exploit it to the full, and this means firstly meeting the immediate demand for the brand. A trial missed can be very expensive, the prospective consumer may not come back, her regular brand may be able to 'stock her up' and then it will be necessary to tempt her to the new brand all over again.

Beyond the immediate need, it is important to ensure that the follow-up promotions are fully geared to the new potential, and are used positively to consolidate the gains which have been made. The follow-up promotion will be, for many consumers, the beginning of the all-important consumer regular buying habit, and it will be essential to have a satisfactory level of brand stock in the stores to meet this demand.

All sections of the business are involved, and the difference between the results obtained by the very good operator, and by one who is just average, will again play a major part in the progress of the brand.

Business operations in general

The above analyses refer to the value of effective operations in specific circumstances. While effective operations can have a special value at these times, it is in the day-to-day running of the business that operating efficiency can have most effect.

Competitive advantages provide the 'extra' so necessary if a business is to go forward to achieve an outstanding business success. However, such a success will only be possible if the competitive advantages are backed by a sound 'everyday' operating performance.

Effectiveness and efficiency in operations are founded on a very high degree of skill, together with a willingness to work hard, from people right through the business. It also requires an acceptance of the need to provide the most suitable capital resources in the form of plant and equipment.

However, while the really effective operators do have very high skills, considerable energy, and are well equipped, they also have an additional quality which in certain respects is even more important. This quality is an attitude which in every aspect of the business sets a standard at the highest level of performance, and then sets out to beat the standard.

There is always a better way. The whole organization, every part of it, is under a form of continuous review. The review searches for a 'better way', and when it is developed, action is taken to put it into operation. The people of the organization not only accept this approach, they are very much part of it, they are the people who are looking for the 'better way'. The various value analyses, cost effectiveness, profit improvement, and similar programmes now employed in many business organizations, are all part of the search for the better way.

An approach of this kind, pursued actively right through the business, can bring a very high level of effectiveness in operation, and this can represent a very worthwhile competitive advantage in itself when the opposition is only of average standard.

6 In the UK soaps and detergents market during 1974-83 the leading contestants – Lever and Procter & Gamble – were both working aggressively to gain a competitive advantage through improved efficiency in operation.

Lever had a series of value analysis and cost effectiveness projects running through the period and they covered all the various parts of the business. One of the very rough guides to productivity performance used by the company was the measure of 'output per person employed'. The total tonnage produced in a given year was divided by the number of people employed. The company was able to achieve an increase of 80 per cent in this rough measure over a period of 10 years, and at the same time the total output of the business increased substantially.

In its published progress report for 1983 Lever stated: 'These improvements in productivity have been a vital factor in our success and have enabled us to provide job security, and fair rewards for our employees.'

P & G was also working along similar lines to improve its productivity. The report of the Price Commission on P & G published in November 1978 commented on cost saving: 'Each department is required to put forward annually a financial target of savings which it intends to achieve in the next 12 months by changes in methods or, for example, production, distribution and use of materials. In general the company looks for a saving of an average of 5 to 6 per cent of costs each year.'

In this highly competitive industry a major leap forward in productivity, in a short period of time, would have been necessary to have obtained a significant competitive advantage. However, if either Lever or P & G had relaxed their efforts and failed to achieve an advance in any given year they would have fallen behind in the competitive race. Not to have improved productivity for two or three years would almost certainly have provided the opposition with a competitive advantage. **,**

Operations and company morale

There can be little doubt that the standard of operating efficiency in a business is always higher when the morale of personnel is good.

Company morale is often difficult to define and to evaluate accurately. When morale in a company is riding high it is very evident and easily recognized. It is equally easily recognized when morale is very low—at the intermediate levels it is much less prominent.

Company morale is linked to a whole series of factors including the style of management employed within the business, management leadership, the way people within the business are treated, the degree of success achieved by the business, and the level of confidence the people of the business have in its future. Anyone who has worked in a business engaged in a vigorously competitive market will know that high morale is essential for real success, and skilled and successful top management will take active steps to ensure that good morale is developed, and maintained, within its business.

' In the 1950s and 60s Procter & Gamble in the UK established an enviable reputation as an effective and efficient business unit. It launched a number of successful brands. Its operations were invariably well planned and carried through in a very positive manner. P & G trained personnel were greatly sought after by other UK companies.

Through this period Lever carried out a number of company reorganizations. In many respects the performance of the business was at a high level, but at this time Lever was outshone by P & G in the UK.

In 1969 P & G was able, for a short period, to claim leadership of the important UK washing powder market. Morale in the Lever business was at a low ebb, and this had an effect on the operational performance of the company. Reports coming from P & G were of buoyancy and high morale.

During the 1970s Lever engaged in a conscious effort to rebuild company morale. The exercise became a top priority for senior management and every suitable occasion was used to talk with the staff throughout the business, to discuss company problems, to explain the opportunities available, and to outline the action necessary to develop and exploit the opportunities.

At the same time Lever began to record a number of notable achievements. A series of new brands was launched with considerable success, market leaderships were gained, and profitability improved. Company morale certainly improved, and now Lever people were in demand.

During this period P & G's published statements showed a decline in profitability, and the company was certainly experiencing a more difficult time in the market-place. Rumours were coming through to Lever that its competitor was having morale problems.

From this experience it is clear that a high level of company morale can be a most valuable asset – it can definitely help in the development of an efficient operation. It is also clear that success can be a tremendously helpful factor in building a high level of morale, and success requires a winning strategy.

Success and high morale are complementary. Management must aim to build both and to ensure they are maintained at a constantly high level. The two great dangers, complacency and over-confidence, must be guarded against at all times.

Company morale and company culture are certainly linked. They are not the same thing, however, and indeed, it is possible for a company culture which has become unduly harsh, or otherwise misdirected, to have an adverse effect on company morale.

Company culture

Company culture has received considerable attention from business researchers and consultants over recent years, particularly in the USA. Culture is 'the pattern of human behaviour in speech, thought, and action that is concerned with man's capacity for learning and passing knowledge to others'. Company culture is about 'what we believe in, and how we do things in this company'.

Many of the early leaders of American industry were excellent businessmen. They believed implicitly in their brands and products, they worked very hard, and they took active steps to ensure that their employees shared in the progress and development of the business. They each believed that a certain basic approach, or series of approaches, was fundamental to the success of their business. For instance, one leader stated, 'our service back-up is the very best' – and he would have taken active steps to ensure that everyone in the business knew this, and that the service actually was of the highest order.

Business leaders of this kind were also present in Europe and they also built strong cultures within their companies. In simple terms these men built a pride in the business and in its performance. The basic approaches they followed were linked to operations and were invariably key to the performance achieved by the business. If you sell complex machinery, a service back-up that is the very best is an important selling point. If you sell consumer brands, listening to the consumer makes good sense. And if you sell products which are perishable, 'a reputation for the very best in freshness' is helpful.

The early business leaders also mastered the art of simple communication. The people who worked with them were informed on a regular basis, of the business progress. The importance of getting the basics right was stressed continually. Beyond this the early leaders had the good sense to ensure that those who worked with them shared in the rewards which came from the progress of the business.

From this it has been reasoned that the development of a strong company culture is a vitally important factor to the success of a business. Indeed, some enthusiastic advocates of this approach argue that culture is the key factor.

> ❛It is interesting to note that the two leading companies in the UK soaps and detergent industry – Lever and Procter & Gamble – were both founded and developed by men who clearly believed fervently in the importance of a strong company culture.
>
> P & G was founded in the USA in 1837. From its early beginnings the company established a reputation of paying scrupulous attention to its customers and their requirements. William Cooper Procter, a descendant of one of the founders and president of the company from 1907 to 1930, introduced both profit sharing and guaranteed employment into the P & G business at times when benefits of this kind were rarely, if ever, seen in industry generally. At the same time, as a good businessman, Procter emphasized that profits had to be earned before they could be shared.
>
> The Lever Bros business was founded by William Hesketh Lever (later Lord Leverhulme) in the UK in 1885. He also believed deeply in the importance of the customer, and in the quality of his products. His introduction of co-partnership in 1909 was a move in employee participation well ahead of its time. Lever believed passionately in the welfare of his employees and this included providing them with housing. The village he built at Port Sunlight was widely recognized as an enlightened development. William Lever was also a very good businessman. He was equally

emphatic about the importance of running his business in an effective, efficient, and profitable manner.

When Lever made a determined effort to enhance morale within the company in the mid-1970s it re-introduced a number of the approaches originally used by William Lever. This included the chairman talking with every employee at least once each year to explain the progress and results of the business.

,

There is little doubt that the development of a sound company culture can be a major strength for the business concerned. However, it is important that this should not replace or in anyway be confused with the need for a successful business strategy.

Company culture, while led from the top, concerns everyone in the business. It permeates the whole company, and in the strong organization, is shared by everyone in the business. Strategy formulation and planning, in particular decision making, is likely to concern very few people within the business. Indeed, at its highest level it concerns just one man — the Chief Executive. While he may receive help and guidance from his colleagues, as the business strategy should concern the whole business, so the final key strategy decisions should rest with the man who is responsible for the whole business — the Chief Executive. The majority of people in the business just do not have the necessary information available to them to make sound strategy decisions, and in all probability, it would be impractical to involve them.

The vitally important task of putting the agreed strategy into operation, however, will concern everyone in the business. Here the company culture plays a significant part. If the wrong decisions have been taken in the strategic planning, however, and the wrong strategy adopted, then the existence of the strongest company culture is unlikely to bring success. Given the right strategy, a strong company culture can certainly play an important part in its exploitation.

The probability is that the early American business leaders and their counterparts in Europe, who were wise enough to build a strong and sound company culture, were also wise and shrewd enough to ensure that they had a winning business strategy.

CHAPTER 16

Sales Force, Distribution – the Trade

There was a time when the support of a large and well organized sales force was essential if a brand was to make any real impression in a major consumer goods market.

It is often said that in the late 1940s with the development of synthetic detergents (as distinct from soap) the big oil and chemical companies were keen to enter the retail soaps and detergents market. They were certainly well equipped technically and financially to do so, but it was the big soap operators who had the sales and distribution organizations and were able to make the retail synthetic detergents market theirs. No doubt there were other factors involved, but the possession of a well trained and organized sales force was important.

In most developed countries the retail trade has changed dramatically over the last 30 years. The many thousands of small retail stores, each one owned by the trader and thereby requiring a separate negotiation, have been replaced by a limited number of super stores. Some small stores remain, but in number and influence they no longer occupy a position of major significance.

The sales force

The sales force is normally considered as an operational rather than a strategic factor. This is understandable, but as with many operational factors it does also have a part in strategy formulation.

It may appear that the value of an effective and efficient sales force has diminished through the period of change. This is not the case but it has been necessary to make changes in the structure, size, and skills of the sales organization, to ensure an effective performance.

Basically, the three requirements of the sales force have changed little over the years:

1. Store distribution of the brand
2. Brand feature, ie prominent display in appropriate positions within the stores
3. Competitive brand pricing.

Store distribution

A satisfactory level of consumer penetration is vitally important to a brand. The most effective way to increase brand sales volume is to increase brand penetration. Consumer brand penetration is invariably linked directly with brand store distribution. The brand advertising may have been very persuasive, the brand promotion may have been both exciting and attractive, but if the brand is not available in the store where the consumer carries out her shopping then she is unlikely to become a buyer.

At one time obtaining satisfactory store distribution for a brand required a personal call on many thousands of small shopkeepers, each one having to be persuaded that the brand represented a sound business proposition for him. This necessitated a large and well trained group of salesmen. With the dramatic change in the structure of the retail and wholesale trade, the requirement now is to convince a much more limited number of businessmen that the brand represents a sound proposition to occupy space in the retail stores which they control. A limited number of salesmen is now required, and their skill needs to be of a more sophisticated kind. However, the requirement is the same: if the brand is to be successful it will need a satisfactory level of store distribution.

In his negotiations for brand store distribution the salesman will be helped by the record of the brand in testing, both with the consumer and in the market-place, by the level of advertising and promotional investment which is backing the brand, by the various trade offers he may have available, and by the profit earning potential it has for the trader. The skill of the salesman in presenting the brand and its support will be an important factor in gaining the necessary distribution for the brand, and in gaining it rapidly.

Brand store feature

Of course, the real aim of the manufacturer is more than just store distribution. He wants his brand stacked in the right quantity, at the right price, and in the best position within the store. The aim is that the consumer will be unable to miss seeing it, and will be tempted to pick it up and drop it in her basket or trolley. The manufacturer wants his brand 'featured'.

Features are normally agreed after negotiation between the salesman and the store manager/store chain buyer. The salesman's skill in negotiation will again be extremely important.

Competitive in-store pricing

When resale price maintenance was practised generally the manufacturer set the price at which his brand should retail, and in the main, this was followed throughout the retail trade. This still applies in a limited number of markets and countries, and for certain specific brands. However, in general, manufacturers now accept that the retail price should be set by the retailer.

It can be argued that the retailer invests his capital in space and stock, and by recording rates of brand movement he can readily decide the level of margin he should take on any given brand. Rapid brand movement should mean a relatively low margin, and slower brand movement a higher level. In practice many retailers do carry out calculations of this kind. However, the position is rarely clear. The various special offers, consumer promotions, periods of heavy advertising, competitive pressures etc tend to confuse the position. It follows that the skilled salesman can have a marked influence on the level of price at which his brand is retailed, and this can have a considerable effect on the brand's chances of becoming the consumer's 'best value' choice.

The recent retail trade developments have tended to help the smaller manufacturers as it is no longer necessary to have a large sales force to get satisfactory brand distribution. The developments have placed a particularly high value on the skills of a limited number of salesmen.

A sales force which can ensure a satisfactory level of brand distribution, a preferential level of brand feature, and competitive brand pricing, will most certainly have made a very real contribution to a brand's progress. A sales force of this calibre could well constitute a competitive advantage.

From a strategy formulation viewpoint it is important that the real strength and capability of the sales force should be recognized. Equally the strength, or weakness, of competing sales organizations should also be recognized. The comparative positions need to be taken account of in strategic planning.

The fact that only a relatively small number of salesmen is now required to obtain national coverage in a developed country, such as the United Kingdom, is of considerable significance to a competitor entering an entirely new market. The investment, and the time, required to build an effective sales organization has been greatly reduced.

How many brands can a salesman sell?

This is an additional sales force consideration which is often debated by sales and marketing executives and it is one that can have a place in strategic planning. The operative word is 'sell' as opposed to just booking orders.

The question can be important because as a company grows so does the list of its brands. Anyone who has had experience in the marketing department of a multi-brand company will know of the continuous fight which goes on among brand managers for the 'priority' spots in the salesmen's presentation each sales cycle. Only if a brand is on the priority list will it be 'sold', only if it is on this list will it be considered for 'feature'; off the list it will get only a 'top up' order. There is also the psychological point claimed of buyers. They will only give one manufacturer a limited number of feature spots each month, and two or three spots is the maximum you get, no matter how good the offer. This point is difficult to prove, yet experience tends to confirm it.

It is from reasoning of this kind that the concept of having a number of sales divisions, each one carrying only a limited number of major brands, has developed.

The economic case for the sales divisional approach is that the manufacturer will increase his brand sales volume, and thereby increase brand contributory profit margin by an amount which more than covers the cost of the divisionalization.

For a growing business, the new sales division will provide 'sales force capacity' for new brands under development, and at the same time avoid any detraction from the effort put behind established brands. As the number of major selling points has decreased so the cost involved in mounting an additional sales division has fallen, and the approach has become that much more attractive.

6 In the period immediately following the 1939-45 war the grocery trade in the UK was composed of over 100,000 mainly small, often independently owned, shops.

Through the next three decades the number of these small independent shops reduced as the multiple chains and the wholesale buying groups took an increasing share of the total grocery business.

During the period 1945-60 Lever had three selling units in the UK, each one carrying a very limited range of soap, detergent and household cleaning brands. One of the basic reasons for maintaining three sales forces was the fact that selling to the smaller traders required a direct personal approach with a very short sales interview. This meant that the number of brands the salesman could actually 'sell' was strictly limited.

In the early 1960s, when the change in structure of the UK grocery trade greatly reduced the number of buying points, Lever found it appropriate to concentrate its selling effort into one sales force. The businessmen who were now running the grocery business required a very different selling approach from that which had been successful with the small independent traders.

There is a view that into the 1990s it may well be advisable for companies such as Lever to consider a move back to more than one sales force. The number of important buying points will be very limited and so the number of salesmen required will also be very limited. With only a short list of brands to sell a highly skilled salesman should be able to concentrate his effort and simplify his approach. It is reasoned that this should allow him to obtain much more than the marginal extra sales necessary to pay for his keep.

,

This whole question of how many brands a salesman can really 'sell' and the concept of additional sales divisions, is debated at length by professionals in the sales area. It is difficult to produce conclusive test data on the subject, and it remains an area where good judgement is at a premium.

Physical distribution

The cost of physical distribution has risen rapidly over recent years and it now forms an appreciative part of the total cost of the majority of branded goods marketed in developed countries.

The aim of the manufacturer in this field is basically very simple: it is to get his finished product, that is his brands packed in appropriate cases or trays, from the end of his production line to the point of sale, efficiently and at as low a cost per unit as possible, within the delivery approach he has chosen to follow.

Efficient operation is clearly essential. It is an area where the question: 'Should we do it ourselves or should we hire?' needs to be raised.

Volume can be an important factor in the cost of physical distribution, although its advantages are not so obvious as in the field of production. Normally a full truck, as large as possible, will be cheaper to operate than a series of small loads. If the truck can be full of one brand, better still of one size of one brand, then there should be further economy.

The cost of running heavy goods vehicles is the most visible cost within the physical distribution scene. However, it is important to recognize that there are a number of other significant cost factors. The mere act of picking up a number of cases and then putting them down again is a costly business — costly in terms of the personnel and handling devices which will be necessary, in the storage facilities, and in the capital tied up in the stock. The ideal is for the product to move directly and automatically from the production line to the transport, and then again into the retail store. In this way handling and storage costs can be held at a minimum level.

The manufacturer has a 'tool' available to him which can markedly affect his whole physical delivery system and this is the structure of his price-list. The price-list structure is a 'policy tool' for not only does it affect the delivery system, it also helps the salesmen to obtain orders at particular types and sizes of retail outlets.

The manufacturer should decide, as part of his marketing strategy, which retail and wholesale outlets he wishes his salesmen to call on, where he wishes them to book orders (as distinct, for instance, from making a merchandising call) and where he wants his vehicles to make delivery.

He can attempt to call on many of the smaller stores should he wish, or he can decide to call only at head offices and deal exclusively with the very large wholesale and retail operators. Of course he may take up positions between the two extremes.

In many countries the manufacturer will have complete freedom in the structuring of his price-list, the various stages will not necessarily have to be linked to his costs. Indeed, if he wishes, he can have special terms for his bigger accounts so that he may achieve the desired economy of moving his brands directly from his production lines to his customers' stores.

In other countries, there may be certain legal requirements, such as linking terms with costs, which the manufacturer must follow. Even in these circumstances he will be free to decide on the terms intervals within the price-list.

The manufacturer needs estimates of the probable cost of the various delivery approaches. It is important that the costs should be total costs, that is, the items such as the various handling and storage charges, and the cost of tying up capital, should be included.

The final decision as to the terms structure within the price-list is a policy one, and it should be made within the wider context of a total marketing strategy. However, as the costs of physical distribution are now invariably substantial, they should play a material part in the considerations which lead to the policy decision.

Having decided on his delivery approach, the manufacturer should take every action to ensure that it is carried out effectively and efficiently in just the same way as he should with his production performance. A truly efficient operation will be valuable as large sums of money are likely to be involved.

It is not easy to obtain a significant competitive advantage in the field of physical distribution. However, when efficiency in operation is linked to a shrewd approach to the wider issues of sales force callage and the price-list terms structure, a worthwhile advantage will often be possible.

The trade

Customers are defined here as the people to whom the manufacturer actually sells his brands; for the products we are primarily concerned with they will be either retailers or wholesalers.

The manufacturer can trade directly with consumers through door-to-door selling, direct mail contact, or local agents. However, the products of by far the majority of manufacturers of branded goods reach consumers through the wholesalers and retailers who are generally termed 'the trade'.

There is a continuous movement within the trade. The decline of the independent sector and the growth of the multiple chains have already been mentioned. Over recent years in the United Kingdom there has been first the growth and later the decline of the consumers' co-operative movement. The growth of the cash and carry wholesalers, and the development of the large superstores, have been two other recent developments.

‘The table below gives an indication of the development of the UK grocery trade through the 1970s. It demonstrates the importance for a manufacturer of forecasting such a development accurately, and also of providing for its exploitation in his strategy formulation.

1. Through the 10 years 1973-82 the multiple section of the UK grocery trade was making great progress:

UK Grocery trade

	1973	1982
	Market share	
	%	%
Multiples	51	72
Others	49	28

2. However, within the multiple section some concerns were making considerably more progress than others:

Company	UK Grocery trade 1973 %	Market share	1982 %
Tesco	7.5		14.0
Sainsbury	8.0		15.0
Asda	3.0		8.5
Other multiples	32.5		34.5
	51.0		72.0

Probably the most important 'trade' business strategy consideration for manufacturers is the developing strength of the big chain retailers and the effect of this on their relationships with manufacturers.

In a country such as the United Kingdom in the late 1940s it was quite common for a major manufacturer to deal directly with some 75,000 or more retailers. No one of them would have more than 2 or 3 per cent of his business. Today in the UK two retail chains are reported to hold well over 60 per cent of the packaged grocery market in the London region, a region which totals some 30 per cent of the UK market. If a brand is to have any chance of real success in this London region it must be stocked by the two chains, and success in 'the region' is essential if the brand is to be a national leader.

The growth of the major retail chains is not slowing down. In fact it is accelerating. The bigger operators have access to the necessary finance and management to lead the movement into superstores and other new retailing developments. Retail trade movements of this kind have been taking place in a similar way to that in the UK, sometimes at a faster rate and sometimes slower, throughout the countries of the developed world.

All of this means a great change in the relationship between the manufacturer and the retailer. Clearly, in the earlier periods, the balance of strength was with the manufacturer. When he launched a major new brand and communicated directly, and persuasively, with the consumer the small retailers were almost forced to stock it. And if some of them stood out and decided not to stock, their volume was so small it really didn't matter unduly to the manufacturer.

Today if one of the major retail chains refuses to stock a brand the loss in revenue to the manufacturer can be most damaging. If three or four of the top retail chains refuse to stock a brand, the effect could possibly kill it. Deciding how to handle this new position is an important strategy consideration for the manufacturer.

Trading pricing policy

In earlier chapters the point has been made that the strength of the retail trade should be a major factor within the broader business strategy planning. Here it is proposed to consider it on a narrower front. The major retailers can be crucial to the success of a brand — how should they be handled?

There are a number of factors which can enter into the negotiations the manufacturer has with his major customers. However, either directly or indirectly, the negotiation will be concerned primarily with the price the major retailer is to pay for the manufacturer's brands.

In a number of countries the law specifically requires that the manufacturer should employ what is generally known as an 'open price-list'. It means that the one price-list and the terms within it must apply for all customers. It does not mean that they will necessarily all buy at the same price, as the list can make allowances for volume within its terms structure.

The legal requirement for an 'open price-list' does not apply in all countries. For instance, it does not apply at the present in the United Kingdom. This means that the supplying manufacturer can, if he wishes, have a differential pricing approach. Under this approach special terms are made available to selected customers as the manufacturer considers appropriate.

Should a manufacturer in the United Kingdom, or in any country where the law allows, follow a differential pricing approach, or should he insist on using an open price-list?

If he follows the differential approach he may keep a good position with his major customers for a period. However, he must face the fact that his 'secret' terms are unlikely to be a secret for very long. Buyers change their employment, some of his own staff may move to competitors, and so on. Soon details of his special terms will be known to other retailers who will want their share of the special terms. If he is clever in his dealings, the manufacturer may be able to sustain his position for a reasonable period. Nevertheless, he could well find himself eventually giving 'special' terms to all his major chain customers, and then the biggest of them may look for even better terms to restore their preferential position.

He can opt for the more straightforward 'open terms' approach. Of course, he may need to face the fact that some of the major retailers will prefer to stock the brands of his competitors who are prepared to meet their preferential term requirements and not stock his brands. However, a major benefit will be that he will avoid the continuous 'play-off' of a trader complaining, and possibly taking action, because he believes one of his retail competitors is obtaining special treatment.

There are, of course, positions in between these two extremes. For instance, the price-list can be an 'open' one and additional payments made under headings such as 'merchandising', but paid only to a limited number of traders who meet a particular requirement.

An 'open price-list' which makes due allowances for the cost savings of volume is probably the most desirable for the manufacturer if, and this is very important, he is strong enough to make it work. The strength really refers to the manufacturer's brands and just how many consumers consider them to be best value, when given an opportunity to buy. There is little doubt that in this negotiation the market strength of his brands is the manufacturer's key bargaining tool.

The terms as set out in the 'open' price-list will of themselves be a form of compromise on cost. They are, for instance, unlikely to take into account the cost differences incurred as a result of the varying distances between the manufacturer's plant and the individual warehouses. It is possible to build in allowances for these costs but it makes the price-list very complex.

When he decides to average within his terms, the manufacturer should be clear that he is subsidizing some deliveries and penalizing others. If there are extremes within the data on which the average is based, the manufacturer could place himself at a disadvantage in some instances, as compared with a competitor who does not average.

The small manufacturer with relatively weak brands will probably be forced to practise some form of discrimination in his trade pricing if he wants his brands to live. If he is skilful, he will use the discrimination very carefully, avoiding the pitfalls and always working to ensure that his expenditures bring worthwhile results.

It is advisable that a manufacturer should, from time to time, check the cost of doing business with his various individual customers. He may not wish to use the information to change his price-list, but at least he will know his position and where he may eventually wish to make changes.

In arriving at his costs he should be careful to eliminate the many 'cost allocations' which tend to be used in this area. When allocations are made on a basis such as 'percentage of total trade' they are invariably very misleading.

The national promotion plan—for and against

The manufacturer with strong, leading brands will generally attempt to keep his national operations programmes intact. He will wish to coordinate closely his manufacturing plan, his deliveries to the trade, and his advertising and promotional investment. He will reason that only with complete coordination on a national or regional basis can he expect to get the full advantages that the synergy should bring.

The weaker manufacturer will have long since dispensed with national operations. His smaller brands will be much more at the mercy of the retail and wholesale trade. He will tend to be opportunistic and to ride in with individual traders as openings come up (this will apply particularly where he is practising discriminatory pricing).

Is there a way between the two extreme positions? Where the law allows discriminatory pricing there can be a way through. It is necessary for the manufacturer to have a basic national operation, and then on top of this to make individual offers to particular customers at varying times through the year. The manufacturer would need to be sure that all his major customers are covered, and that the support offered to them over the year is at least roughly related to their total purchases.

Moves of this kind can cause problems with the various retail chains each one of whom will be convinced that his competitor is receiving priority treatment. This is why it is often necessary to link the support directly to volume purchases.

The compromise can have the advantage of allowing for an investment with a major customer to be in a form preferred by the customer, and at a time which links with his programmed activity.

For a leader to use a compromise approach may prove difficult but certainly not impossible. His prominence will most probably mean that all his moves will be studied closely, and his prices will be noted. For him to discriminate could bring about troublesome relations with his major customers. However, for a smaller manufacturer the position is very different: the compromise could represent a real opportunity to develop his brands.

Trade development

It is important to maintain a continuous review of trade developments. As in all fields, there will be winners and losers, and it is important for the manufacturer to be moving with the winners. If the United Kingdom trade position in the grocery market is studied, it is very obvious that through the period 1970-80 the major multiple chains made substantial market share gains at the expense of other traders.

For the manufacturer intent on the growth and development of his brands through this period there has been a requirement to ensure that his operations are sensibly aligned with the growth sector of the grocery trade, ie with the multiple sector. Again, within the multiple sector there have been particular chains which have progressed very rapidly, and others which have been static or in decline. Manufacturers have needed to maintain a close alignment with the progressive retail operators. Constructing a realistic forecast of the development of the retail trade, its form and structure, and within the forecast to decide which retail operators can be expected to develop and progress, should be part of the strategy formulation process. Plans can then be made to ensure that such factors as delivery arrangements, price-list structure, case sizes and packaging, and similar items are developed in such a manner as to exploit the trade developments.

Where a manufacturer distributes his brands through a series of retailers with whom he has exclusive distribution agreements covering given areas, or possibly a distribution agreement which is linked to the provision of certain servicing facilities, then a very different set of circumstances exists. In this case it is necessary to build a chain of distributors appropriate to the need of the brands, and then to ensure that it is maintained at a satisfactory level of effectiveness. There will be opportunities to widen distribution as the new form of retail outlets, such as the superstores, develop. There may be problems both to hold the existing distributors and to take in the new, and strategic decisions as to which are the most important for the future may be necessary.

The rapid development of the retail and wholesale trade, and within it the progress of the successful traders, can provide very real opportunities for manufacturers. For those who are skilled in forecasting this development accurately, and who follow through and exploit it to the full, it can provide a significant competitive advantage.

Indeed, for the smaller brand hoping to grow and to challenge the leader, a shrewd exploitation of the trade will be essential for success. For the leader, the development and use of his brand strength with the trade will also be very significant.

CHAPTER 17

Capacity

There is a statement often quoted in strategy discussions which argues that 'The time to make your big effort to stop your competitor is before he buys his capacity, not after he has purchased it.'

The implications behind this are that once the competitor has purchased capacity, say a new plant, there will be many fixed costs which will accrue to him automatically. He will incur these costs whether or not the plant produces. The incentive to get the plant working will be a strong one, and so he will make strenuous efforts to obtain the market share which will provide the necessary volume. His selling prices may not cover all his costs, but he will be better off using the plant and making a contribution to profit, rather than have it standing idle. This will probably mean a price and/or a promotional battle in the market, and considerable loss of profit for the man already holding the market.

The statement clearly contains much business sense. If a possible competitor can be convinced that it will not be worthwhile for him to invest in plant, the man holding the market may be saved considerable effort and expense.

How important is capacity?

There are, of course, some markets where additional capacity can be obtained rapidly and with only a limited level of investment—for instance, capacity in the form of a mixing bowl and a filling line. There are also occasions when the capacity for one market may be switched to another quickly and with only a small investment. In cases of this kind capacity is unlikely to be a key factor in strategy formulation.

(In many markets, however, capacity *is* an important factor. It requires careful planning and preparation, a period of time for installation, and a relatively high level of investment.)

The first question the manufacturer needs to answer then is, 'Is capacity an important factor to me or to my competitors in this market?'

If capacity is significant it is important to have a clear indication of the investment level, the running costs, and the output potential over various time periods, for various sizes and types of plant. From estimates of this kind a reasonable indication of unit output costs, for various volume levels, should be obtainable.

It is important that these estimates should provide for modern and fully effective plant and equipment, and if there is an economy in size then details should be included. In particular, if new and more economical processing methods are available they should also be included in the calculations. The importance of including the most economical process is that the manufacturer may then know just what competitors are capable of mounting, and also have a comparison with his own current costs. If his own costs are out of line he may need to consider new plant investment for his business, even if his current plant is relatively new.

Should the industry be one where capacity can be added a piece at a time, while leaving the whole fully effective and economical, then the manufacturer is fortunate. More frequently the position is that capacity needs to be added in units, and the size of the unit added is a key factor in its effectiveness and in the unit cost of output.

Who has capacity?

One of the basic questions the manufacturer needs to ask of his industry is, 'Who currently has capacity, what is the extent of the capacity, and what condition is it in?'

The manufacturer must firstly identify which of his competitors has the ability to produce (if they are merely selling agents, then who has the ability to produce for them). Secondly, he must quantify how much each competitor is capable of producing over given periods of time. Thirdly, he must ascertain the condition of the capacity — is it a modern and fully effective plant, or is it an old and worn out facility?

These questions, and the answers to them, can be crucial in strategy formulation. To be short of capacity when a market in its growth stage makes a rapid move forward, could mean the loss of brand position, the transfer of volume and possible leadership to a competitor, and the loss of a major competitive advantage.

Equally, if the manufacturer is the only competitor with vacant capacity available, and the market is capable of considerable growth, then an opportunity may be available to him should he stimulate rapid and immediate growth.

Capacity frequently has to be planned and committed a long period ahead, possibly a number of years, before it comes on stream. There is always a risk involved in the provision of capacity—a new development may render the current form and type of product out of date, a major increase in the price of a raw material may force a strong price increase causing volume to fall, and so on.

The manufacturer's stance on capacity should be straightforward. It is to ensure that he has his own capacity in line with his needs and with the market development. The capacity should be capable of production at costs which are, at equal volume levels, at least as low as any in the market, and preferably lower than any competitor. This may mean that he will need to face some expensive replacements for older plant—better this than he should become a high cost producer.

As far as he can, he will want to ensure that his competitors are short of capacity when it is needed most. If he is the market leader he can, by the level of unit margin he applies, discourage them from new investment. Beyond this, he has a very strong interest in attempting to convince any potential new competitors that they should not invest to enter his markets. Again, the level of the unit margins likely to be available within the industry would be a key factor in dissuading them.

With regard to his own capacity, the manufacturer will have his market movement estimates for the period ahead. They will probably be in ranges showing both his lowest and his highest volume market expectations. He will know of his own product developments and will need to make estimates of the impact they may make on the market, and on his share and volume.

Also, he must consider his competitors and their likely moves in terms of brand developments and market shares. From these various considerations the manufacturer can build a 'most likely' estimate of his volume requirements, together with a range of upper and lower limits. From these estimates can follow statements covering the capacity position he faces, the probable level of activity of his existing plant, and his possible need for additional capacity.

> ❝ It is important to appreciate that the significant capacity is that which can produce the specific product as required to meet the particular market demand. This does not necessarily mean capacity to produce a general product for the market. It follows that the key capacity consideration is often the ability to make or to process a particular ingredient.
>
> In the UK in 1968-69 Procter & Gamble launched a successful enzymatic

washing powder. Lever was very keen to reply immediately to this competitive activity with an enzymatic product of its own. However, one of Lever's problems at the time was a lack of capacity – not an inability to make washing powder, but a lack of facilities to process the enzyme ingredient and to inject it into the washing powder. **,**

The provision of new capacity is a policy investment. It is an investment which should be viewed and justified within the strategic plan for the business as a whole. Policy investments should be measured ultimately in terms of profit and loss for the whole business, as distinct from operating investments where the justification can be, for instance, the saving of cost in the performance of a particular function within a sector of the business.

It is noticeable that in many business organizations the examination of proposals for what are termed as capital projects, such as new plant and equipment, is much more rigorous than for revenue projects, such as brand advertising and promotion. In the big companies this can often mean delays as head office specialists are consulted and estimates questioned. No one wants to be labelled 'the man who built the plant that has never worked at more than 25 per cent capacity'. The cost of being short of capacity at the 'wrong time to be short' can equally be very costly, possibly much more costly than excess capacity.

In considering capacity investment proposals the important figure is the actual net cash payment to be made. At the present time there are many special taxation allowances, regional grant payments, etc made available by government and regional bodies who may be anxious to attract investment. The actual cash outlay is the cost of the plant. Of course, if there are any disadvantages associated with a particular investment then they should also be included in the calculations.

It is always important for the market leader to appreciate that if he allows it to be known that he is, or is likely to be, short of capacity, he may well encourage others to invest. Once they have invested, they will want to use their plant. When a leader invests in capacity before he really needs it, he will at least have made his position clear to others viewing the market. It is possible for an action of this kind to dissuade a competitor, or potential competitor, from investing.

Carrying over

Getting market and brand volume estimates exactly right is almost impossible. Similarly, new plant is not always ready for production on the planned date.

When new plant is to come into operation it is desirable that there should be an adequate production volume available right from the start, adequate, that is, to provide for an economic operation. This may require that, for a period, existing plant should be run at well over its 'normal' level.

Plant engineers in general have three levels of plant operation. What they term as 'normal' is a level which allows a fully adequate time for maintenance, cleaning etc plus an allowance for safety. It is at this level that they usually prefer to operate. A 'full' level provides for a limited amount of overtime running and removes the major safety allowances. 'Full capacity' is a level which works the plant full-out with maximum overtime and with all the safety valves removed. The names may differ but such levels do seem to exist in all plants. Engineers are always understandably most reluctant to see the safety cover removed. The safety cover referred to is concerned with plant breakdowns and not human safety. It follows that before the new plant comes on stream it may be necessary to 'overload' any existing plant.

Efficiency in the production process is always important. During a period of 'carry over' it is especially so. A plant producing at 95 per cent efficiency produces over 25 per cent more in the same time period than a similar plant running at only 75 per cent.

When the issue of a business possibly requiring new capacity is first raised, the initial move should be to consider the loading and efficiency of existing plant, and ways in which both may be improved. There is a production 'safety-valve' available to a manufacturer in these circumstances and that is to buy production from another supplier. This may be possible in certain industries although it has the drawback of requiring publication of the brand formula and production process; this would not be acceptable to many manufacturers.

Another 'safety-valve' approach is to arrange 'importation' of the brand from an associate. This approach tends to be favoured by multinational operators. It avoids publication of the brand formula and process, but it can involve considerable extra cost.

It is important that these various 'carrying-over' techniques are kept in mind during strategy formulation. They can alleviate the problems of product shortages, they can help in the running-in of new plant but they can be expensive and if they are needed for a lengthy period, their total cost can be significant.

PART 4

CHAPTER 18

Ownership, Management, Finance

Owners differ in their approach, in their style, and in their concern for the business they own. For some, the business has developed from years of hard work and many struggles, their heart is in the business, it is very much part of them. For others, the business is merely a financial invest-ment, to be traded at the right time in the future.

Some owners are also managers of the business and are closely involved in its day-to-day activities. Other owners employ professional managers on a salaried basis, they rarely meet, and the results are their only con-cern. Yet again, other owners take their managers into shared ownership, they meet and discuss progress regularly.

Knowing who owns the businesses that compete in his markets, how they are managed, and their financial position, can be vitally important to the Chief Executive in his strategy formulation. It is equally import-ant, of course, that the Chief Executive should know the owners of his own business, and should be clear as to what they expect from it.

Ownership

Ownership of a business can take many forms. In those countries follow-ing the free enterprise approach, the law invariably permits a whole series of different forms of business ownership: here it is necessary to generalise. Our concern is with the possible effect of ownership on the strategies followed by various competitors, and so the discussion is focused on the different types of competitor:

- Sole ownership

- Local company
- Conglomerate
- Multi-national
- Distributor.

There is one very important factor which is common to all: the business may be in private or public ownership. Public ownership implies that the business has its stock quoted on a public stock exchange, there is buying and selling of this stock, and the company is required to publish full details of its financial record at regular intervals and at least once each calendar year. A private business is defined as one that does not have its stock quoted publicly, and does not have to publish its financial record.

The difference from a strategic planning viewpoint will be clear. The public company may find it very difficult to live through a period without trading profit, or without paying a dividend; the effect on its quoted share price could be disastrous. Further, financial problems, such as an acute cash shortage, are much more difficult to hide when it is necessary to publish detailed financial statements.

With a private business the same problems will not necessarily apply. For instance, it is possible for a private company to go a number of years without making a trading profit, and dividends may be suspended over this period. These facts need not receive any publicity, and the share value will not necessarily change.

Frequently a parent company is a multi-national or a conglomerate and is a public company, but the operating units in the various countries around the world remain private companies. The detailed financial records of the parent company are readily available but the records of the operating units are not published. In these circumstances acquiring accurate financial data on the operation units can prove extremely difficult.

Sole ownership

In this instance the business is owned by one person, or possibly one family, and it will almost certainly be a private company. Businesses of this kind were once numerous within the various markets; they are now much more limited in number, but some have survived and grown into major international operations.

Where the founder of the business remains in charge, his role will frequently be a dominant one. His personal private wealth may be such that he is not necessarily concerned with short-term profitability. His business has probably been built on certain basic principles, for example: 'You get market leadership and then you hold it irrespective of the short-term cost.' Frequently, the founder will hold a number of basic principles on, for instance, product quality, production processes, or employee relations. These principles are rarely disregarded by the business. Similarly he may believe his brand success is founded on always following a limited number of key actions. He will tend always to take these actions, repeating them from time to time with all his new brands. This is all very understandable—a successful record can be a very powerful support in any business argument. It applies particularly when the man who built the success also owns the business.

When competing with this type of business it is important to know of the principles and actions, to know how they have been applied, and to keep them very much in mind when formulating strategy.

It is also important to know the personality of the founder, and his attitude and approach to particular competitive situations. His personal independence may enable him to take unexpected action, possibly action which in the shorter-term may not appear to be good business sense.

> ❜During 1961 Lever Bros acquired (through Unilever) the Domestos business which had been founded in 1929 by Mr Wilf Handley. Working initially from his home in Newcastle upon Tyne, Mr Handley had gradually built the business into a strong national operation. He continued to own the bulk of the company and was the main force in its development.
>
> During the early period of the business growth, as he moved his brands into wider distribution throughout the country, Wilf Handley is said to have often suffered as the result of 'cash shortage' problems. He believed that the major reason for these problems was that many of his customers were slow in settling their outstanding accounts.
>
> After one such problem period he resolved that he would henceforth only sell his products on a basis of cash on delivery. This was to apply to all sales, including those to the largest and most prestigious of the retail grocery multiple chains. This ruling is said to have been strictly enforced throughout the business.
>
> While not necessarily an important factor in their strategy formulations, those companies competing with Domestos would surely have found that this particular 'rule', enforced by the founder and owner of the business, could provide a valuable 'tactical' opportunity from time to time. ❜

Businesses of this kind often pass through difficult periods when the strong and dominant leader leaves. Sometimes members of his family will feel just as he does about the company and will have developed many of his business skills. Frequently this form of business has succession problems and during a change-over period it is very vulnerable. Those who follow the 'old man' may not have his stomach for a tough market fight, or be willing to forgo short-term profit and dividends. Similarly, partnerships, where two or three men have founded and developed a business together, can be very vulnerable when the original management is forced to break up.

Personality factors, succession problems, considerations of this kind tend to be of particular significance in the sole ownership type of business and should be watched with great care. Knowing just when, and how, to attack such a business is clearly of importance. A detailed knowledge of the business, and of its owner, may highlight a very worthwhile business opportunity.

Local company

In the majority of markets there will be a number of local companies who are active competitors. Here the term 'local company' is used to describe a business which is formed and operated fully in only one country. The business may have an export trade but this will usually be operated through selling agents. This should not be confused with the multi-national business where the parent company operates internationally and its local subsidiary operates in one country only.

Local companies of this kind can be either public or private. Frequently they are businesses which were first to move into a particular market, and the management has had the skill to hang on to a strong position despite the multi-national attacks.

This type of business is usually very limited in its research and development effort. In fact, it rarely engages in research and normally concentrates solely on development. In new brand introduction, or for existing brand re-launching, it tends to be an imitator, picking up ideas and giving them a different presentation.

Local companies must keep a balanced product portfolio. One or two very bad years in terms of trading profit can bring severe problems. Probably the most important strategy consideration for the local company is that it makes the right decision about where to compete within the market. Frequently, it is better equipped to compete in the specialist sectors where its limited research investment can be concentrated, and where its inability to finance extensive advertising and promotional programmes is not a major drawback.

The local company can often prove to be a dour and stubborn defender of its market position. Much of its defence will tend to be with 'below the line' activities—individually directed trade offers, case bonus offers, special consumer packs, and so forth. It is understandable that the local company should fight this way—one of its strengths should be its flexibility. It is also understandable that it should be a stubborn fighter for often it can be a matter of life or death for the business and for the people in it.

A particular form of local company is the producer co-operative, as frequently found, for instance, in the dairy industry. Often controlled by committees, this form of competitor may find it difficult to move rapidly in either new product development or in general operation. Their strength is usually concentrated in the more rural areas. Normally they are led and managed by producers, and so their reasoning and approach are often those of the producer rather than of a consumer orientated business. The co-operative type of business is often able to wield considerable political influence. This can show through in the form of state subsidies and the use of pricing regulations.

Conglomerate

A conglomerate is defined here as a holding company which controls a series of subsidiary companies of various sizes and types. The subsidiary companies may compete in a series of different industries. The holding company's control is primarily a financial one.

Conglomerates differ from company to company in the way they are managed. Usually the holding company exercises very strict financial control and selects the senior executives for its subsidiary companies. Beyond this, the units are allowed to follow their own way, although there is often a very clear requirement that a given level of profit and cash be produced. The conglomerate does not normally consider itself tied to a particular industry, and it is quite prepared to trade operating companies whenever it considers this advantageous.

It is difficult to comment on the conglomerates' major influence on strategy planning as so much will hinge on the individual organization and how it is managed. In general, the conglomerate is more likely to be interested in getting results over the short to medium term rather than the long term. The financial pressures on the subsidiary will often be shown clearly by the results of the holding company. If the holding company has liquidity problems then the subsidiary will be expected to contribute cash.

Multi-national

A multi-national is a large scale operator, normally in a major country, who has subsidiary companies operating in many countries throughout the world. The base company, in the home market, will frequently act as a 'feeder' to the subsidiaries.

The multi-national will tend to restrict its operation to a relatively small number of markets in a limited number of industries. In these fields it will become something of a specialist.

Recent years have seen considerable growth in the activities of multi-national companies. In particular, there has been a spread of USA based companies into Europe and other parts of the world.

The multi-national parent will normally be a public company and its stock will be quoted on one or more of the major stock markets. Its subsidiaries around the world will usually be private companies.

Probably the major business advantage accruing to the multi-national is that the wide spread of countries in which it operates can add up to a very large market. This market can support a strong research effort, and the research developments can be exported rapidly around the world. Similarly, improvements in production processing techniques, marketing, selling approaches, and so forth, can be developed in one country and then introduced worldwide.

Multi-nationals differ in their management styles. Some are highly centralized with a large head office staff, requiring that almost every decision of any substance should be referred back to this staff. Others are more relaxed and give their local executives considerable autonomy.

The multi-national can run a portfolio of its companies, attempting to develop market share in certain countries, and paying for this with cash withdrawals from others. This means that a local company can have periods without trading profit, and this will not necessarily cause the business problems.

The need for lengthy consultations with head office can often slow down the operations of the multi-national's subsidiary units. At times they can become unduly ponderous. The assumption that what has been received well by consumers in the home base country will automatically have the same reception throughout the world, can on occasions prove very wrong. It is an assumption which would appear to cause problems for many multi-nationals.

Within some of the multi-nationals the parent company will have formulated clear rules, or disciplines, with regard to the operation of the business. The local companies will often have to follow these rules irrespective of whether or not they make good business sense in the local situation.

It is valuable in strategy compilation to know the rules of a multi-national competitor, and also be aware of how much autonomy the local subsidiary management has. It can also be very worthwhile to know of the executive who is responsible within the parent company for the subsidiaries who are your competitors: his training, his personality, and his approach, may be important factors in the behaviour of the multi-national competitor.

Distributors

The distributors referred to here are the various retail and wholesale chains who sell a wide variety of own label brands, brands which carry the trade name of the particular retailer or wholesaler.

This group of competitors has a very special position in that they are invariably both customers and competitors.

The whole subject of distributor brands within strategy formulation has been considered in more detail in Chapter 13, but it is worth re-emphasizing a few salient points.

Over recent years, particularly in the United Kingdom and Continental Europe, but also in other parts of the world, 'own label' brands have recorded a remarkable growth in both volume and market share. In many of the big consumer markets in Europe distributor brands can have over a 25 per cent share of the market.

The distributors rarely move into the manufacture of their own label products; they use either the available specialist manufacturers, or the normal branded goods makers who are prepared to produce own label brands.

It should be clear that the distributors are indeed competitors. The thought that 'they have their sector of the market, and we have ours' is unsound, and into the long term can bring major competitive problems.

The owners of the distributor brands are the proprietors of the retail and wholesale businesses. They will vary widely in their approach. For some the own label is not of any great significance, merely a means to cover the lower price sector. For others the own label will be viewed as very important. The brand will be seen as part of the long-term future of the business.

Knowing just how a particular retailer or wholesaler views his own label activity can be of value in strategy formulation. The current size and standing of the trader, and his potential for the periods ahead, is a factor which will need to be examined. By summarizing the views of the major traders it should be possible to obtain a useful insight into the likely activity and presence of own label brands in the future.

It is always possible for the manufacturer to produce for the distributors. As we have already seen, this can be an opportunity for some, but for others it may well be an opportunity best ignored.

Management

The sections above have considered ownership. In certain instances the ownership and management of the business will be the same, certainly in the case of the dominant sole owner. However, many owners do not manage their businesses, they do not make the strategy, and they do not control the operations. They appoint a group of managers to carry out these tasks for them. In effect, they appoint a small group often known as the 'top management' who formulate strategy, and operate the business.

It can be argued that this produces a less complex position in that the managers will work in the interest of the owners, and they will therefore be concerned to improve the share value, and increase the dividends. To achieve this they will concentrate on maximizing the profits of the business, certainly over the longer term.

In the main, by far the majority of top managers do have the interests of the shareholders very much in mind as they manage the business. However, top managers are human beings, and business organizations are made up of active people who are subject to the ambitions, the prejudices, and other human reactions which are present in all groups. It is important to recognize this fact for it can play a major role in deciding the 'real' strategy a competitive business may follow.

The human considerations are just as relevant to the top managements of the conglomerates, and multi-nationals, often described as 'inhuman' and 'computer controlled', as they are to the smaller local operations. The frequent, and very costly, attempts to revive a brand which has been a major success at home in the base country but has failed elsewhere, is one example of the effect of such forces. The formula ingredient employed widely, primarily because it is one that the president originally developed, but which has never really delivered, is a further example, and there are many others.

The basic point is that these human considerations depend on the personalities of the people who manage the business. These people take the key decisions in the 'real' strategy their business follows. Normally, for most concerns, the personality traits are limited in their effect and are balanced within the internal management. However, even in the most correct businesses personality strengths will from time to time show through. These occasions can be periods of opportunity for competitors.

It follows that it can be worthwhile getting to know who really takes the important decisions in competitive organizations and then building up a record on each individual. Their history, their training, their successes (and failures), the promotions they are likely to be looking for, and when, and any other appropriate details. The record can always be supplemented by personal evaluations.

This part of strategy formulation does not lend itself to a simple expression in precise figures. Indeed, many of the details mentioned may be recorded only in the mind of the Chief Executive and not included in written reports. However, it is information which may, on specific occasions, prove to be of considerable value in the formulation of a successful strategy.

It can also be worthwhile finding out how competitive managements actually operate. Do they have to refer to an office in another country to get a decision on a relatively small capital investment? What is their budgeting period? Can they ever get a budget changed? The answers to these, and similar questions can provide useful information which may be of value in specific competitive circumstances.

Finance

'Businesses go under through lack of cash not lack of profit. A shortage of profit may be one of the reasons they are short of cash, but it's the actual cash shortage which brings the downfall.' This statement, or one close to it, will often be heard when a business is under some form of financial suspicion, or there are rumours that it is likely to fold. It is basically true.

There is an argument that the most important financial statement a company issues each year is not its orthodox balance sheet, or its profit and loss account, but its cash fund statement (sometimes named the source and application of funds statement). The argument may not be fully accepted, but it is a fact that the statement can be most revealing in terms of the company's cash position. It shows how operations have been financed, where the finance has come from, and can give an early indication of possible cash problems.

There are a number of basic financial questions which should be asked during the strategy formulation exercise:

- Has our business adequate access to funds to carry out our proposed strategy?
- Are we covered if we are outstandingly successful? Are we covered if we are very unsuccessful?
- Are any of our competitors likely to be troubled by a shortage of funds through the period? If so, can we turn their problem into an opportunity for us?
- In the financing of our business is there any way in which we can obtain our funds whereby we get a competitive advantage over our competitors?

Other, more detailed, questions will naturally be added to these.

The contention that 'a good successful management will always be able to raise funds' is probably correct. However, even for a very successful management, funds raised in a big hurry can prove very expensive. If cash has to be raised, then better it be done at a favourable time, and in a manner which has been chosen as the most acceptable.

The accepted business strategy should be backed by an estimated funds statement. It may be that additional funds should be invested in the business. Within the conglomerate, or multi-national, it may be necessary to 'sell' the growth plans to head office. For local companies it may be necessary to raise new outside funds. Often there will be a need for a degree of flexibility in the business strategy, and also in the funding plans which go with it.

The decision on how to arrange any necessary additional funding can be complex. So much will depend on such factors as the prevailing economic climate and the forecasts for the periods ahead, the position of the company, and any overriding views held by the owners.

This particular part of the financial function is one where skilful application can be very rewarding, and mistakes very expensive. To raise finance by increasing gearing can often appear particularly attractive—current owners do not forgo, or have to share, the high rewards that success can bring. However, higher gearing entered into at the wrong time, with high interest rates, can be expensive and even crippling in the event of a downturn in business.

Raising capital is a competitive issue, and so it is important that it should be raised as cheaply as possible. In calculating business costs, an issue of new shares may appear more attractive than increasing debt. The servicing of the debt will be classified as a cost to be taken as a charge before arriving at the profit figures, while dividends will be classed as an appropriation of profit. However, from the existing shareholders' viewpoint the issue of new stock could prove expensive. Not only will a new issue of stock mean a sharing of capital values, but also in many countries the servicing of debt is a charge before tax, while dividends are in effect an after-tax charge.

It can be further argued that a competent management should be prepared to carry a reasonable amount of debt, and should be concerned to obtain it at the lowest possible rate of interest. Higher gearing can bring a degree of risk; an important issue is how much risk of this nature it is wise for the business to carry.

It would seem to be unreasonable to consider a requirement for additional finance to cover both a major success and a big failure. However, the two possibilities should be covered in planning, for either can necessitate extra funds.

It is often both wise and very necessary to reinforce a major success, and in this way ensure that it is a firm success, before competitors have the opportunity to strike back. A major success, particularly within a rapid growth market, can mean a need for additional finance to fund such items as extra raw materials for product stocks, work-in-progress, finished stock, and debtors. With a failure, the planned revenues will not be forthcoming but much of the plant capital and up-front advertising and promotional expenditures will have been committed, and so a deficit is possible.

From an analysis of their various financial statements, and a close observation of their current trading, it should be possible to draw up a reasonable forecast of the financial position of any competitor. It may be more difficult with private companies, but even here a worthwhile rough estimate should be possible.

A competitive financial weakness is likely to bring opportunities in two ways—market share, and a possible acquisition. A business with an acute shortage of cash is unlikely to be able to defend its brands should they come under attack in the market. It follows that there could be an opportunity for an aggressor to obtain market share cheaply. A business acutely short of cash must be a potential take-over target, and one which could be obtained at an attractive price.

CHAPTER 19

Acquisition and Disposition

Often viewed as a last resort ('We failed to develop our own brand and so we had to go out and buy') acquisitions can in fact be a very positive factor in the formulation of a progressive business strategy.

For success, acquisitions need to be approached with caution, and negotiated and handled with great skill. There are a number of companies which have clearly mastered the art of buying other businesses and integrating them successfully into their own operations. They have prospered and have grown at a much faster rate than would otherwise have been possible.

However, it should be recognized that a very high proportion of acquisitions, probably a good majority, are unsuccessful. The main problems would seem to centre on inadequate examination and preparation, poor negotiation, and an unsatisfactory follow-through when once the acquisition has been made. Knowing just when, and how, to dispose of a company, a brand, or a group of brands, can also be key to a successful strategy.

Acquisitions

The basic reason for making an acquisition is that it will enable your company to achieve its strategic objectives more effectively than by alternative approaches. The alternative normally considered is that of internal development.

For present purposes, acquisitions are considered under two broad headings:

- Financial
- Operative.

A 'financial' acquisition is one made primarily for financial reasons. The buyer has no real knowledge of the technology of the business he is buying or of the markets in which it competes. He does not necessarily have ideas on how it should be developed but he has recognized that it represents a good financial buy. He may well sell his purchase within a very short time if a buyer willing to pay the right price should appear.

An 'operative' acquisition is one in which the buyer has made his purchase because he believes it will enable him to progress towards a particular strategic objective more effectively, and in which he intends to manage the purchase. He believes that he can bring to the purchased company certain strategic and operating skills which will enhance its development and, in turn, the purchase will contribute to the greater strength of his own business.

Of course, it is always possible for an 'operative' acquisition to represent a very good financial buy. It is accepted that in practice, in many instances, the difference between a financial and an operative acquisition can be very fine.

Financial acquisitions

For success in acquisitions of this type management needs a high level of financial acumen, the ability to appreciate a bargain, and a willingness to move decisively to realize the bargain. The major skill of the people who are likely to make a success of this form of acquisition tends to be of a financial nature. In particular they need to have a finely tuned ability to recognize where particular assets are undervalued. They also need a great skill in selecting, and then motivating, the managers who are to operate the businesses they purchase.

A number of major businesses have been formed and developed by this type of acquisition. It is a form of development which was particularly prevalent during the 1960s and the earlier part of the 70s. The successful operators in this field invariably maintain very strict financial control of their companies. They may allow their local management considerable freedom of action, or they may impose many restrictions; however, in all cases the financial control is invariably very tight. There is clearly a place for this type of business within the free enterprise society. For real success they require a particular form of management skill discussion of which is outside the scope of this book.

Operative acquisitions

Operative acquisitions may be made for a number of specific reasons. Discussion here is arranged under five possible reasons for purchasing a business:

1. It has one or more brands which have not been fully exploited.
2. It has a major brand, possibly a market leader, and is available at what is considered to be a reasonable price.
3. It is believed that the purchase will provide a valuable 'learning experience'.
4. An effort to limit competition.
5. A move which represents a form of vertical integration.

A brand has not been fully exploited

In many markets a relatively small operator can discover a new consumer purpose for a brand, or develop a special ingredient which brings a particular consumer benefit, or has some other form of significant competitive advantage, but is unable to exploit it through lack of capital or for some other reason. In some cases the business may not fully appreciate the value of the advantage it has developed.

For a well equipped company to buy such a business, and give the particular brand the backing of a major production and marketing effort, is often a very good investment. Much will depend on the price to be paid for the business, the potential of the brand or brands, and the skill of the purchaser in exploiting the potential.

A systematic search of the markets for 'buys' of this kind should be part of the strategy review process of every operator. There is an art in appreciating the potential of the undeveloped brand, and a skill in negotiating an acceptable purchase price for the business concerned.

The search will need to be international. In particular it should cover those countries which enjoy a high standard of living. Frequently, the brands developed to meet the higher standards travel across national frontiers as the economies develop. The initial aim in the international search could be to buy the rights to the brand for the home country market, and not necessarily to buy an overseas company.

The cost of purchase should always be compared with the investment and effort required to 'grow at home'. The outside purchase will bring both advantages and disadvantages.

A major argument for the ready-made brand is the saving in time. It can mean that the purchaser will have an established position in the market immediately, and the time factor can be important if the market is developing rapidly. A brand developed at home can take possibly three or four years to bring to the market-place if a normal development and testing procedure is followed, and even then success cannot be guaranteed.

A major argument against purchasing outside is that the purchaser will probably have to acquire a complete company, a large part of which he may not wish to have. Sometimes, of course, his new acquisition may give him a pleasant surprise, for he may discover some hidden gems.

However, more frequently he is likely to find a plant, buildings, and possibly staff, which he does not require. Indeed, part of the success of the acquisition may hinge on disposing of the various other assets of the purchase rapidly and at a satisfactory price.

With this type of acquisition it is important that the purchaser should have thought carefully about how he intends to integrate his purchase into his organization, prior to completing the deal. When he first examines his buy from the inside he may find there are exceptional reasons why he should not follow his plan—the reasons should be exceptional and not just based on 'local opposition'. If he intends to leave the new acquisition as an independent operation, then this should be made clear, and if it is to be integrated into an existing unit this should also be made clear. For the people and the brands of the acquired business, the most unsatisfactory position is to be left floating without any real direction.

A major brand is available

When the proposed purchase involves an established brand which is already a major force in the market, the considerations tend to be of a wider nature.

In a market where, say, four brands, A,B,C, and D, are locked in a battle for leadership and each has approximately 20 per cent of the market, then the whole competitive position can be changed dramatically if A should buy either B,C, or D. If it is an industry where there are very real economies in volume production, then A will immediately have double the volume of any other competitor. The lower unit production cost should apply to all of the 40 per cent market share that A will control. No doubt A would prefer the 40 per cent share with one brand; however, if he can get the production economies with two brands this may be a very good second best.

With this new total volume A should have a significant competitive unit cost advantage which he may use to move for a higher company market share and outright brand market leadership.

For an operation of this kind to be fully successful it is necessary that production unit costs are of consequence, and the buyer has the necessary vacant capacity to take up the extra volume. He must also take appropriate steps to remove the costs, both production and distribution, which he will have taken over with his purchase.

The very simple example used above quoted four brands. The effect can be even more dramatic when three brands lead a market and one is taken over by a competitor. In this case, the buying company would have a dominant market share and twice the volume of its only major competitor.

When a market is growing, and the forecast is that it will continue to grow in the long term, then buying an established major brand is a way for a manufacturer to ensure that he has the opportunity to grow with the market. By buying a ready-made brand he will avoid the time delay and the risk of failure involved in starting from scratch.

The key considerations are:

- Skill in forecasting the size and rate of growth of the market;
- The ability of the brand, backed by strong and skilled management, to grow at (or preferably above) the rate of the market growth;
- The level of contribution the brand can be expected to make to profit; and
- The purchase price required.

It will be necessary to consider the place proposed within the buyer's organization for the company to be purchased. If it is to be integrated, then the action to remove surplus costs will need to be carried out effectively.

> ❝ When an acquisition brings together two companies which have very different backgrounds, management styles, and methods of operation, great care is necessary to ensure that the 'values' acquired are not lost.
>
> In 1961 Lever Bros, through its parent Unilever, acquired the Domestos business. The two companies were very different in many ways. Lever Bros was a large business with a well developed marketing and sales approach. For many years the Lever business has been managed by professional managers as distinct from the owners. Domestos was a relatively small business, built and managed by the owner. Its marketing was more basic in approach and it used van-selling extensively.
>
> The acquisition and eventual merger was managed with considerable skill and great care and was a successful operation. However, the difference in the approach of the two companies affected the fortunes of the Domestos brands when they joined Lever.
>
> The Domestos company had three brands – Domestos, Stergene, and Sqezy. Domestos, the household bleach, was a strong brand in the premium sector of the market at the time of the acquisition. It responded particularly well to the additional research and development effort that Lever was able to provide, and it also benefited from the higher level of marketing investment that it received. In the 20 years following the acquisition the Domestos brand strengthened its position in a market that grew appreciably, it became a dominant market leader and one of the outstanding brands in the UK grocery markets.
>
> Stergene, a light duty fabric washing product, was a small brand within the Lever scene. It continued as a small brand which made a useful contribution with a limited resource backing. Stergene would have probably made better progress in a smaller business where it would have warranted a higher priority within the company operations.

Sqezy, the Domestos company washing-up liquid, was well positioned as No 2 brand in the UK market at the time of the acquisition. The brand had a reasonable level of performance (below the market leader Fairy Liquid) and sold at a lower price. It was particularly important to Lever at the time as the Lever brands in this market were faring badly.

Lever was clearly never happy in its management of the Sqezy brand and had difficulty in clarifying its positioning, performance and pricing requirement. Over the years, in a market which expanded threefold, Sqezy lost both share and volume. In retrospect, the brand would have probably fared better if its performance limitations had been both recognized and accepted, and the importance of it having a very competitive price more fully appreciated.

When a major manufacturer in a market has, for some particular reason, missed a significant development in the market growth, buying an established position may be his only way of having a part in the future of the market. If he has the production and marketing resources in position and ready for action, then it will clearly be advisable to buy brands with volume and potential, provided the purchase price is right.

A valuable learning experience may be provided

When a manufacturer believes the skills he has acquired in his traditional markets will enable him to operate successfully in a particular new market, and yet he accepts that he lacks the detailed experience of the new area, he may purchase a business which already trades there to obtain a 'learning experience'.

In these circumstances the purchase would normally be of one of the smaller companies operating in the market. A number of senior personnel from the new parent company would join the acquisition. They would have the job of both acquainting themselves with the detailed workings of the industry, and building the company into the right shape to mount a major attack on the market.

An effort to limit competition

It is quite permissible for one company in a market to attempt to buy one of its competitors to reduce the level of competition in the particular market. Where there is considerable surplus capacity in an industry it is not uncommon for a company to be purchased primarily to remove its capacity. As competition is at the very heart of the free enterprise system, it is understandable that a purchase of this kind may have to be reviewed and examined by a regulatory body.

Acquisition to provide vertical integration

The consumer goods manufacturer who uses a very large number of cartons may well be tempted to move into printing; the manufacturer who uses large quantities of plastic bottles may similarly be interested in moving into bottle manufacture. One way to get into this form of vertical integration is to acquire a printing business or a producer of bottles.

A move for vertical integration needs to be approached with great care. It is sometimes true that 'it is always cheaper to do things internally', but not always. Is the supplying industry a truly competitive one? If it is then there is unlikely to be any outstanding gain from vertical integration.

When a manufacturer makes an acquisition which moves him into a technology which he does not fully understand, and therefore he cannot manage with full confidence, he may meet a number of hidden problems and with them extensive hidden costs. Frequently, astute buying can get the same results as integration promises without the problems, and resources can then be invested in those fields where the manufacturer has superior skills.

There are, of course, many other reasons for making acquisitions. For instance, a business may have a strong cash flow position that is likely to continue over a number of years. Another company may have an extensive new brand development programme and an urgent need for cash. An acquisition by the cash rich business could make good sense. A business looking for rapid international expansion could find that a series of acquisitions in appropriate countries is the best way. There may be problems, and it will often be difficult to find suitable companies to buy, but an acquisition can provide immediate access to the market and there is likely to be less risk than with an operation that has to start from scratch.

It is important to recognize that the successful handling of a series of acquisitions, or even just one, which is out of the normal line of a company's business, requires a special management skill.

The number of companies who have been successful in their own field, who have then made an acquisition in an entirely new industry, and have failed badly, is indeed very high. Frequently as the acquisition goes astray, the time and attention of the top management are distracted, and soon the base business is also in trouble.

It is rather like a good and successful operating management in a consumer goods market deciding that it should engage in what has been described in this book as a financial acquisition. The skills required for success are very different, and moves of this kind are rarely fully successful. The advice 'never buy a business you cannot manage' has much to commend it.

Dispositions

Acquisitions are frequently mentioned within the strategy formulation discussion, while dispositions rarely receive attention, yet from time to time during its development practically every business could benefit from a disposition review.

Dispositions may be considered under two headings:

1. The sale of a company, a group of brands, or a brand, which no longer fits into the business strategy.
2. A sale to raise cash.

Sale of an asset which no longer fits the business strategy

A business may need to face the fact that a change in its strategy is necessary. The market which appeared very promising and well suited to the company five years ago is no longer considered either promising or suitable. A business which was purchased to provide an entry to a particular market is now a problem. When a major acquisition was made some years ago it had attached to it a small unit specializing in a product well removed from the company's normal business—the unit has continued ever since to trade at roughly the same very low level of profitability. Instances such as these are typical reasons for companies finding themselves with businesses and brands which do not fit. The danger is that these units will be allowed to continue in the business without any real adjustment. It is likely that they will be heavy consumers of top management time and effort, and also possibly heavy consumers of cash resources.

By far the major problem is the management time and effort such units consume. They tend to require very special attention, they require a different approach, and while the concern may produce many highly skilled managers for its own type of business, they are not necessarily skilled in the manner required by the specialized unit.

This problem can often be seen in large companies which hold a leading position in a major market with a limited number of fast moving big brands which have attached to them a small unit selling a large number of minor and slower moving brands. The operating approach required for success in the large unit is totally different from that necessary for success in the small, so there will invariably be difficulties as the successful managers from the large unit attempt to introduce their management approach to the small unit.

Similar problems, but on a different scale, can arise when a large company has within it a few major leading brands and also a number of very small brands. Invariably, the small brands will demand, and get, service and attention from the organization's 'general assets' (the management, the sales force etc) which are out of proportion to their current or potential level of contribution to profit.

If the key factors in management, of concentration and simplification, are accepted, and their important contribution to business success recognized, then the small units and the small brands mentioned in the previous paragraphs should be considered for disposition. In the case of a management skilled in the handling of specialized units, or small brands, they could be very successful. It is possible that the realizable value of the small unit, or brands, would be a very worthwhile amount and the funds so raised could be put to a more profitable use.

Exactly the same remarks can apply to the 'out of place' unit which has been acquired within a major acquisition. Rather than being allowed just to drift along, it should be considered for disposition.

A sale to raise cash

In the above remarks the major concern has been the effect of the unit, or brand, on the strategy of the business. The raising of cash may, of course, have been important, but it was not the first priority. There may be occasions when the raising of cash is the first priority. The sale of a unit and with it a group of brands, or the sale of an individual brand, is a way of raising cash.

It is necessary to decide on the best way, from the company's viewpoint, to raise the required amount of cash. There are usually a number of cash raising methods open to a business—bank borrowing, an issue of new shares, the issue of loan stock, and so on. The selling of company assets is clearly one more.

There is no one correct way to raise cash. So much will depend on the particular circumstances ruling within the company, and the business environment at the time the cash is needed.

If a brand, or a group of brands, is to be sold then the timing is crucial. The competitive position of the brands in their market, and their current level of profit contribution, are factors of consequence. For instance, it would be better for a manufacturer to sell before he becomes involved in a fierce market-place battle which he cannot expect to win, than to sell during or after the encounter.

PART 5

CHAPTER 20

Organizing for Strategy Formulation

How should the business organize for strategy formulation? Successful strategies have come from companies where there is no strategy staff at all, equally successful strategies have come from companies with highly organized strategy units. There is no one correct way to organize for a successful strategy formulation. So much will depend upon the approach of the Chief Executive and the management style of the business.

The size and form of the business will clearly be a major factor in deciding how it should organize. For the large international business it is quite common to have a corporate development unit, staffed by a team of specialists. Smaller organizations may have one individual manager who gives his full time to servicing the Chief Executive in strategy. For very small business units the position may be that a member of staff is seconded to strategy work from time to time as considered necessary. The size, structure, and the position of the strategy unit within the business, is not necessarily the most significant consideration.

It *is* important, however, to appreciate certain key factors with regard to the business strategy:

1. It is vitally important to everyone in the business that a successful strategy should be formulated.
2. The Chief Executive must ultimately take responsibility for the business strategy.
3. The Chief Executive will need to be serviced with a series of facts and estimates. The facts will need to be accurate, and at times they may be required in a hurry. On occasions the Chief Executive may need his information on a strictly confidential

basis—he may not wish to alert the whole organization to the particular line of enquiry he is making.

4. The Chief Executive is responsible for taking the key strategy decisions. It is important that he has a means of communicating these decisions to selected people within the organization at the time and in the manner he considers appropriate. Whether he decides to make explicit statements of strategy to his staff or not, the Chief Executive will need to ensure that his staff are 'with' his strategy, and that means backing it with commitment and enthusiasm.

The Chief Executive must communicate with his staff. He may do this through the formal organization, by direct address himself, or by 'walking about and talking'. The point is, he must do it.

A business strategy drawn up by a group attached to the Chief Executive, without consultation with executives in other sectors of the business, is unlikely to be successful. It is likely that the business in a subtle (or perhaps not so subtle) way will react against such a strategy. Highly polished plans may look good, but the all-important results come only when the plans are successful in operations and for this it is vital to secure the full support and commitment of management right through the business.

On the other hand, if strategy formulation is turned over in any considerable extent to line management, there is always the great danger that it may take second place to next week's operations. After all, line management know they are more likely to be judged on short-term actual results, than they are on their long-term reasoning which may, or may not, apply.

There would seem to be a good case for a Strategy Manager (sometimes called a Corporate Development Manager) with a unit or department as appropriate, with direct responsibility to the Chief Executive, but also having direct liaison with the various line sections.

Should the Strategy Unit report directly to the Chief Executive, or through another director, such as the Head of Finance? The case for a direct line to the Chief Executive is indeed very strong. If it is accepted that the provision of a successful strategy is one of the most important responsibilities the Chief Executive has, then there would seem to be every reason for a direct responsibility. If reporting should be through some other line director there is always the danger that, first, the importance of strategy formulation may be downgraded and, second, that a 'departmental' bias may come through in the formulation process.

The Strategy Manager should take direct responsibility for the coordination of all data, and for the preparation of all outside forecasts, such as the population, the economy, consumer spending, national productivity etc. The internal departments of the business should prepare all data on current positions within their particular fields, and also the forecasts for the years immediately ahead.

An approach of this kind ensures that all the line functions are involved in the process of strategy formulation, and yet they are not so deeply involved that all their attention is taken for a lengthy period away from the basic job of running the operations of the business.

One of the most important considerations is the computer system maintained within the business. A well designed and well applied computer application can ensure that data collected throughout the company, and also certain appropriate data from outside the company, can be available to management rapidly, as required.

A Chief Executive who is active in strategy formulation will want to examine carefully the key estimates his staff have compiled. He will listen to the various views of the market growth, new sector development, production unit cost movement etc, and he will form his own views. It may be necessary to check the estimates and prepare alternatives.

A major contribution of the Strategy Group will be the analysis of competitors, their cost structures, financial positions and details of their other developments such as personnel changes, new capacity, and sales force organizations. In the case of the multi-nationals a record of their developments in other countries, particularly in their home base, will be helpful.

The search for possible opportunities in new markets will require detailed studies from both home and overseas. Similarly, the search for suitable acquisitions both at home and overseas will require studied attention. Here the detailed work could be carried out by the Strategy Unit liaising with appropriate line executives and, as appropriate, outside advisers.

It is possible to buy much of this information from specialist consultants. However, an active Chief Executive is unlikely to find that a link with outside consultants will meet his needs completely. He will frequently just want to talk around a possible opportunity, using his staff as a sounding board. Often he will wish to take a 'rough look' at a particular situation, always considering possible opportunities, dropping many and concentrating on a limited number which appear most promising.

In many companies an annual budget procedure is firmly established, and this is linked to the production of a longer-term plan. Possibly once every two or three years, a five-year plan is produced.

There is no reason why production of a longer-term plan should not be turned into a strategic planning exercise. It is quite possible that a well formulated business strategy will be maintained basically intact for a period well beyond two years. However, it is important that it should be reviewed frequently as competitive circumstances change and new opportunities become available.

The search for new business opportunities should certainly not stop at the close of the bi-annual strategy review. It should be a continuous process. Accepting that 'there is always a better way' means that the search for new opportunities never stops.

An active Chief Executive is likely to find that an effective strategy unit, reporting directly to him, is invaluable in providing him with appropriate information so that he may concentrate on getting the key strategy decisions for his business *right*.

CHAPTER 21

Should Strategy be Made Explicit?

Should a company take active steps to involve its management widely in strategy formulation? Should the company follow this with a detailed statement of its business strategy to all its management? Or are there other, better ways, of handling strategy formulation and information within the business? Is it possible to maintain management commitment and enthusiasm without detailed strategy statements and consultations? Does the involvement necessarily provide for a better strategy?

These are live questions in many business organizations. They should be, for it is vitally important that the business should have a winning strategy, and that its management should be committed to it, and follow it through with skill and enthusiasm.

The case for making strategy explicit

There are two major reasons for making strategy explicit within the business, and involving a good spread of managers in the formulation process:

- If involving a good spread of managers in the formulation process means that a better strategy is produced.
- If by making the strategy explicit to them, the commitment and enthusiasm of the management throughout the business is ensured and strengthened.

Will a better strategy necessarily follow the involvement of a wider spread of management? Strategy is concerned with the use of all the resources of the business, and it must use them fully to get results. In particular these resources should be co-ordinated to provide for total company action.

The 'wider spread' of managers will, in the main, be concerned with particular sectors of the business. They are unlikely to be familiar with the wider scene with which strategy must be concerned.

On the trends and behaviour of costs, in given circumstances, and for their particular sections of the business, they may be well qualified to comment, and it could be very wise to consult them. However, their contribution would relate to a specific sector of the business and not to the total overall business policy. This particular group of managers is unlikely to have had the opportunity to study the relevant reports and data for the total business. It would probably be both costly, and time-consuming, if the detailed reports were to be supplied and explained to them.

There must be considerable doubt as to whether this wider involvement would necessarily produce a better strategy, and the opportunity costs involved in terms of management time could certainly be very high.

Normally, if people have been involved in the construction of a particular plan, they will have more commitment to it than if it is presented to them as a *fait accompli*. However, as regards the total business strategy it must be asked if such a process would be worth the cost and effort involved. It is worth repeating, though, that it is important that responsible managers should be consulted on specific aspects of the strategy for which they may have a special knowledge, and 'feel'.

Making an already formulated strategy explicit to managers is a different proposition. There will be a cost involved in actually preparing and making presentations—in particular the cost of management time may be high—but within the total context this cost should not be extensive.

The task of getting an agreed strategy committed to paper is invariably much more difficult than it sounds. However, it can be argued that the discipline of having to write the key considerations down into a strategy paper is a worthwhile task in itself.

The argument for this exercise often leads with the point that once such a strategy document exists 'everyone in the business knows where they are, and where they are going'. The priorities of the company become everyone's priority. The production manager with a material supply problem, who must decide which of a number of brands his plant should make, can take his decision knowing the priority of the company. When once managers understand the company strategy they will comprehend the need for urgency on specific projects, and with this understanding they will be better leaders and motivators.

Strategy and the longer-term plan

Before discussing the case against making strategy explicit it may be helpful to consider strategy and the longer-term plan.

Longer-term plan compilation became a widely adopted procedure throughout the business world during the 1960s. It is still practised extensively. Normally the plans cover up to five years, although this period tends to vary from business to business.

Isn't the formulation of a longer-term plan exactly the same as the formulation of a strategy? The answer is that it depends just how the longer-term plan is compiled. It is possible but most unlikely that it will take the form of a strategy formulation.

Longer-term plans frequently become a form of accounting document. In their compilation they tend to continue current trends, they concentrate on what the company proposes to do, and rarely consider possible competitive moves seriously. Invariably they show profits rising over years four and five. It takes a brave man to put forward a plan which shows that after five years of his management the business will be in decline.

Longer-term plans often contain calculations of return on capital where sunk capital is mixed with proposed new investment. From these statements 'average' rates of return are compiled, and these can be misleading in strategy considerations.

A particular problem can arise where the longer-term plan is integrated into a wider set of plans, and when agreed, is viewed as a management commitment. Such a position must almost guarantee a plan which provides just enough progress to keep everyone happy, but certainly no more. Longer-term plans of this kind tend to major on the production of an acceptable level of trading profit, and a satisfactory level of profit return on invested capital, over the five-year period.

Perhaps the worst feature of 'accounting' style longer-term plans is that they encourage rigid thinking. The feeling that 'we have expended great time and energy on this plan, and so now we are going to stick to it and make it work' may seem reasonable, but it can also be dangerous — dangerous in that it can mean an outstanding opportunity is not exploited to the full, and dangerous in that a competitive move may not be countered as vigorously as it should be.

It can be argued that the traditional form of longer-term planning is more valuable to a business in terms of the 'ancillary' reviews it normally requires, rather than the financial results on which it tends to concentrate. For instance, the reviews of factors such as company personnel, plant capacity, and operating efficiency, can play a valuable part in ensuring company progress.

The case against making strategy explicit

In September-October 1967 the *Harvard Business Review* published an article which has since been recognized as a classic of its kind. The article was by H Edward Wrapp and was entitled 'Good Managers Don't Make

Policy Decisions'. In the article Wrapp sets out five skills or talents which his researches had shown him to be common characteristics among successful managers. This is what he writes about the fourth skill:

> The fourth skill of the successful manager is knowing how to satisfy the organization that it has a sense of direction without ever actually getting himself committed publicly to a specific set of objectives.
>
> This is not to say that he does not have objectives — personal and corporate, long term and short term. They are significant guides to his thinking, and he modifies them continually as he better understands the resources he is working with, the competition, and the changing market demands. But as the organization clamours for statements of objectives, these are samples of what they get back from him:
>
> 'Our company aims to be number one in its industry.'
> 'Our objective is growth with profit.'
> 'We seek the maximum return on investment.'
> 'Management's goal is to meet its responsibilities to stockholders, employees, and the public.'

In my opinion, statements such as these provide almost no guidance to the various levels of management. Yet they are quite readily accepted as objectives by large numbers of intelligent people.

Wrapp goes on to ask the question, 'Why does the good manager stay away from precise statements of his objectives for the organization?' and he answers:

> The main reason is that he finds it impossible to set down specific objectives which will be relevant for any reasonable period into the future. Conditions in business change continually and rapidly, the corporate strategy must be revised to take the changes into account. The more explicit the statement of strategy the more difficult it becomes to persuade the organization to turn to different goals, when needs and conditions shift.

In these comments, Wrapp has in fact, made the main case for not making strategy explicit.

There will be many occasions when the Chief Executive can see, say, five major opportunities opening up for his business, but he will need time before he is able to decide which ones are really right for his company. Gradually the opportunities will be sorted out, some will fall by the wayside, others will open up, and eventually one, or possibly two, will come through as the ones for action.

Conveying information of this kind to a large number of people can be particularly difficult and could be perplexing. It could give the impression that the top management is confused, and in this way defeat the purpose of the exercise.

As is so often the case with issues of this kind, whether or not to make strategy explicit can be very much one of degree—it is not a black or white issue, but one where there can be a shade of grey. The successful executives Wrapp writes of would probably have followed a course whereby some of their staff would know of the executive thinking on various parts of the strategy. For instance, the operating board of the business would know of the major alternatives open to the company and of the decision timing plan which has to be followed. Equally, senior executives would know which market opportunities the business is following and how each one is progressing.

Can the management morale and enthusiasm be held at the right level under this approach? Much will depend on the skill and the leadership of the Chief Executive. His ability to give his staff the feeling, backed by results, that the business is making progress, will be all-important. He will be greatly assisted by a successful previous record, as well as success in the current operation.

A Chief Executive who has the ability to make this form of leadership work will gain many additional benefits. He will avoid the policy straight-jacket problems which invariably follow the publication of a detailed strategy document. Similarly he will avoid the need to write a detailed company manual, or detailed statements of corporate objectives, or highly detailed organization charts with job descriptions. Demands for statements of this kind normally accompany a request for an explicit statement of strategy. Wrapp's successful executives avoid all of them. They are probably aware that they are heavy time consumers in terms of compilation, and even heavier when it is necessary to sort out the differences of interpretation which usually follow their publication. The time can be much better spent on productive pursuits.

Wrapp has made the case for not spelling out business strategy in great detail. His successful managers were able to achieve fully acceptable results without publishing the detail of their strategy reasoning and planning. For anyone experienced in the practical management of a business, especially one competing in very active markets, it is not difficult to appreciate the many benefits of an approach which, while it appears to be rather loose and 'easy going', in fact, requires a considerable skill and leadership ability in application.

Many successful companies take a different view. They do attempt to keep all their senior management, and many of their middle management, very well informed of their strategy, and they do try to set out this strategy in a series of written statements.

It is important to appreciate that this chapter has been concerned with the publication of the business strategy. This should not be confused with the publication of a statement of general objectives. Many companies discuss and publish their general objectives within the business but a statement of general objectives is not a business strategy.

CHAPTER 22

Financial Measurements and Guidelines

The shrewd operator uses 'the figures that are right for the occasion'. In many places this would be greeted with a wry smile, as the remarks of a man who is just a little too clever.

In strategy formulation figures have a significant part to play. They are a vital part of the whole process of quantification, and the various measures can have a material influence on the final decisions.

It is clearly important that the 'right' figures should be used at the 'right' time. For instance, to have any real meaning in business 'costs' need further definition. There are opportunity costs, replacement costs, historic costs, and so on. One of the major skills of a good commercial man is knowing which costs to use at any given time. Similarly, it is important to use the 'right' measure for the particular requirement. Profit return on total invested capital may be right for a certain occasion, and profit return per share at another time.

As far as strategy formulation is concerned, the shrewd operator is undoubtedly correct—he needs the 'right' figures for the particular occasions. Of course, the term 'right' is used to describe figures drawn up under the correct concept for the particular circumstance, and not figures manipulated to provide a desired result.

The production of 'orthodox' periodic financial accounts has become a well organized operation in many companies. Linked to budgeting, the production of the four-weekly, or monthly, accounts is established as an important part of the management control system.

From a management viewpoint, part of the strength of such a system is that it is directly linked to the periodic report which has to be made to the shareholders, or to the senior managers at head office who will be representing the shareholders.

A well managed system of budgeting control and periodic reporting, provided it does not become unduly complex and is produced in good time, can be a very helpful tool to management. Frequently, the installation of a tightly controlled financial approach into a loosely managed business has been enough, in itself, to turn a loss position into profit. The discipline that such an installation brings with it can be a key factor in changing the management thinking and approach.

However, there appears to be a tendency in many companies to attempt to make the figures produced by the periodic accounting system serve many purposes, and this includes playing a prominent role in strategy formulation. It sometimes appears to be a case of 'We have a system that requires considerable investment to maintain, and so we intend to use it to the full.'

This can be a dangerous approach. Many of the figures, and values, coming from the 'control accounts' are not suited for strategy formulation. Beyond this, the reasoning which the control approach fosters is not necessarily suited to the longer-term considerations often required in the strategy exercise.

In this chapter just three of the more common concepts, often encountered where periodic reporting is strongly enforced, are questioned: percentages, costs, and return on investment.

Percentages

Percentage levels seem to have a mythical attraction for some managements. 'Get your percentage right, and it will come good', is a typical approach.

A percentage level control is often used to cover such widely different items as advertising, waste control, brand margins, and sales promotions.

In part, the attraction for the use of the percentage comes from the executive's need for a familiar guideline, one with which he is experienced, and which he associates with success.

Managers are always looking for 'trusted guidelines', measures against which they feel they can make worthwhile comparisons, measures which give them a 'feel' of control. They are happier when these guidelines are familiar to them. When the guidelines represent a *new* concept there is often a period of suspicion, of reluctance to accept, and possibly a period when there is a lack of confidence. If the guideline is associated with a lengthy experience, however, and this experience has been a successful one, then it is indeed in a powerful position.

This approach is very understandable. Particularly the points about 'experience and success'. There can be little doubt that skilled and successful managers do develop a 'feel' for many of the important factors concerning their brands and their markets. The percentage guideline often appears to fit well with this position. 'We were very successful when we used this percentage level with Brand X, so why don't we use it again with Brand Z?' Managers challenged on this stance will often ask 'Can you give us a guideline which is better suited, or more reliable?' Nevertheless, the very widespread use of the percentage guideline must be questionable, for there are some instances where its use could be damaging.

There is a view that for success in certain markets your brand should have a gross margin of a given percentage. The gross margin would in this instance be the difference between the unit ex-works cost of production and the unit selling price. The margin would be expressed as a percentage of the selling price. Experience may argue that you need a margin of say 30 per cent to go on to make a satisfactory level of brand profit.

Does the level of 30 per cent remain constant at any time during the brand and market development? Is it constant through the growth stage of the market, during maturity, and also during decline? And does it remain at the same level during the launch of a new competitive brand, or during one of its own major re-launches? If there is a strong increase in the price of a major ingredient should the unit price of the brand be raised to ensure that the 30 per cent margin is maintained? What if competitors do not use a 30 per cent rule, and so move differently? Business common sense would argue that the brand unit gross margin level should be allowed to change in each of these circumstances. Management must ask if this gross margin percentage guideline really is a valuable tool.

There is a strong argument for considering brand margins in terms of money, and also in terms of a total amount of money rather than on a unit basis. Normally, the important consideration will be the volume $\times$ unit margin, rather than merely the unit level. The aim should be to ensure that the brand is contributing as high a level of monetary contribution as is possible, while at the same time meeting its other objectives in terms of such factors as market share, growth, penetration, and brand franchise strength.

Similar questions apply to a percentage guideline which is set for brand advertising appropriations or for brand promotional investments. They should move in relation to the opportunities available to the brand, and should vary depending upon such factors as the market growth and competitive developments.

When an overall percentage level is used to control waste levels for product formula ingredients, or packaging materials, a misplacement of effort and resource can result. A 3 per cent waste level may be acceptable for an inexpensive material but it certainly will not be for a very expensive ingredient, particularly if large quantities are involved. Again, it is better that the control be centred on the amounts of money concerned, rather than a somewhat arbitrary percentage level.

These notes have not put forward an alternative guideline to the percentage except to suggest that the *sums of money* concerned should be critical, and that for many purposes the total sum of money (ie volume × unit) is the one that really matters.

The desire to find a simple guideline which will apply in all circumstances is fully appreciated. However, it must be questioned whether such a guideline does in fact exist. When money values are used they at least tend to concentrate attention on the major issues.

Costs

The idea that the costs as reported in the periodic accounts are suitable for use on all occasions is clearly erroneous. There is a whole series of cost concepts and the most suitable concept should be selected for each particular occasion. Economists have dwelt at length on this topic, and it is not proposed to attempt a review of all the various costs concepts here.

Probably the most important concept is that of opportunity cost. It is never recorded as such in the financial accounts or costing records, but the concept and the reasoning its use enforces, is crucial. If it is accepted that opportunity cost takes the form of the price a particular item, or combination of items, would command in the best alternative use which has been sacrificed, it follows that the opportunity cost concept should be applied continuously in all business organization.

Management should ensure that there is always competition between its various brand and project proposals for the use of the limited resources of the business. The opportunity cost of accepting a particular plan for operation is the profit contribution which could be obtained if the resources concerned were put to the best alternative use. A management which is conscious of the opportunity costs concept automatically considers alternative approaches and the return they are expected to bring. Rather than restricting its thoughts to what the business is doing, it also considers what it is *not* doing.

In practice, replacement costs are normally much nearer in value to opportunity costs than are either current or historic costs. There is a strong case for using replacement costs in all brand and other cost statements, and this applies particularly during periods of high level inflation. Many manufacturers continue to use historic costs in their calculations at all times, and this is probably one of the reasons why prices have frequently failed to keep pace with the rate of inflation.

Allocated costs

Always take great care when considering 'total costs'. This applies particularly where an allocation of general costs has taken place in building up
the total cost figure. A simple example of this may be seen when selling
expenses are considered. Account A is a major retailer with many branch
stores. All business is negotiated by the head office buyer. Manufacturer
X has a large sales force which calls on a whole series of retailers. Part of
the cost of maintaining this force is allocated to the 'cost of servicing
Account A'. Manufacturer Y deals only with the head offices of major
chains, and does not have a large sales force. There is no allocation for a
cost of servicing Account A.

Under the allocation approach Manufacturer X will record a much
higher cost for the servicing of Account A than Manufacturer Y. If
Manufacturer X allows this allocation approach to influence his pricing
he could put himself at a serious disadvantage.

The basic rule for such costs is to charge against the particular operation only those costs which are directly attributable to it. The general
costs should be kept to a minimum level commensurate with the provision of an effective performance. If a cost allocation is necessary, then it
should be charged only to those projects or units where the service is
actually provided, and an attempt should be made to ensure that the
charge for the service is a realistic one.

Return on investment

If asked to produce one figure, from the records of an operating company,
which is considered to be the best guide as to how well the company is
managed, many observers would reply, 'profit return related to the capital employed in the business'. Others may carry this further and say the
measure should be 'profit return related to shareholders' capital'. The
shareholders own the business and so the real judgement should centre
on the return made on their capital.

The major difference between these two measures is that the second
approach accepts that some of the capital invested in the business may be
represented by debt. If the managers have been skilful in both their financing and their management, they will have paid less for the use of the debt
than the profit they have been able to produce from the capital it has
provided.

It is also worth mentioning that for a branded goods company probably
its most important assets are its brands. Much of its skill, energy, and
resources are given over to building and strengthening its brands—the
brands do not normally appear anywhere on the balance sheet. It should

also be noted that the assets rarely include people, and yet skilled people are vital if the other resources are to be used effectively.

There is also the problem of measuring the profit made during a particular period. If the aim is to provide a record of management performance then it may be appropriate to rule out any 'windfall' profits, ie profits that have arrived by pure chance rather than by management action.

Despite the problems and limitations, 'return on capital employed' remains probably the best general guide to how effectively management is using the funds available to it.

It should be clear that this is using the 'return on capital employed' measure as a guide to the owners of the business to how their appointed managers are using the shareholders' funds. When the use of capital is considered within strategy formulation very different values may need to apply. For strategy formulation purposes there is a very big difference between capital already invested and capital to be invested.

Capital already invested

Here the strategic approach should be led by the question 'Are we using this resource in the most profitable manner open to us?' Detailed calculations of the percentage return on capital, irrespective of how the assets concerned are valued, are of very little use. The important consideration is how to use the resource to obtain a higher level of profit.

The only valuation of already invested capital which is of consequence in these circumstances is the resale value. Can the items concerned be sold and the cash proceeds used to obtain a higher level of profit contribution?

This is a very simplified approach, but it sums up in a straightforward manner the strategy position with 'already invested' capital. Of course, in practice it is rarely as simple as this. For instance, in considering the use of the resource, both the short and long term need to be viewed. The plant may be idle for the present but if, in two years' time, it is expected to make a major contribution to a new project, this will need to be allowed for.

Capital to be invested

In this context calculations of the return on capital the project is expected to produce are very important. Before the investment all dealings are with cash values. There will always be alternative avenues for the investment of the limited resources and management should decide which ones it wishes to follow. There will be a number of guiding factors—the rates of return the various projects are expected to produce will be one of the main considerations.

It is understandable that managers may wish to bring together into one plan the proposals for both 'invested capital' and for 'capital to be invested'. If, in the future, the managers are to be judged on the 'return on investment' figures produced from the orthodox accounting statements, it would seem reasonable that they should wish to consider the figures which are expected to appear.

However, if strategy decisions are to be taken on proposals where the figures are combined, and these figures are influenced by 'return on investment' calculations, then the decisions could be unsoundly based. For instance, a business may have been showing a particularly good rate of return on its invested capital, and proposes a series of projects for which the investment is heavy and the return, by current standards a very good one, is below the level shown on the already invested capital. The combined figures for the future will show a downward trend. To reject or delay the new proposals because the rate of return is falling could be a wrong decision. A problem of this kind can often arise where the already invested capital is included on an historic cost basis.

So the shrewd operator is quite correct in demanding the right figures for the occasion. New investment proposals should be judged on their merit. If, after full consideration, a proposal is judged unable to provide an adequate level of return then it should be rejected. In deciding what is an adequate level of return the alternative avenues open for investment should be assessed. Management should consider the opportunity cost of the proposal.

CHAPTER 23

Strategy Formulation

A winning strategy is vitally important for the well being of the business and of all the people associated with it. In view of this it has already been argued that the key strategy decisions should be taken by the Chief Executive. Just how he decides to carry out his strategy formulation will be very much a personal matter. Much will depend on his management style and approach.

Highly formalized procedures have been known to get good results—they have also been known to go astray, and to be overcome by bureaucracy. It is equally possible to cite many winning strategies which have come from a simple 'muddling through' approach.

There is no one correct way to formulate a winning strategy. Ultimately it is a matter of the people concerned, their skill, their judgement, their attitude, and the way they like to work. It isn't the quantity of the ideas and the figures produced, it's the quality that really matters.

The size, the extent, and the complexity of the particular organization are likely to be the considerations which decide the approach to strategy formulation followed within it. The 'back of an envelope' approach could well be quite satisfactory for the small general business, or indeed for the small single product branded goods manufacturer. For the multi-brand business, operating in a number of markets, something more formal would be essential. For a multi-national organization with many brands, in a number of markets, in various parts of the world, a detailed co-ordination of strategic plans and investment proposals, together with the consideration of exchange rates, taxation complications etc will be necessary.

This chapter suggests a simple seven-step approach to strategy formulation. This approach may be considered unduly formal for some smaller businesses, and unduly simple for the bigger operators, but we are more concerned with the reasoning behind the approach, rather than actual procedure.

Within the seven-step approach two factors are of fundamental importance. Firstly, it is essential that the approach should be kept simple and straightforward. Strategy decisions which are taken as the result of the formulation exercises must later prove to be 'right' in terms of producing a successful business. Undue complexity, and a mass of data which cannot be fully appreciated, is unlikely to help the task of decision making.

Secondly, the approach attempts to get all of the more senior managers in the business associated with the strategy formulation exercise. However, this should not be taken to mean that all senior managers are necessarily to be involved in actually taking key strategic decisions.

If a strategy is to be successful it will need the enthusiastic backing of all managers, and ultimately all members of the staff. One way of helping to ensure this backing is to give the senior individuals concerned the opportunity to contribute to the formulation process. If the senior managers feel that the strategy is in part theirs, then they are likely to be better leaders and motivators of their own staff.

The length of time a particular strategic plan should cover varies from business to business depending upon the form and nature of the products, and on the development periods involved. In some cases it may be necessary to cover a period of at least ten years. In other cases a time period as short as one year may be appropriate. For present purposes a period of approximately five years is typical.

The seven stages in the strategy formulation process are:

1. General forecasts
2. Specific forecasts
3. Common assets review
4. Opportunities review
5. Selecting opportunities for action and forming the strategic plan
6. Deviation from plan
7. Plan for action.

Stage 1: General forecasts

Here we are concerned with what might be termed the basic and more general forecasts which will form a background through the period to be covered by the strategic plan. In the main, the items covered will be outside the direct influence of the business. In a small way the business may contribute to these various basic items but in practice it will have to accept them and work accordingly.

Economic forecasts should contain projections on such items as:

Population trends
Gross national product growth
Consumer expenditure
Unemployment levels
Wage and salary developments
Number of houses to be constructed.

Other factors to be covered within the general forecasts include:

- *Media trends and costs.* The cost of advertising space and the movements in prices between the various types of media.
- *Household durables and electrical appliances.* Estimates by quantity, by value, and by types.
- *Research and development.* New discoveries and other technological developments likely to become effective during the period. Those fields which are closely associated with, or likely to affect, the markets within which the company competes now or may possibly compete into the future are the primary concerns.
- *Legal considerations.* Any likely changes in the law which are expected to have an impact on the business, for example, changes in the law relating to the packaging of products, or to product formulations.
- *Environmental isssues,* for example, government moves to change certain manufacturing processes or to require particular safety precautions.
- *Taxation and special grant changes,* for example, the introduction of a new tax, such as VAT, or the provision of a special development grant for certain activities.

If necessary, many of these forecasts can be supplied by specialist consultants. It is important to be sure that they are basically sound and provide at least a reasonable degree of accuracy. Some experience of their form and the building of a track record, will be necessary before the forecasters can expect to command full confidence.

All of the various forecasts enumerated above can be developed to an appropriate level of detail.

Stage 2: Specific forecasts

With the general forecasts submitted, considered, and agreement reached on the expected levels and developments of the key items over the period, the business is ready to move to the second stage of the strategy formulation process.

Here the concern is with specific forecasts, ie forecasts which are specific to the industry and the markets in which the business competes.

They should start with a factual statement of the current position, and should show how this has been developed over the previous five years. In some cases it may be worthwhile to go back over a longer period. This set of forecasts should also contain statements outlining the present position of competitors, and their development over previous periods. The specific forecasts in effect fall within the general forecasts, and will be greatly influenced by them. Among the more important specific forecasts which should be covered are:

Market development

A forecast of the developments expected over the period for each of the markets in which the company competes.

It is most important that within the total market all the various market sectors should be covered, and the trend of their development outlined. Within each market, and market sector, the movement of the individual brands should be plotted.

Frequently it may be wise for these particular forecasts to cover more than five years. It can be helpful if an estimate is provided showing the expected size of the market and within it the various market sectors when it reaches its expected full potential.

Accompanying each of the market development forecasts should be the latest consumer research findings on the market. This research should cover the existing brands in the market, their purpose, their performance levels, their price positions, and their strengths and weaknesses. There should also be a research statement setting out the consumers' feelings about existing brands in the market (their personalities), their criticisms of them, and their future requirements. A separate statement should cover the brand formulations, production costings, sales volumes, selling prices and gross margins.

The aim is to build up a factual view of the current market, and the brand positions within it, and a consumer research based view as to where the market is likely to move into the future.

In addition to considering the development of the home market, it is advisable to have available a general review of what is happening in the other similar leading markets of the world. Such reviews can be purchased from specialized agencies or obtained via associated companies.

Research and development

A statement covering all the various research and development projects within the business, their progress, and when they can be expected to be ready for practical use.

In some cases the researchers will not be completely sure that they can deliver against a particular requirement, in other cases they may be confident of delivery but in doubt as to the time of completion. The aim should be to provide a realistic assessment of the progress and potential of every project.

Production

A statement of the company's detailed production capacity, the extensions to this position which have already been committed, and the dates when the new capacity will be available for production. A statement should also be prepared showing the capacity position within the industry.

Financial position, ownership and management

A statement covering the current financial position of the business with all the outstanding commitments listed. Also required is a statement covering the financial position of competitors together with any known outstanding commitments they may have. Where the competitor is part of a multi-national or conglomerate, a statement of the financial position of the parent company should be added. Notes on the owners, and top managers of competitors should be included. When there has been a change in management, or a change is expected, this should receive special attention. Details of the new men, their training, and previous experience should be noted, together with any known preferences they may have for particular approaches to business.

A review of customers

In the businesses with which this book is primarily concerned, this will mean a review of appropriate retailers and wholesalers. An analysis of the current position—just who is doing the retail and wholesale business, with an analysis by type of store, and by owner. Recent trends should be accounted for, and forecasts provided of the developments likely over the period ahead. This analysis will need to be developed on both a regional and a national basis.

The specific forecast may be extended as appropriate to cover other subjects which are considered significant to the particular business concerned.

Stage 3: Review of the common assets

Here the term 'common asset' is used to describe those assets which service all the various brands and projects, and are not specific to any one.

Beyond this, the term 'asset' is used in a wider sense than is normal in that it is intended to include items such as the sales force, marketing department, commercial department, and indeed the business senior management. An important section that should be included in the review is the research and development department.

The main requirement at this time is to have details of the service provided, the number of people involved, and the other costs incurred. The probable development of each sector over the period of the plan should be outlined, together with an estimate of the cost.

At this stage the business will have the three basic sets of papers on which it must work to formulate its business strategy.

Two additional sets of papers should also be provided by the strategy unit at this time:

Proposals to move into new markets
Proposals for acquisitions and dispositions.

The notes should set out in detail the case for moving into the new markets, and include proposals for the manner of entry. The proposals for acquisitions should make clear the areas in which searches are concentrated, and also state the various take-over targets that the company is studying in detail. The case for disposing of any brands, or companies, if appropriate, should be stated and the proposed method of disposal outlined.

Much of the work on the general forecasts will have been carried out by the strategy unit or by specialist consultants. The specific forecasts and the statements on the common assets can be provided, in the main, by the personnel concerned within the business aided by the strategy unit.

The company is now ready to move forward to the opportunities review. All sections of the business are involved, and this stage is at the very heart of the strategy formulation process.

Stage 4: Opportunities review

It has already been stated that successful business is concerned in the making and taking of business opportunities. At the centre of the plans to exploit a business opportunity will be the development and use in operation of a worthwhile competitive advantage.

It follows that the opportunities review is concerned firstly with defining and evaluating the various business opportunities which are thought to be available to the company, and secondly, with the development of the competitive advantage which will provide for the exploitation of the opportunity. The need for everyone in the business to be fully aware of the requirement to develop and exploit competitive advantages has already been stressed. The major drive should be for the development of the big, truly worthwhile, competitive advantage which can be used to make a successful new brand, or take an existing brand to dominant market leadership. Of course, the smaller competitive advantages certainly have their place, and when totalled they can go to make up a truly effective and efficient operation that is, in itself, a very worthwhile competitive advantage.

It is at this stage that the Chief Executive can get all of his managers involved in the strategy formulation process. Since 'there is always a better way' *every* section of the business has a part to play. Each should consider its position, consider the forecasts, and set about answering the question 'How can we do better?' — 'better' in whatever measures are accepted as reasonable guides to the level of efficiency applying in their particular functions. For the production units this may be cost per case, or output per hour. For the distribution section the measure may be cost per delivery drop, or cost per thousand cases delivered — other sections will have their own measures. It may be advisable to form special task forces, or on occasions to use specialist consultants, to help in the departmental reviews. All sections of the business are involved in the search for opportunities but the main drive for the major competitive advantages which can be directly related to the brands will tend to centre in the marketing, and the research and development departments.

Discussion of the opportunities review falls here into six categories:

1.   existing brands
2.   new brands
3.   acquisitions
4.   new markets
5.   capacity: plant and equipment
6.   the common assets.

Existing brands

Here the need is to take a hard look at the forecasts, both general and specific, and to ask questions such as: What are the opportunities for our existing brands? Where we already have a competitive advantage, are we exploiting it to the full? If we do not have a brand competitive advantage, where is it possible for us to develop one, and then go on to exploit it?

There is also a requirement to consider probable competitive developments, and to prepare to defend and counter-attack, wherever it is appropriate for existing brands. Estimates should be prepared which provide an indication of the costs of the defensive action. The possibility of moving ahead of the competitor and thereby turning defence into a form of attack may be worth examining in detail.

The research and development units will be feeding the brand discussions with data on possible new formulations and new packaging alternatives. However, the examination should concentrate first on the consumer. Among the questions which need answers are: What does the consumer really feel about the brands in the market? What, in her view, are their strengths and weaknesses? What further developments in the brands would the consumer appreciate most? When a brand is already the market leader, the questions should be: How do we make this brand a dominant leader? What will provide the brand with a major move forward?

If the market is a growth market, and the brand is already the leader, then the questions could be: Are we using our volume strength to the full? Are we getting all the cost advantages which should be ours? If not, why not? Should we take a more aggressive price position? As the market grows unit costs should be moving down, and prices should fall—should we take a strong lead by bringing our price down ahead of competition?

If the company brand is second or third in the market, then the questions could be: How can we build in a worthwhile performance extra, and then go back to the consumer for re-trial? Would we be better advised to develop a more specific appeal that has shown promise in testing with the consumer—could we ultimately turn the specific appeal into a more general position, and in this way move up on the leader?

The brand's reaction to advertising and promotional support should be considered: Is there an opportunity to increase penetration with the right level of support? Can we increase consumer consumption by presenting an additional use for the brand?

At this stage a rigorous and positive review should highlight the opportunities open to each brand. This should be followed by a consideration of the brand competitive advantages which will be needed to open up the opportunities. It will also be necessary to appraise the ability of the business to develop the necessary competitive advantages, and how long this is likely to take. In addition it will be necessary to have a reasonable indication of the costs and revenues expected to result from the exploitation of each opportunity.

New brands

Reference should again be made to the market forecasts and the detailed consumer researches. The leading question should be, 'Is there a marketing opportunity in this market which we believe we can fill successfully and which warrants a new brand?' It may be a new brand with a purpose that differs significantly from existing brands, or it may be a consumer performance requirement which is markedly in advance of existing brands and which will require a much more costly formulation, and probably a higher unit selling price.

The organization's ability to meet this marketing opportunity should be examined in detail. Can the business develop the required competitive advantage? What is the time period involved? What are likely to be the costs and revenues? These are among the crucial questions although, of necessity, in many instances, the answers may be only very rough estimates.

With both the development of existing brands and the introduction of new brands, it is most important not to underestimate the strength and extent of the probable competitive counter-attack. One of the most frequent errors in strategy planning is an underestimate of a competitor's desire to retain his leadership position, and the price he is prepared to pay to hold on to it. To make a bold and extensive attacking move, with either an existing or a new brand, and then to have to fall back through a lack of the necessary resources to sustain the attack, can be devastating.

Acquisitions

Can any of the marketing opportunities be better exploited by the purchase of an existing brand, or by purchasing the company that owns the brand or a series of brands? Details of the possible candidates for acquisition should be noted, and the prospects of being able to purchase any one of the companies listed at a reasonable price examined in detail.

New markets

Proposals to enter entirely new markets should be treated separately. New market brand proposals will, of course, have to compete with existing market brand proposals for the limited available resources. It is probable, however, that the new market proposals will have been compiled by a separate staff, and they may possibly involve special production facilities, with a new selling and distribution organization. If a 'learning approach' is proposed then an acquisition may be necessary.

Capacity: plant and equipment

With the various brand forecasts for the future available it is important that the business considers its production capacity. This review should include:

1. A consideration of the existing plant buildings and equipment. Are they outdated? What sort of savings are available if they are replaced with new up-to-date facilities? The important

consideration is that frequently it can be advantageous to replace plant and machinery well before it is completely worn out.

2. A statement covering the new plant and equipment which will be necessary if the various brand and project plans are accepted for action. Any new plant and equipment specifically required for a new venture would be part of the cost of the venture, and should be considered within its total business proposition. It is frequently necessary, however, to provide new facilities which are not allocated to any one project but which are essential to provide services to a plant site and in turn to a series of projects.

The common assets

The common assets should also receive a thorough review for they, too, can present opportunities. The reviews should cover the whole general operation and administration of the business, and include all the service sections such as marketing, and the sales force. The service sections should keep pace with the changing developments of the business in a sound and economic manner. In particular, the business must keep a sensible control on its service costs and not allow itself to become over-administered.

Often, when a business gets into trouble it suddenly finds it does not really require its expensive head office building. The need for the expensive head office should be questioned whether or not the business is in trouble. All the various service and administrative costs should be part of a regular review process. The questions asked should include: Do we really need to continue with this approach? and Is there a better way?

Once a process of strategy formulation is established within a business much of the basic work described above will take the form of reviewing and adjusting previous forecasts. Keeping a close watch on the key trends within the various markets and linking these with the forecasts is an important part of the exercise.

The success of the opportunities review will hinge, almost completely, on the ability, and attitude of the personnel concerned. A high degree of skill is always important but, in many respects, the attitude adopted by the people involved is equally crucial. A positive, sensible, aggressive attitude is often essential for the best results. It cannot be overemphasized that 'there is always a better way' — the record shows that this statement is most certainly correct. If really worthwhile results are to be obtained, the atmosphere and approach applied within the business and the lead given by the Chief Executive will be crucial.

Stage 5: Selecting opportunities for action and forming the strategic plan

At this stage the Chief Executive and his strategy team will have available to them 'opportunity' proposals for existing brands, new brands, acquisitions, new markets, capacity—plant and equipment and the common assets.

Now it is necessary for the Chief Executive to review these proposals and decide which should go forward to form his business strategy.

Firstly, there will be a need to bring judgement to the proposals. For instance, some proposals may be considered unduly ambitious in the sales volumes they propose, and others somewhat pessimistic. The Chief Executive has the responsibility to adjust the proposals as he considers appropriate. Enthusiasm is vital for a successful operation but it should never be allowed to overcome the need for a realistic assessment of the various opportunities and business propositions.

Secondly, he should bring to the formulation process the other basic strategy considerations which have been covered in the earlier chapters. Often there will be views held, or judgements made, by the Chief Executive or his senior advisers, which they find difficult to commit to a detailed written statement. For instance, a particular market situation may be developing and the reaction to this situation by the owner of a major competitive business may fit a particular pattern. This should be taken into account in strategy formulation even though the competitive reaction may not appear to be very logical.

Financial factors can also have an important part to play at this stage. If any major competitors are meeting cash problems or are known to be under pressure to produce short-term results, such considerations should be taken into the strategy reasoning. Similarly, if competitors are known to be changing executive personnel and this is thought to be significant, it too should be noted. Issues of this kind can, at certain times, be critical; at other times they may be inconsequential. The ability to judge just when they really matter is not a skill to underestimate.

The Chief Executive will also know of the demands that are likely to be made on him by his owners. He will know if he needs to plan his brand portfolio with great care to ensure that funds are available for a high level of dividend payment, or if he can plan for a period when his short-term results may be allowed to ride at a lower level.

The selection of opportunities for action is very much the judgement area of strategy formulation, and good judgement is paramount for success.

As the Chief Executive sifts through the various proposals his strategy will begin to form in his mind. A sound practice is to begin with the key established brands. These will be the lead brands of the company, normally they will be the major profit and cash contributors, and the first requirement is to ensure their continuation as strong contributors. Appropriate action to keep these brands strong is likely to be the Chief Executive's priority.

After this he may begin to think in terms of his support brands. Which ones have the ability to grow and become leaders of the future? Or should he accept that they be used primarily as cash contributors over the coming years?

The proposed new growth brands will need careful attention. Out of, say, five runners at the early stage it is probable that only one, or possibly two, will make it to the national market.

It is important to ensure that a project's progress is checked frequently and that it is removed if it fails to show real promise. Flexibility in planning is essential. As a project's progress becomes clear, so it can begin to take a firmer position in the strategic plans.

In this way a plan for proposed activity in existing markets can be built up. There is a requirement to consider capacity, and where appropriate ensure that it is covered. The opportunities review may have shown that new plant can bring worthwhile savings in production costs. This development and its effect on capacity, should be taken into account.

At this stage it should be possible to build up a plan dealing with existing and new brands in the established markets, for the period concerned. The plan should be a 'positive' one, that is it should take a realistic view of prospects for the business, and avoid either undue pessimism or extreme buoyancy.

When a plan covering proposed capital expenditures on buildings, plant and equipment is added, together with statements covering working capital movement, it should be possible to calculate the probable cash position of the business throughout the period. Proposals for entry into new markets, for acquisitions and dispositions have yet to be added. When they have been finally agreed and included, the business can have its first look at its likely position in terms of both trading profit and liquidity—this assumes that the actual results achieved are close to those set out in the plans.

These initial plans are unlikely to be completely satisfactory. There will probably need to be a number of revision meetings. The timings may be unbalanced with too much activity planned for one particular year. There may be capacity problems or a need to balance the cash position. However, out of the revisions and replanning should come a basic plan that is acceptable to the Chief Executive.

Of course, it is likely that the actual results will not be exactly in line with the plans—they may exceed them handsomely, or they may fall below them, and so it is necessary to move to the next stage.

Stage 6: Deviation from plan

If the actual results differ from the plan to any great extent the deviation will probably have happened for one or more of the following reasons:

1. The actual results of one or more of the company's major projects exceed plans by a considerable margin.
2. The result of one or more of the company's major projects falls far short of the plans.
3. One or more of the company's competitors has made a move (or moves) which has proved to be very successful and this has adversely affected the company's results.
4. There has been an exceptional occurrence within the business environment which has had a particularly adverse effect on the company's business.

There may be other exceptional factors which can have either a helpful or adverse effect on the results of the business. In the main, however, these four circumstances are likely to cover the major risks to the planned results.

The Chief Executive should attempt to estimate the possible effect of the variations listed above on the results of the business. The estimates are likely to be very rough but it is important to have *some* indication of the financial effect, and also have in mind a plan to counter any adverse position.

The embarrassment of success which can follow item 1 should be recognized. If the company is unable to follow up a significant success and ensure that it is exploited to the full, then an opportunity to tie up a major market for a lengthy period of time, possibly for the life-time of the market, will have been missed. Such opportunities are indeed very rare. Plans should be drawn up, rough outline plans, but nevertheless plans which will ensure that the opportunity should it arise, will not be missed.

Despite the very best efforts in planning and execution, it is always possible that a major project, the launch of a new brand, for instance, may not obtain in the national market the results that regional testing has promised.

It is both possible and necessary to estimate the effects of this. Again, they may need to be rough estimates, but the Chief Executive should be aware of the rough cost of varying levels of failure and he should have thoughts as to how these problems can be overcome.

Frequently, when researchers begin to get good results from a particular line of enquiry, competitors somehow get to know about it. Working on the information, by cutting corners, and by good operation, the competitor may win the race to the national market. Alternatively, a competitor may develop an entirely new approach to satisfying a particular consumer need, and this may give him an outstanding success in the market-place.

It would be completely unreasonable to expect estimates to be formed to cover every possible competitive success that may have a marked effect on the business progress. However, every well managed business takes legitimate actions to ensure that it does get advance notice of major competitive moves. The period of notice it gets will vary according to the action. Frequently, it will be known that an attack is coming but pinpointing the exact date may be difficult.

Strategists should prepare estimates to cover these anticipated competitive attacks on major operations. The minor brand re-launch activities will be covered in the normal course of brand development.

If exceptional occurrences are anticipated within the business environment they should also be covered by appropriate estimates. If it is possible to be completely sure of the date, and the extent, then they should be included in the base plan. An example of this form of development could be a particular change in taxation which can have a marked effect on the company's brands—it may have been rumoured, and then talked of publicly by politicians, but the position will be unclear until a governmental announcement is made. (Again the reference is to a significant move and not a relatively minor change which affects all competitors in the industry.)

At this stage the Chief Executive will have:

1. A basic strategic plan which has been constructed on a positive basis.
2. Strategic plans which provide for the company's major projects to be successful and well ahead of plan.
3. Strategic plans which provide cover should the major projects fall well below the planned levels.
4. Strategic plans which provide for a competitor (or competitors) to be successful within the market as the result of particular activities.
5. Strategic plans to cover a possible exceptional occurrence which could have a material effect on the business.

Included within these plans will be proposals for providing additional capacity if this is necessary, and for any other appropriate changes in the structure of the business.

The plans need to strike the right balance, having enough detail to be realistic, without being so detailed that they become a mass of fact and figures which are difficult to comprehend. In compilation the key considerations should be the subject of full analysis but for the many smaller issues, rough estimates will suffice.

Just what is to be regarded as a major issue, and what a minor one, will depend upon the size and extent of the company's activity. For the small business a proposal to introduce a new brand into a major segment of a relatively small market may represent a major project; such a move by a major international business could be a minor project.

Stage 7: Plan for action

The strategic plans will be expressed in terms of actions, in terms of time, and in terms of money. From these plans it is necessary to make a plan for action. In effect, this is a date plan for the progress reviews and decisions required by the strategic plan. From this action plan the Chief Executive and managers throughout the business can make preparations to co-ordinate the necessary action.

In practice it will be necessary to prepare a series of plans. The total company plan should be concerned with the key projects and controls: it is in effect the master plan for the business. Within this total plan, each project should have its own action plan against which the various departmental performances can be reviewed, and further action planned as appropriate. As with all planning procedures, it is important to balance the need for enough detail to make the operation practical and realistic, and yet at the same time not to overburden the operators with unnecessary paper and detail.

When the decision for action has been taken, then it should be activated with skill, determination, and enthusiasm.

Revision of the strategic plan

Strategic planning should not be an exercise which happens once in the year and is then forgotten for another 12 months. When a strategic plan has been developed with skill and endeavour it should normally remain basically unchanged for a reasonable period of time. Many of the projects within the plan will require three, four, or five years to bring to fruition. Frequent alterations can prove particularly costly. However, if there are important changes in consumer behaviour, changes within the markets, new moves in competitive activity, or any other important shifts of emphasis, then adjustments will be necessary. The business of 'making and taking opportunities' is continuous—whenever a worthwhile opportunity is discovered it should be examined and, as appropriate, developed and exploited. The fact that the opportunity was not included in the original strategy is inconsequential.

Strategy formulation, management and business success

Business managers are invariably busy people. Will they have time to follow an approach to strategy formulation similar to that outlined in this book?

If a business is to survive into the longer term it must be successful. Business managers must produce results. They have responsibilities to shareholders, employees, and the community. Each of these groups has a vested interest in the success of the business.

Business success is important to shareholders. It safeguards their investment and provides their dividends. Success is necessary to attract the new capital essential for survival and growth.

Business success is important to employees. It provides job security, just rewards, and opportunity. It is also important to the community that the country's resources are used effectively to increase the wealth of the nation. Benefits which are accepted as part of a developed society, such as education and health care, are supported by successful businesses.

Success is crucial to everyone associated with the business. Success is founded on a winning strategy. If business managers are to be successful they have no option—they *must* give strategy formulation the highest priority in time and effort.

Index